The Do's and Taboos of International Trade
A Small Business Primer

Roger E. Axtell

John Wiley & Sons, Inc.

New York • Chichester • Brisbane • Toronto • Singapore

Copyright © 1989, 1991 by Roger E. Axtell

Published by John Wiley & Sons, Inc.

All rights reserved. Published simultaneously in Canada.

Reproduction or translation of any part of this work beyond that permitted by Section 107 or 108 of the 1976 United States Copyright Act without the permission of the copyright owner is unlawful. Requests for permission or further information should be addressed to the Permission Department, John Wiley & Sons, Inc.

This publication is designed to provide accurate and authoritative information in regard to the subject matter covered. It is sold with the understanding that the publisher is not engaged in rendering legal, accounting, or other professional service. If legal advice or other expert assistance is required, the services of a competent professional person should be sought. FROM A DECLARATION OF PRINCIPLES JOINTLY ADOPTED BY A COMMITTEE OF THE AMERICAN BAR ASSOCIATION AND A COMMITTEE OF PUBLISHERS.

Library of Congress Cataloging-in-Publication Data

Axtell, Roger E.
    The do's and taboos of international trade : a small business
  primer / Roger E. Axtell.
      p.   cm.
    ISBN 0-471-61637-0   ISBN 0-471-54941-X (pbk.)
    1. International trade.   2. Small business.   I. Title.
  HF1379.A96   1989
  658.8'48—dc19   88-35180

Printed in the United States of America

10   9   8   7   6   5   4   3   2   1

To my father, age 94.
For him, the word "international" meant World Wars I and II,
for he fought in both.

To my grandchildren, Emily and Tim, ages 5 and 3.
For them, let us hope the word "international" will mean
worldwide peace
through trade and understanding.

Foreword

It is a genuine pleasure for me to introduce Roger Axtell's book on international trade and the opportunities it offers to both business people and students of the subject. The author has outstanding qualifications to write on this subject from his many years as an international sales executive, and as a special adviser to me and former Governors of Wisconsin on the role that state government should play in the challenging, but rewarding, field of international trade.

Roger was successful in international business, not only because he was a savvy negotiator, but more so because he always approached this subject of international trade first as a student of culture and tradition, and second as a company representative. His earlier book, *Do's and Taboos Around the World,* a guide to international behavior, proves this beyond a shadow of a doubt. Individual cultures must be recognized, learned, and appreciated for any person or firm to be successful in international marketing. Foreign business practices and perceptions are rarely the same as those found in the United States.

Since I became Governor in 1987, I have had the opportunity to take an aggressive sales role in promoting Wisconsin among business executives in many other countries of the world. My efforts focus on personally making the foreign business executives aware that I and my administration are at their disposal to serve as either catalysts or brokers both to start and to close the business deal. My experiences in this effort confirm what Roger has emphasized over the years. A successful long-term business relationship between a U.S. executive and a foreign customer is not possible unless the U.S. executive responsible for the relationship comes to know his or her foreign counterpart as first, "a human being I can trust and respect and whose trust and respect I have earned."

Nothing will ever replace a face-to-face business relationship, not even a fax-to-fax one. The other key ingredient for success is that you *always* treat your foreign customer with the same amount of courtesy and service as you do your best customer in the United States. This demands a long-term commitment on the part of top level executives in the U.S. firm. When paying calls on your foreign customers, you send the same level of executive to Mexico or the United Kingdom, for example, 5 or 10 years into the business relationship as you did when you first met the foreign executive and the firm he or she represents.

It is a dramatic fact of life for all U.S. citizens that international commerce is critically important to the economic well-being of our nation. The world economy has only a few major free market economies, namely, regional ones in Europe and Asia and the Western Hemisphere. However, the single largest market is still the United States. This will become even more important as the U.S.-Canada Free Trade Agreement enters into force. This could have a significant impact on your individual business situation.

International trade is a major factor in the national economy, both in terms of the dollar value of our commercial trade and the amount of foreign industrial investment that has entered the United States. It also is significant in the percentage of our labor force whose jobs depend on free trade. Agriculture, manufacturing, finance, and the service industries all rely heavily on favorable conditions for the free flow of capital and commodities between the United States and other nations.

Wisconsin, as a microcosm of the United States, is proud of the accomplishments in international trade achieved by its business community. However, it is abundantly clear that there simply are not enough of our smaller firms in the international marketplace. Barely 10 percent of all the firms in the United States export and an even smaller percentage export on a regular basis. This is the paradox! All of us recognize that historically we did not really have to export. We were a self-sufficient market. If you were a success in the U.S. market, that was an achievement in itself. Now, that is no longer sufficient. We must convince more firms, especially smaller ones, that if they really want to develop a successful strategic marketing plan, it had better include an international sales component. Furthermore, as Roger's new book demonstrates, the difference between the efforts of many firms in other countries as opposed to many of those here in the United States is that the foreign firms do not look at export sales as "a nice incremental sales factor." They look at their export sales as a matter of business survival. Granted, for many foreign countries exports have always been extremely important to their economic stability and growth. Now, the United States is in that same category.

During the economic slowdown in the early 1980s, many Wisconsin firms heavily involved in international marketing were at least able to keep their existing labor force. They owed this to their international marketing efforts, which at the time of a strong dollar required innovative and deeply committed efforts to hold on to their existing foreign customer base. This contrasted sharply with those firms that had no export sales in a receding U.S. economy. Many of them had to reduce their labor force, in some cases at a traumatic level. To re-emphasize the point, if you can see your way to a real commitment to international sales, no matter the initial investment on your part, you as a business executive will first ensure your company a better future, and second, provide the key ingredient for our nation to reclaim its position of being a net exporter, with a favorable balance of payments position. Keep in mind, as Roger shows, there are a lot of sound business reasons why export sales are important to your company's future.

I can speak for almost all the other governors of the United States, that as a group we are acutely aware that international commerce is a vital factor to the economic future of our respective states. My colleagues are all becoming active in establishing or expanding an international trade program and opening representative offices abroad. The individual states as a group are today playing a more important role than the U.S. government in promoting foreign trade and attracting investments, particularly among the small business community. The premise for this activity is that there is more direct and personalized service from a bureaucrat in your own state responding to your request for assistance than what you will get from a bureaucrat in Washington, DC, who has to handle inquiries from firms all over the United States.

The United States is the world's largest economy, the largest single market, the leading importer, and is among the leading exporters. However, our merchandise trade deficit is intolerable. Today, only about 2,000 U.S. companies account for more than 70 percent of U.S. manufacturers' exports. These exports account for about 5 1/2 million jobs in the United States, but many more of you must get into international marketing if we are to overcome our trade deficit and ensure continued growth for your firm and for our national economy.

There are many ways to get involved in the international marketplace (e.g., export sales, licensing, joint ventures, establishing subsidiaries). Depending on the specific country and local economic conditions, one or more of these techniques can be successfully implemented. There are also many specialists in the private and public sector who deal with the mechanics of this subject, namely documentation, financing, transportation, and contractual drafting. This book will provide you with a great opportunity to avail yourself of help where and when you need it most.

Roger's book will not only make this exciting venture called international marketing easier for you, but also more rewarding to your firm and more enjoyable for you personally.

TOMMY G. THOMPSON
Governor, State of Wisconsin

Acknowledgments

As I travel the United States presenting seminars and after-dinner programs on international trade, cross-cultural communication, behavior, and protocol, one of the first things I urge travelers to do is to learn how to say "thank you" in the language of the country they are visiting. It is such a simple, enjoyable gesture. In keeping with my advice, at the very outset of this book I want to express my thanks and appreciation to the group of people who assisted me in this endeavor.

I say a sincere "thank you so very much" to Governor Tommy G. Thompson of Wisconsin for contributing the Foreword to this book and for his personal dedication to international trade and investment. It was no accident that I first met Governor Thompson in 1980 when we literally bumped into each other in the doorway of the magnificent Grand Hotel in Taipei, Taiwan. He was there as a state legislator learning first-hand about the benefits of trade, and I happened to cross his path while there on business. From that first contact, we became allies to the cause and I am pleased to serve him now, on a dollar-a-year basis, as a policy advisor and Special Assistant for Business. Governor Thompson is a leading example of the new breed of state leaders who fully recognize that exporting and reverse investment not only create jobs at the city and county level, but bring coveted new investment capital into a state. Governor Thompson also serves as chairman of the National Governors Association Task Force on U.S.-Canada Trade. The State of Wisconsin is benefitting directly from his tireless campaign to increase exports and encourage investment. If his salesmanship and personal zeal could be exported to every state, the United States would soon tip the balance of trade back where it belongs.

Patrick A. Willis is District Director of the U.S. Department of Commerce in Milwaukee, WI, and, being located in a good, solid German community, I say (phonetically) *danka-shane*. Pat supplied valuable resource material, checked and rechecked the manuscript for accuracy, and provided support and encouragement with the affability and conscientiousness he brings to all his tasks. He is a credit to public service.

A brotherly "thank you" to my older and wiser brother, Dean R. Axtell, for his counsel in writing Chapter 7 on Pricing. Dean is not only a CPA, but currently president of Trak International. He is a former executive vice president of the Overseas Private Investment Corporation under President Jimmy Carter, and organizer of a Swiss trading company for Amca International, a giant American-Canadian conglomerate.

Harold E. Tower, former treasurer of The Beloit Corporation, largest U.S. exporter of paper-making machinery, assisted me in the review of the Chapter 8 on Financing and Payments. Hal has traveled the world financing export sales, including the challenge of India, so I say a Hindi *dan-ya-wad* to him.

Robert E. Collins is that rare lawyer who can explain the law without speaking legalese. He helped substantially with Chapter 6 on the Law. Bob is also a wise and intelligent counselor whose friendship I value highly. To him I say, Thank you. You are a true party of the first part.

The S.C. Johnson Co. (better known as Johnson Wax) reportedly sells more than 60 percent of its products outside the United States. This is, I am certain, largely because of the hard work of Larry M. Greb, who for 27 years traveled the world in international sales for Johnson. Larry worked with distributors on five continents and made valuable contributions to Chapter 10, Managing and Motivating the Distributor. His favorite region was Latin America. To my old high school buddy I say *gra-cee-yas, mee a-mee-go*.

Ralph H. Graner labored for 32 years with the U.S. State Department in postings all over the world and is now the able director of the Bureau of International Development for the State of Wisconsin. For that reason, I turned to him for assistance on the advice in Chapter 11 on Language and Communication. In China, the word "Mandarin" refers not only to one of the major languages spoken there, but also to a highly placed civil servant within the Imperial family. So to Ralph, I express a Mandarin *shey-shey*.

Professor Sol Levine, an expert on Japan at the University of Wisconsin, kindly offered counsel on Chapter 12, Dealing With the Japanese Mystique. A senior member of the faculty of the School of Business, Sol is respected on both sides of the Pacific. At dinners hosting Japanese visitors he is wont to honor them with a lusty *Banzai,* being one of the few to know that word is *not* only a World War II warcry, it is also a joyous shout of congratulations and goodwill comparable to "Hip, Hip, Hurrah!" To Sol, *bahn-zy* and *du-omo ah-ree-gha-toe.*

Shu-kran is the Arabic word for "thank you" and is therefore an appropriate choice for anyone who must do business in the complex Middle East. Del Brahm is an instructor and professional international freight forwarder who does a great deal of work in the Middle East. Del helped me edit Chapter 9 on Shipping. *Shu-kran,* Del.

Congressman Toby Roth (R-Wis.) is not only a vocal stalwart for small business but a leader in Congress for the promotion of international trade. I am grateful to him for his dedication and support on all international trade issues. Since the Portuguese were historical leaders in world trade, it is appropriate to thank Toby with a Portuguese *ohb-ree-gha-doh.*

Scott M. Cutlip, Robert Williams, Arthur W. Foster, and Richard W. Holznecht have been mentors and valued friends both now and throughout my career. Each of them has provided encouragement and counsel. I say to them *gracias por todo.*

A special thank you to Steve Ross, my editor at John Wiley & Sons, Nancy Marcus Land of Publications Development, and to Sally Wecksler my literary agent, all of whom literally made this book possible.

Ian Kerr is not only a "veddy proper" British gentleman, but a kind, considerate, and highly competent professional public relations counselor in Greenwich, Conn. To him I say a clipped but warm British "Kew."

Peter Diotte is a bright young computer/word processor consultant and teacher who also, incredibly, has accumulated business experience in South Korea and elsewhere. His patience and assistance throughout this project plus his cures for computer hiccups earned my well-deserved applause. So, "bravo" Peter.

I say thank you, with sincerity and humility, to all of the following people: Professor Robert Aubey, School of Business, University of Wisconsin; John Roethle, Milwaukee-based consultant and contributor of valued information on World Trade Centers; James L. Arndt, Wisconsin Department of Development, for his advice on trade exhibitions; David Hammer of the Wisconsin Department of Agriculture, for information on U.S. Department of Agriculture services to exporters; Francis E. "Bud" Bowen, retired advertising professional and collector of advertising bloopers; Barbara Moebius, head of the Waukesha County Technical College's international training programs; Samuel P. Troy, Greensboro, NC, southeast Regional Manager for the U.S. Department of Commerce; Robert H. Letzing, Wisconsin Department of Development; Rolf Wegenke, Division Administrator of Economic Development, State of Wisconsin; Denise M. Dey, National Association of State Development Agencies, Washington, DC, for the list of NASDA members; Ingeborg Hegenbart, delightful fellow panelist and expert on international banking with the Southern National Bank, Charlotte, NC, who also helped edit the chapter on payments; Eugene Theroux, attorney and expert on the People's Republic of China, Baker & McKenzie, Washington, DC; James Wroblewski, Bank One, Milwaukee, WI, for supplying various financial documents; Lewis Griggs and Lennie Copeland, authors of the excellent text *Going International* (Random House), for permission to reprint the excerpts found in Chapter 1; Robert C. Floyd, founder and president of Fitz & Floyd Inc., Dallas, Texas, probably America's most creative designer and supplier of fine china and giftware; and Steve Renk, Renk International, Sun Prairie, WI, energetic and creative booster of exports and trade.

Finally, I owe profound thanks to my wife, Mitzi, who successfully kept home, hearth, and family together when we first lived abroad and then for many succeeding years when, because of my extensive business travels, it just seemed like I lived abroad.

Contents

Introduction

The question "Why haven't more American businesses become involved in international trade?" has been called "an enigma wrapped in an irony."

That question is an enigma for several reasons. First, there is money to be made in international trade. American businesses can profit from new markets larger than the United States, from incremental profits and sales, and as a counterbalance to cyclical swings in the U.S. market. Second, American business people take pride in their reputation for aggressiveness, marketing ingenuity, and their action-oriented culture. In spite of all this, less than one in five American businesses is involved in international trade. The U.S. Department of Commerce estimates that there are 175,000 companies in the United States capable of exporting but not doing so. The riddle is: "If international trade can produce extra sales and profits for American businesses, and if those businesses possess a special reputation for aggressiveness, why then have they seemingly shunned exporting and trade?" That's the enigma and the first half of the total question.

Now, what about the irony. The irony is that there is no one *opposed* to exports. There is not one public or private body that stands against exporting. The government favors it, indeed, vigorously promotes it. Labor unions support exporting because they know it creates new jobs. (The Department of Commerce estimates that every $1 billion in new exports creates 20,000 new jobs.) Local communities, state governments, trade associations, chambers of commerce, and every port in the United States strongly support trade and exporting. Even businesses, at least those one-in-five who are actively engaged in international trade, will stand up and urge their colleagues to become involved. Contributing to the irony

1

is that the economy of the United States desperately needs more businesses to become involved in exports and world trade to help reverse the balance of trade deficit which we will say more about in Chapter 1.

Why do the majority of American businesses, large, medium, or small, apparently turn their backs on international trade? The reason, as we are told by government observers and specialists, is "fear of the unknown." The enigma wrapped in an irony persists: Businesses are not involved in trade even though they should be, no one is opposed to it, even our national well-being is involved . . . and then we find that the explanation is as disturbing as it is un-American. Fear.

For almost 20 years, I have participated in classrooms, workshops, seminars, and one-on-one counseling trying to wipe away those fears and encourage American businesses of all sizes to examine the opportunities in international trade. I did this for several reasons. First, 33 years ago I happened to join a company that, early in this century, discovered the values of world trade. Second, the management of my company encouraged me to contribute my time proselytizing others because they knew the multitude of benefits to both individual companies and to the nation in the form of profits, expansion, new jobs, and even world peace. When I joined the Parker Pen Company I heard our Chairman, Kenneth Parker, express a now often repeated truism: "Countries that trade together rarely go to war with one another." I therefore inherited an appreciation for international trade unencumbered with any apprehensions or fears about doing business overseas. Starting in 1902, Parker built an enviable reputation overseas. By the 1980s, over 80 percent of Parker's sales came from *outside* the United States. When I was in college in the early 1950s, I remember being asked in a study group "What are the four best-known American brand names in the world marketplace?" We all could guess General Motors and Coca-Cola, but the other two names were surprises: Parker Pen and Singer Sewing Machines. The Parker brand name was so well-known that the Thai word for "pen" is "Parker." Also, in some countries with high illiteracy, consumers bought only the caps of Parker pens to display in their pockets because this signaled they were not only literate but had the money to buy such an expensive imported pen.

As I urge fellow business managers to expand into exporting and trade, my theme is simple: If one relatively small company located in the heartland of America, in the tough and competitive business of consumer goods, can become a highly respected, successful and well-known name in the world marketplace . . . why can't you?

Yet the riddle has continued through the 1970s and into the 1980s. As I speak at seminars and workshops and talk with my colleagues in international trade, the conclusion is inescapable. The presidents and CEOs of thousands and thousands of businesses across the United States are simply not taking the time to examine exporting and trade as a new business opportunity. At first they rationalize that the American market is large enough and challenging enough to fully occupy their time and energy. Yet on further questioning one discovers their reluctance is really tied to apprehensions about "How would I get paid?", "Would I have to modify my product?", "I don't understand shipping and documentation for overseas destinations," and finally "I don't understand the language or the strange customs overseas." What they are exposing is a natural human reaction that says: What I don't understand, I don't like, and besides that, I don't want to be embarrassed in the process.

These are the roots of the enigma wrapped in an irony. Yet there are increasing signs of change. We needn't look too far to find stimulating success stories, and those successes should bring pause to the most doubting of Thomases. Leading the crusade for more international trade is the U.S. Department of Commerce and its International Trade Administration (ITA). As you will learn, the ITA staff can be your mentor and leading support group in finding ways to penetrate overseas markets. Commerce offers a bundle of services, all of which are described in Chapter 2. Economic development agencies within your state government may also offer valuable advice and assistance. As you read in the Foreword, a new vanguard of state leaders appreciates the multiple values of trade and are using their offices to lead results-producing trade missions abroad. All of these initiatives are generating new momentum, new successes and more American brand names appearing in marketplaces around the globe.

WHAT DOES "INTERNATIONAL TRADE" INVOLVE?

The operational phrase throughout this book is *international trade*. Those two words encompass many things.

International trade involves exporting, importing, licensing, joint ventures, direct investment overseas, so-called "reverse" investment (where foreign companies invest in the United States), and barter and countertrade. This book has useful information for all those activities.

The most common entry to international trade is through exporting—the exporting of goods or services from the United States to some other country. For this reason, much of this book concentrates on exporting. The next two most common forms of international trade are probably licensing and joint ventures. These are also explained, along with the pros and cons of each, but their permutations are so many that it is difficult to dwell on them in detail. Direct investment overseas can mean investing in a joint venture, but it customarily means building a distribution center or factory or some other major enterprise outside the United States, and is more common among the Fortune 500 companies than among medium and small businesses within the United States. Direct investment of that type is highly complex involving local tax laws, employment contracts, and a host of other complications and therefore is difficult to present in a fundamental book on trade.

For readers interested in how to begin an import business, I recommend *Building an Import/Export Business* by Kenneth D. Weiss (Wiley). This is an enjoyable and comprehensive guide concentrating mainly on importing which will be a valuable addition to any business manager's research.

Whatever form of international trade interests you, there is considerable information and advice in this book to help. For example, Chapter 2 describes how *foreign trade zones* work; this is valuable information for both the exporter and the importer. Chapter 3, among other things, tells about world trade centers and of a unique network service for buyers or sellers in international trade. Chapter 4 titled "The First Handshake" is helpful whether you are in export, import, licensing, direct investment overseas, or simply entertaining customers, clients, or prospective investors in this country. The same applies to Chapter 11 on "Communications," Chapter 12 "Dealing with the Japanese Mystique" as well as the final chapter on "Barter and Countertrade."

Most important, it is hoped that this book will dissolve some of the enigmatic clouds and ironic mysteries that seem to pervade international trade. If that happens, we all stand to benefit. American business benefits from new growth and new profits earned through expanded trade. The nation benefits because global inter-dependence is a reality and, during the current decade at least, the United States is woefully out of kilter because we are buying more than we are selling. Other countries, other competitors in this global interdependence, view international trade differently. Lew W. Cramer, Deputy Assistant for Trade Development in the Commerce Department, visualizes American babies being rocked in their mothers' arms to the tune of "Rockabye Baby," while Japanese mothers sing the tune "Export or die."

The potential is there for the taking. American business managers need only do their homework, obtain a passport, pack a briefcase, and fly overseas in search of new markets. And that is exactly what some successful American firms are doing. When a Columbus, Ohio exporter can sell sand to Saudi Arabia (because of the high silicon and moisture content), it raises images of cartoons showing salesmen selling refrigerators to Eskimos (now more properly called *Inuit*, just one of the many new stereotype-busters you will learn in this book.) And what would you think are the chances of selling wooden chopsticks to the Orient? That is precisely what a Minneapolis manufacturer is doing, by the millions, each year. Other American businesses are selling perfume to France, bows and arrows to the Japanese, ginseng to Hong Kong, beer to Germany, and chicken feet to Hong Kong.

CAREERS IN INTERNATIONAL TRADE

What about careers in international business? For the new generations, anyone from grade school to graduate school, a career in international trade must be considered as a career in a growth industry. With the United States' dismal record and the compelling national need to internationalize, a new corps of globally minded young people will be required by both manufacturing and service industries. The portents are already appearing. Colleges and universities are slowly adding more courses, undergraduate majors are being offered in different aspects of international business, centers for international business are being established, and language departments are joining with business schools for joint programs. At the junior college and technical institute levels, a new awareness is spreading with courses being offered in everything from general cross-cultural communication to the technical aspects of freight forwarding, documentation, and shipping. There is even a high school in Long Beach, California that not only teaches Russian, Chinese, and Japanese languages but graduates young people fully qualified to take threshold positions in trading firms in the bustling Los Angeles harbor area.

Men and women alike would be wise to consider careers in international trade. Furthermore, a career in international trade need not be limited to marketing or government relations. Engineers who can also work easily and comfortably with other cultures and within foreign systems will be in increasing demand. Lawyers can specialize in international law and thereby add a whole second dimension to their career. Finance and accounting majors can hardly function in the corporate world today without a knowledge of foreign exchange, international accounting standards, and cash flow in hyper-inflationary countries.

A number of schools in the United States are now offering highly specialized training for careers in trade. The American Graduate School for International Trade in Glendale, Arizona, also known colloquially as "Thunderbird," offers a one-year graduate course in international business and has acquired a special cachet for training young people for careers in international trade. Students there can specialize in marketing, finance, or government relations with emphasis on one of three major geographic regions: Europe, Latin America, or the Pacific Basin. As more and more Thunderbird graduates fill important international business positions, they return to Arizona to recruit graduates for careers in trade. Educators in international trade tell me that five other universities offer excellent graduate programs: University of Miami, especially for Latin American studies; University of South Carolina, Columbia, SC; New York University; University of Southern California; and the University of Hawaii, especially for Pacific Rim studies. At other colleges and universities, a combination of courses in international business, cross-cultural communication and, of course, the study of languages is an excellent platform on which to build a career. As one educator advised, "If you think you are interested in an international career, start taking every course you can find that begins with the word international."

Unfortunately, learning another language is, by itself, not sufficient to qualify for a job in international trade with most international firms. Knowing another language fluently is an excellent skill to have but business training, and especially international business training, is required before most firms will considering hiring an applicant.

Finally, a growing number of student-exchange programs are sending more and more high school and college students overseas for periods of months, semesters, or even a full year. These young people return with a whole new appreciation of the world they are inheriting and are better equipped than any previous generation to work effectively with other cultures.

Toward the Year 2000

Whoever coined the phrase "timing is everything" could well be describing international trade in the decade of 1989 to the year 2000. Dollar exchange rates are more attractive to foreign buyers than they have been during the past decade. You can now offer your product or service to most hard currency countries at half of the dollars they would have had to pay out 8 or 10 years ago . . . without losing a penny of your own profit.

Another reason for timeliness is we are on the verge of a new *common market* between the United States and Canada. If you are not already doing business with Canada, imagine the opportunity when all impediments to free trade are removed.

A third timely reason to consider expanding beyond our borders is that the year 1992 could well be an historic year in Europe where "the common market" is scheduled to transform itself into "the unified market." That means that the members of the European Economic Community (EEC) and its so-called common market would advance further toward unification by adopting common banking and taxation rules and procedures, by agreeing on certain product standards and specifications, and possibly even adopting a common currency. This will offer a more homogeneous market than before, one equal in size and opportunity to the whole North American market.

Finally, the new generation is traveling the world more than any prior generation. This causes them to move freely and comfortably from culture to culture and be more prepared than any prior generation to accept this legacy of global trade and global interdependence.

If international trade is beginning to sound timely, opportunistic, and attractive, then reading this book will also be timely, opportunistic, and attractive.

My motivation in producing this book was generated by two factors. First, I refuse to accept that American business managers will continue to allow apprehensions and insecurities to prevent them from venturing overseas. The American spirit of enterprise and success in business is much too strong. Second, the cure is in information and education. Famed educator Glenn Frank stated it succinctly: "We all too often underestimate the intelligence of the public and overestimate their stock of information." Thus, an intelligent and informed business public will brush away misunderstandings and fears and get the job done.

That is what is desperately needed in the United States today. We must resolve the enigma, brush aside the irony, and get the job done. In my view, there is absolutely nothing wrong with being profitable *and* patriotic at the same time.

1

The Setting

It's not a game out there. It's World War III,
a war of economies.

International Businessman

"Export or die" was a slogan in Europe in the 1920s and 30s when countries there began to realize that trade and the interdependence of economies were fundamental to economic survival. Yet three centuries before, Great Britain realized that an island nation's survival would depend on becoming a manufacturing locus when it sought to capture the world's natural resources through giant trading companies. This gave birth to the famous Hudson Bay and East India Trading companies who gained control of the raw materials that were then shipped back to England for production of goods.

The Japanese were also forward thinkers on this subject and about that same time realized its modest size—a gnat among the elephants of world trade—would require concentration of production within the country plus control of both imports and exports to stay economically healthy. This was the beginning of the now ubiquitous *sogo shosa*, or general trading companies who established footholds around the world and brought orders back to the network of nationally controlled manufacturing businesses in Japan.

Today in the United States the cry of "export or die" is just as timely and just as critical as it was in Europe six decades ago or in Great Britain and Japan three centuries ago. The so-called playing field of current global trade has become the site of what observers are calling "World War III—The Economic War."

Never before has this country been faced with such huge trade deficits. More than any other time in our history, the United States needs a gigantic upwelling of vitality to sell our goods and services overseas.

That process starts with you—the business person, the student, the manager, the entrepreneur, the sales executive, the corporate strategist, the neo-exporter, and especially the chairman, president, and chief executive officer of corporate America.

This is assuredly a national problem. The French define the word problem as an "opportunity," and so should we. Any national problem automatically means it is a problem for every segment of business in the United States—large or small, agricultural or manufacturing, plus the entire service sector. There is opportunity for almost any business to compete on an international level.

But first, how did we get in this predicament? And where exactly are we now? In this chapter, we will examine the answers to both of those questions; subsequent chapters will tell us what to do about it and how.

HISTORY OF THE PROBLEM

1945 TO 1971

For more than a quarter century, from 1945 to about 1971, the United States was the sole dominant power in the world economically. The United States represented 50 percent of all world production. It was the largest foreign trader, while at the same time it put less than 12 percent of its gross national product into foreign trade—that means exports *plus* imports. We were banker, supplier, and technologist to the entire world while essentially living within our own national economy.

But in that same 25-year period, America's power base was challenged and countered overseas by the creation and development of the European Common Market and by Japan's determined drive to become "exporter to the world." Here is an example of that determination:

The head of one of what is now one of Japan's largest trading companies was a young executive in the 1950s when his employer sent him to Argentina with the instruction "Live there for a year. Don't worry about doing business. Learn the language. Learn the culture. Then, after one year, tell us what products we should introduce in Argentina."

He did as he was instructed. After a time, he observed that the Argentines liked to sew and they liked music. As simplistic as it may seem, he notified his parent trading company to supply him with prototypes of sewing machines with built-in radios. They were grabbed up on the market, and a new export and a new foothold was discovered for Japan.

Note the key ingredient here: patience. The Japanese, it is said, think in terms of years and decades, whereas Americans think in terms of weeks and months. But more about that in Chapter 12 when we examine the unique success and possible mystique of the Japanese.

THE 1970s

In the decade of the 1970s, U.S. economic dominance was replaced by a tripartite rulership between the United States, Europe, and Japan. The U.S. dollar and other major currencies abandoned the gold standard, exchange rates began to fluctuate, and a new era in world trade began. By the end of the 70s, instructors in long-term corporate planning and strategy took delight in saying, in effect "There is no one alive with more than a few years experience in corporate planning because all the rules of the game changed the moment after the Bretton-Woods agreement on the gold standard and currencies was abandoned." And, for America, the decline began.

Higher costing oil imports, lowering productivity rates, less innovation in high and medium technology all created a steady series of balance of payment deficits for the United States. Inflation climbed. Short-term profit-taking ruled. By 1980, the gross national product (GNP) of the United States was 32 percent of the total GNP of the free world, down from 50 percent in 1950.

But in the sacred measurement that every business school and every product manager worships—market share—the news was even worse. From 1959 to 1979, in the arena of world trade the share of manufactured goods among the largest three trading bodies between 1959 and 1979 changed:

> ▸ United States: down from 22 percent to 16 percent
> ▸ West Germany: up from 12 percent to 21 percent
> ▸ Japan: up from 7 percent to 14 percent

THE 1980s

In the early 1980s, the United States experienced a recession, high interest rates, and an overvalued dollar. All of these contributed to a steady declining balance of trade. The worst year was 1987 at $171.2 billion in imports over exports of manufactured goods, followed closely by 1986 at $156.2 billion. In 1988, the deficit is expected to be around $135 billion.

Since 1985, U.S. economic news has been dominated by three critical measurements: a seemingly ever-increasing federal deficit, a declining value of the dollar versus other major currencies in the world, and record-setting balance of trade deficits. One result was October 19, 1987, the historic stock market plunge when those three crucial and worrisome trends seemed to converge and trigger a violent reaction on Wall Street. The deficit ranks as the number one national worry for all business strategists because of its threat of new and additional taxation to help pay for it. The declining value of the dollar, while aiding exports, creates these worries for the American business manager: it attracts a flood of foreign investment in the United States which, translated into U.S. business terms, means possible buy-outs and takeovers; and, imported raw materials, parts and finished goods become more expensive. The trade deficit means more imports than exports, and that translates into reduced production and fewer jobs. From October 19, 1987 and continuing through to the present time, there was great cause for worry and concern about the United States' weakened position in international trade.

WHAT IS THE STATUS TODAY?

Every quarter, the U.S. Department of Commerce publishes the tables on pp. 14–20 showing the current international trade position of the United States. Here are some tips on how to examine these macroeconomic figures:

▸ Look for your basic industry category. Note the trends in trade over the past few years for your category.

▸ Look for the geographic areas overseas where exports are greatest or the weakest.

▸ Study the chart titled "Factors Influencing U.S. Competitive Position." Apply this to your industry or your company.

▸ Note the shifts among basic trading regions in the section titled "Share of World Exports." Note the declining market share of the United States.

The charts on the following pages graphically substantiate earlier points about the United States' declining competitiveness and the seriousness of the trade deficit.

Once you have studied these charts, you will be able to better understand this information when the U.S. government issues new charts and figures each quarter. Also, the U.S. Department of Commerce issues trade balance figures every month and the news media has highlighted that information more and more in recent years. Indeed, on some occasions the figures, whether up or down, have materially affected actions on Wall Street with the Dow Jones Averages reflecting the good or bad news.

You will also now be more sensitive to three key terms that are used repeatedly in these news reports. However, a safe bet is that 99 out of every 100 Americans do not understand them. To be among the understanding 1 percent, study the following:

▸ The *balance of trade* refers to the relationship between inflow and outflow (imports and exports) of merchandise, or manufacturing goods as it is also called. A surplus is when we export more than we import; a deficit is when we import more that we export.

This is too frequently confused with:

▸ The *balance of payments* or *balance of payments on current account* which refers to the flow of payments in and out— the cash flow—of the United States. Many observers consider this index the more important because it includes

Table 1 Current International Trade Position of the United States

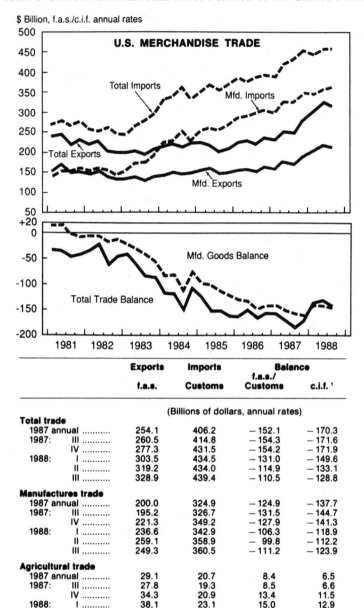

$ Billion, f.a.s./c.i.f. annual rates

| | | Exports | Imports | Balance | |
		f.a.s.	Customs	f.a.s./ Customs	c.i.f. [1]
		(Billions of dollars, annual rates)			
Total trade					
1987 annual	....	254.1	406.2	− 152.1	− 170.3
1987:	III	260.5	414.8	− 154.3	− 171.6
	IV	277.3	431.5	− 154.2	− 171.9
1988:	I	303.5	434.5	− 131.0	− 149.6
	II	319.2	434.0	− 114.9	− 133.1
	III	328.9	439.4	− 110.5	− 128.8
Manufactures trade					
1987 annual	....	200.0	324.9	− 124.9	− 137.7
1987:	III	195.2	326.7	− 131.5	− 144.7
	IV	221.3	349.2	− 127.9	− 141.3
1988:	I	236.6	342.9	− 106.3	− 118.9
	II	259.1	358.9	− 99.8	− 112.2
	III	249.3	360.5	− 111.2	− 123.9
Agricultural trade					
1987 annual	....	29.1	20.7	8.4	6.5
1987:	III	27.8	19.3	8.5	6.6
	IV	34.3	20.9	13.4	11.5
1988:	I	38.1	23.1	15.0	12.9
	II	35.4	19.9	15.5	13.6
	III	35.2	20.6	14.6	12.8

Note: Quarterly data are seasonally adjusted for U.S. total trade.
[1] C.i.f. import values are not shown.

Source: U.S. Department of Commerce International Trade Administration

14

Table 1 (*Continued*)

COMPOSITION OF U.S. MERCHANDISE TRADE

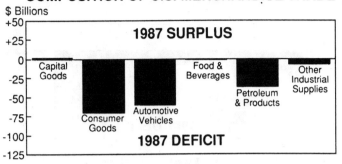

	Exports f.a.s.	Imports Customs	Balance f.a.s./Customs
	(Billions of dollars, annual rates)		
Capital goods			
1987 annual	86.0	84.3	1.7
1987: III	87.0	86.6	0.4
IV	96.2	93.7	2.5
1988: I	103.3	94.7	8.6
II	109.4	101.5	7.9
III	107.1	101.2	5.9
Consumer goods			
1987 annual	17.6	88.7	− 71.1
1987: III	17.9	97.0	− 79.1
IV	18.9	92.0	− 73.1
1988: I	20.6	88.7	− 68.1
II	23.2	90.5	− 67.3
III	23.8	104.3	− 80.5
Automotive vehicles and parts			
1987 annual	24.6	85.3	− 60.7
1987: III	21.3	76.9	− 55.6
IV	27.0	92.2	− 65.2
1988: I	29.7	85.6	− 55.9
II	31.2	90.4	− 59.2
III	26.2	78.6	− 52.4
Food and beverages			
1987 annual	24.2	24.8	− 0.6
1987: III	25.4	24.2	1.2
IV	27.8	25.6	2.2
1988: I	30.3	26.3	4.0
II	30.0	23.6	6.4
III	33.4	24.2	9.2
Petroleum and products			
1987 annual	4.4	42.8	− 38.4
1987: III	4.4	50.9	− 46.5
IV	4.3	45.4	− 41.1
1988: I	4.3	40.1	− 35.8
II	4.4	41.0	− 36.6
III	3.3	39.1	− 35.8
Other industrial supplies			
1987 annual	62.0	68.0	− 6.0
1987: III	61.8	67.3	− 5.5
IV	68.5	72.7	− 4.2
1988: I	78.3	77.2	1.1
II	84.3	79.7	4.6
III	81.7	78.7	3.0

Note: Commodity values do not add to U.S. trade totals because of omission of miscellaneous products.

Notes for tables: Quarterly data are not seasonally adjusted unless noted.   All values in current dollars   f.a.s.—Free alongside ship   c i f—Cost, insurance, and freight.

Table 1 *(Continued)*

U.S. MERCHANDISE TRADE BY AREA

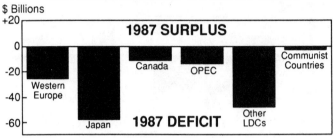

	Exports f.a.s.	Imports Customs	Balance f.a.s./Customs
	(Billions of dollars, annual rates)		
Western Europe			
1987 annual	69.7	95.5	− 25.8
1987: III	64.9	92.9	− 28.0
IV	76.6	104.4	− 27.8
1988: I	87.1	97.9	− 10.8
II	90.0	101.1	− 11.1
III	81.6	95.5	− 13.9
Japan			
1987 annual	28.2	84.6	− 56.4
1987: III	30.6	85.5	− 54.9
IV	32.1	90.3	− 58.2
1988: I	35.3	84.1	− 48.8
II	37.5	86.0	− 48.5
III	39.0	88.9	− 49.9
Canada			
1987 annual	59.8	71.1	− 11.3
1987: III	54.9	65.9	− 11.0
IV	65.3	77.4	− 12.1
1988: I	68.4	79.5	− 11.1
II	74.8	86.2	− 11.4
III	66.2	76.4	− 10.2
OPEC			
1987 annual	11.1	24.0	− 12.9
1987: III	11.2	29.5	− 18.3
IV	13.0	26.0	− 13.0
1988: I	13.3	23.3	− 10.0
II	13.0	23.5	− 10.5
III	13.8	23.6	− 9.8
Other developing countries			
1987 annual	70.6	117.2	− 46.6
1987: III	73.7	123.1	− 49.4
IV	79.3	126.3	− 47.0
1988: I	81.9	123.9	− 42.0
II	93.5	125.5	− 32.0
III	97.8	137.3	− 39.5
Communist countries			
1987 annual	5.7	8.2	− 2.5
1987: III	5.5	8.8	− 3.3
IV	7.0	8.0	− 1.0
1988: I	8.9	9.3	− 0.4
II	9.1	10.1	− 1.0
III	7.5	11.4	− 3.9

Note: Areas are not intended to add to U.S. trade totals.

Table 1 (*Continued*)

U.S. BALANCE OF PAYMENTS
CURRENT ACCOUNT

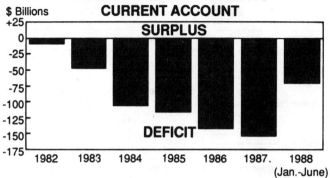

$ Billions

	Exports	Imports	Balance
	(Billions of dollars, annual rates)		
Current account total			
1987 annual	424.8	578.8 [1]	− 154.0
1987: II	401.4	552.3 [1]	− 150.9
III	425.3	593.1 [1]	− 167.8
IV	477.0	611.1 [1]	− 134.1
1988: I	484.5	632.2 [1]	− 147.7
II	493.1	626.5 [1]	− 133.4
Merchandise trade (adjusted, excl. military) [2]			
1987 annual	249.6	409.8	− 160.2
1987: II	239.5	397.7	− 158.2
III	259.6	418.3	− 158.7
IV	272.1	436.8	− 164.7
1988: I	301.2	441.9	− 140.7
II	318.7	438.4	− 119.7
Services			
1987 annual	175.3	155.5	19.8
1987: II	162.0	154.7	7.3
III	165.7	163.0	2.7
IV	204.9	156.8	48.1
1988: I	183.3	177.8	5.5
II	174.5	176.4	− 1.9
Investment income receipts and payments			
1987 annual	103.8	83.4	20.4
1987: II	89.7	82.9	6.8
III ...	93.2	88.9	4.3
IV ...	133.0	82.8	50.2
1988: I	106.2	101.6	4.6
II ...	93.7	100.7	− 7.0
Business-related services [3]			
1987 annual	59.4	56.3	3.1
1987: II	58.5	56.0	2.5
III ...	60.9	57.7	3.2
IV ...	62.8	58.0	4.8
1988: I	66.6	60.0	6.6
II ...	69.5	59.4	10.1
Other services			
1987 annual	12.1	15.8	− 3.7
1987: II	13.8	15.8	− 2.0
III ...	11.6	16.4	− 4.8
IV ...	9.1	16.0	− 6.9
1988: I	10.5	16.2	− 5.7
II ...	11.3	16.3	− 5.0

Note: Quarterly data are seasonally adjusted. [1] Includes unilateral transfers. [2] Exports are valued f.a.s. and imports are customs values. Data differ from those in "U.S. Merchandise Trade" table as they are adjusted to the balance of payments accounting. [3] Primarily travel, transportation, fees, and royalties.

Table 1 (*Continued*)
KEY INTERNATIONAL COMPARISONS
Balance of Merchandise Trade

	Total		With U.S. [1]	
	1987	Jan.-Sept. 1988	1987	Jan.-Sept. 1988
	(Billions of dollars, annual rates)			
United States	− 152.1	− 118.8	− − −	− − −
France	− 5.2	− 5.8 [2]	− 0.8	− 1.5 [2]
Germany, Fed. Rep.	+ 72.4	+ 78.6	+ 13.6	+ 9.2 [2]
United Kingdom	− 16.6	− 32.9	+ 3.1	+ 0.3
Japan	+ 96.4	+ 92.4	+ 52.5	+ 44.7

[1] Imports valued c.i.f.   [2] January-August.

	% Change in Trade 1986 to 1987 *		Exports as % of GNP, 1987
	Exports	Imports	
United States	+ 11.9	+ 11.2	5.4
France	+ 18.6	+ 22.7	16.8
Germany, Fed. Rep.	+ 20.9	+ 19.6	26.1
United Kingdom	+ 22.1	+ 23.0	19.5
Japan	+ 9.2	+ 13.7	9.7

* Based on dollar values.

Share of World Exports

	1970	1975	1980	1986	1987
	(Percent)				
United States	15.4	13.6	12.1	11.4	11.1
France	6.4	6.7	6.3	6.4	6.5
Germany, Fed. Rep.	12.1	11.4	10.5	12.2	12.9
United Kingdom	7.0	5.6	6.0	5.5	5.8
Japan	6.9	7.1	7.1	10.8	10.1

Value and Share of Industrial Countries Manufactured Exports

	Value			Share		
	1970	1980	1987	1970	1980	1987
	($ Billion)			(Percent)		
United States	30	148	179	18.4	16.8	13.9
France	14	84	112	8.3	9.5	8.6
Germany, Fed. Rep.	31	167	264	19.0	19.0	20.4
United Kingdom	17	86	100	10.1	9.8	7.8
Japan	18	124	223	11.2	14.1	17.2

Note: Manufactures include SITC Sections 5 through 8.

Table 1 (*Continued*)
FACTORS INFLUENCING
U.S. COMPETITIVE POSITION

		1987		1988		
	1987	III	IV	I	II	III
	(% change from same period of previous year)					
Industrial Production						
United States	3.8	5.0	5.6	6.0	6.1	5.5
France	2.0	2.0	3.0	5.0	2.6	5.8 [1]
Germany, Fed. Rep	0.5	−0.1	1.7	3.4	2.5	5.2
United Kingdom	3.8	4.3	4.7	4.0	4.0	3.5
Japan	3.5	4.5	8.0	7.1	6.9	5.4
Wholesale Prices for Manufactures						
United States	2.7	4.0	4.3	4.1	4.4	4.8
France	0.2	0.9	2.6	3.2	3.5	
Germany, Fed. Rep	−0.5	0.4	0.9	0.8	1.4	1.8
United Kingdom	3.8	3.6	4.1	3.8	4.3	4.8
Japan	−3.3	−1.7	0.0	0.0	−0.2	−0.4
Value of U.S. Dollar Vis-a-Vis Other Currencies						
13 currencies	−10.8	−6.9	−11.7	−9.9	−8.2	−4.7
French franc	−13.2	−9.5	−12.4	−7.5	−4.1	3.1
German D-mark	−17.2	−11.8	−15.0	−8.9	−5.5	1.5
U.K. pound	−10.5	−8.0	−18.5	−14.2	−10.8	−4.6
Japanese yen	−14.1	−5.7	−15.4	−16.5	−11.9	−9.0

[1] Two-month average.

	1960/70	1970/80	1985	1986	1987
	(% change, average annual rate)				
Productivity in Manufacturing					
United States	2.7	2.3	4.6	3.3	3.4
France	6.7	4.9	3.1	2.2	3.7
Germany, Fed. Rep.	5.8	4.3	3.9	1.7	1.3
United Kingdom	3.7	2.5	3.6	2.8	6.9
Japan	10.8	6.6	5.6	1.7	4.1

U.S. IMPORTS OF PETROLEUM
AND PRODUCTS

	Quantity (Mil. bbl./day)	Value Customs (bil. $)	Price per barrel (dollars)
	(Annual rates)		
1987 annual................	6.8	42.3	17.12
1987: III...................	7.6	50.3	17.99
IV	7.0	44.8	17.28
1988: I...................	7.2	39.6	15.14
II...................	7.4	40.5	15.00
III	7.5	38.7	14.09

Note: Values differ slightly from data in "Composition of U.S. Merchandise Trade" table.

19

Table 1 (*Continued*)

U.S. MERCHANDISE TRADE WITH CANADA

	Exports f.a.s.	Imports Customs	Balance f.a.s./Customs
	(Billions of dollars)		
Total trade			
1986	55.5	68.3	− 12.8
1987	59.8	71.1	− 11.3
Capital goods			
1986	10.2	6.7	3.5
1987	12.7	7.7	5.0
Consumer goods			
1986	2.2	2.7	− 0.5
1987	2.8	3.1	− 0.3
Automotive vehicles and parts			
1986	16.2	24.8	− 8.6
1987	17.6	24.6	− 7.0
Fuels			
1986	1.4	7.0	− 5.6
1987	1.4	7.2	− 5.8
Other industrial supplies			
1986	8.0	20.6	− 12.6
1987	9.4	21.5	− 12.1
Other products, including food			
1986	7.3	6.5	0.8
1987	9.5	7.0	2.5

Note: Total exports are adjusted to include undocumented exports to Canada valued at $10.2 billion in 1986 and $6.4 billion in 1987.

U.S. MERCHANDISE TRADE WITH THE EUROPEAN COMMUNITY

	Exports f.a.s.	Imports Customs	Balance f.a.s./Customs
	(Billions of dollars)		
Total trade			
1986	53.2	75.7	− 22.5
1987	60.6	81.2	− 20.6
Capital goods			
1986	23.4	21.3	2.1
1987	27.1	22.4	4.7
Consumer goods			
1986	4.1	14.8	− 10.7
1987	4.9	15.4	− 10.5
Automotive vehicles and parts			
1986	1.0	12.8	− 11.8
1987	1.3	15.2	− 13.9
Food and beverages			
1986	5.3	4.8	0.5
1987	5.5	5.0	0.5
Industrial supplies			
1986	14.8	18.6	− 3.8
1987	16.2	19.0	− 2.8
Other products			
1986	4.6	3.4	1.2
1987	5.6	4.2	1.4

Note: Trade with the 12 member countries including Spain and Portugal.

nonphysical transactions: investment payments, tourist expenditures, fees and royalties, and all the income from the multitude of service industries.

▸ The capital inflow and outflow account is equally important for it registers just what the name implies, the flow of capital. For the United States, since 1982, outflow has exceeded inflow, still another discomforting trend.

As a result of the current and capital account trends in recent years, the United States has become a "net debtor" country with respect to the rest of the world. What this means is that the value of all foreign public and private investments inside the United States is larger than the value of our investments, or claims, outside the United States. Furthermore, it means we must pay interest or dividends or other remittances on those foreign investments and that means more cash flowing *out of* the country than flowing inward. As for the trade deficit, it is expected to continue well into the 1990s. A new major trade reform law was enacted in mid-1988 designed to strengthen the negotiating powers of the government and help reduce the deficit, but the full benefits will not be felt for 10 to 20 years. One of the main features of the law is that it requires the government to take retaliatory measures against countries who are employing unfair trade practices. In a word, it forces our negotiators to get tougher.

All this is pretty heady stuff unless you have a penchant for economics. For the average business person, it is difficult to relate these macroeconomic issues with individual business concerns such as next quarter's per share earnings or, indeed, even meeting next month's payroll. Nonetheless this prologue sets the stage for the story that follows.

WHY EXPORT

The question is divided into "Why should the U.S. try harder to export?" and "Why should any individual business either explore or expand exporting?"

WHY TRY HARDER?

Let's look at the national reasons first. As we said earlier, the U.S. Department of Commerce calculates that every $1 billion in exports of manufactured goods creates 20,000 jobs. That's a pretty solid reason right there. The Department of Commerce also reports that in the past five years nearly five million new jobs in manufacturing were export-related. Presently, one of every six manufacturing jobs is directly dependent on foreign trade. Clearly, exports are vital to a healthy economy.

Heading the train of exports is capital goods such as aircraft, super-computers, or heavy machinery, followed by industrial supplies and material, then food, feed, and beverages. Until recently, agricultural exports have been the winner in the U.S. export competition. About one of every three acres of American farmland is harvested for export. However, embargoes placed for political reasons in the past decade or so have caused buying nations to either become more self-sufficient or else to find other sources, with the result that U.S. agricultural exports have been hurt.

While exports are clearly vital to the United States, we are doing a poor job in comparison to other nations. In this decade, exports account for about 8 percent of the U.S. GNP; but in Japan, exports represent 13 percent of GNP; in Great Britain, 22 percent; and in West Germany, 24 percent.

How does the vaunted American marketing machine do when it comes to exporting? The answer, in baseball terminology, is "about 22 games out of first place."

Consider these facts as determined by the U.S. Department of Commerce:

- ▶ Only about 35,000 U.S. firms are now actively exporting.
- ▶ Five times that many—some 175,000—U.S. firms are capable of exporting, but are not doing so.
- ▶ Less than 1 percent of American firms, or about 2,000 firms, account for 70 percent of manufactured exported goods.
- ▶ 100 U.S. companies account for about 50 percent of all exported goods.

Back to market share for a moment. Take the total of all trade done in the world and picture the United States in 1960 as accounting for one-quarter, or 25 percent of all trade. By 1970, the U.S. share of that market had slipped to about 16 percent. In 1986, the U.S. share was 11 percent. Any business with that dismal a decline in market share should be scrambling for solutions.

Is there a connection between that declining share of world trade and the fact that hundreds of thousands of medium- and small-sized American businesses are ignoring trade and exports? The answer from almost all observers is a resounding "yes."

Consider another related fundamental marketing term—competition. The U.S. National Foreign Trade Council estimates that about 80 percent of all U.S. industry now faces international competition. America, whose shores have never been invaded successfully by hostile forces in our 200-year history, is now host to our foreign competitors in a bloodless battle for sales and profit. Lennie Copeland and Lewis Griggs, in their excellent book *Going International* (Random House), described the incursion this way:

> International no longer means outside the country. So many foreign firms operate here that foreign is as close as across the hallway. For the first time a non-U.S. company, Germany's KNU subsidiary of Siemens, has won a contract to manage a U.S. nuclear plant. We are buying Japanese cars and electronics, Korean ships, Philippines underwear, Hong Kong watches, Taiwan clothing, and Malaysian calculators. No black-and-white television sets sold in the United States are made in the United States. Foreigners now own such American symbols as Howard Johnson's, Baskin-Robbins Ice Cream, Saks Fifth Avenue, Alka-Seltzer, Chesterfield cigarettes, Bantam Books, and the *Village Voice*. A Saudi Arabian owns a majority interest in the National Bank of Georgia and Mainbank of Houston. Australians have bought Utah International. Kuwaitis own Santa Fe International. A Canadian company owns Paul Masson wines. Swiss Nestle's acquired Libby and Stouffer Foods, and more recently doubled its presence in the United States by buying Carnation. A French firm owns a major portion of the A&P food chain.

And if that isn't startling enough, as Griggs and Copeland point out, the fourth largest exporter in the United States is actually a Japanese company, Mitsui USA.

How has this happened? Why are we so poor at trade and exporting? Again, Copeland and Griggs offer this evidence:

> Fewer than 8 percent of U.S. colleges and universities require knowledge of a foreign language for entrance. Fewer than 5 percent of America's prospective teachers take any courses in international subjects as part of their professional training. Some years ago a

UNESCO study in nine countries placed American students next-to-last in their comprehension of foreign cultures. Only a few years ago, 40 percent of high school seniors in a national poll thought Israel was an Arab nation.

America's labor and management pool is critically deficient in skills required for competence today. Only 3.4 percent of MBAs major in international courses. Curricula have not been internationalized to provide American graduates with the knowledge today's manager needs to maintain a competitive edge in the international arena. Nor are multinational organizations bringing managers up through the international divisions. Nearly two thirds of the presidents and chairmen of the largest international firms are guiding those companies without having had any experience in the international divisions or overseas.

Meanwhile, other nationalities tend to be better informed about Americans. Mitsubishi has 650 to 800 employees in New York simply for the purpose of gathering information about American rivals and markets. One of the Japanese businessmen in the *Going International* films had been sent by his company to St. Louis to do nothing for the first few years but learn to understand Americans.

The Japanese are not alone. The so-called sleeping giant, The People's Republic of China, is hardly asleep when it comes to preparing its new generations for international trade. Television analyst and commentator Robin MacNeil reports that there are presently more people in China studying English than there are *people* in the United States.

WHY ARE WE SHUNNING TRADE?

The penetrating question is: why are American businesses, especially those critical medium- and small-sized businesses, shunning international trade?

The Department of Commerce and other counselors offer this simple but shocking answer: fear of the unknown. It is human nature that what we don't know or understand, we dislike . . . even fear. When confronted with proposals to export, American business people throw up their hands in protest, saying "How will I get paid? I don't understand foreign currencies and I don't want to get paid in pesos that will be worth who knows what. Also, I don't know anything about how to ship overseas—all that special documentation and insurance. And what about licenses to export? What about duties and tariffs? And besides that, they deal in metric. And if that isn't good enough reason, I don't speak any other language. No, sir. It isn't worth the trouble."

This attitude is understandable, myopic, but understandable. We live in the largest, wealthiest and most competitive country in the world. Succeeding in the U.S. market is an achievement in itself. Many medium- and small-sized companies have yet to enter certain regions within the United States, so why venture abroad?

Seeking answers to that question, some 7,500 independent businesses in the United States were surveyed in 1985 by the National Federation of Independent Businesses to determine exactly what prevented them from exploring or expanding into exports. The replies were as follows:

- ▶ Obtaining adequate, initial knowledge about exporting (72%)
- ▶ Identifying viable sales prospects abroad (61%)
- ▶ Understanding business protocols in other countries (57%)
- ▶ Selecting suitable target markets on the basis of the available information (57%)

What about those few small businesses that do venture into exports? How do fledgling exporters get pushed out of their comfortable American nests? Again, the survey by the NFIB showed that most frequently:

- ▶ The initial order was unsolicited. The international buyer found the U.S. supplier.
- ▶ The initial order was of modest size.
- ▶ The initial order came from an English-speaking country.

THE ADVANTAGES OF EXPORTING

Thus far, we have examined some of the history of international trade and its implications on the U.S. economy. We learned how we got "in this fine mess," as Oliver Hardy would complain to Stan Laurel, and we have examined the present status. The case for "why export" has been presented and a self-examination showed why we Americans tend to be poor performers in international trade.

Now it is time for the *Big Question:* "What's in it for me? What are the advantages for me and my company?"

Here are some of the answers:

1. *Increase profits.* Repeated studies have shown that companies that export grow faster and also profit more than companies that do not export.

2. *Spread overhead costs.* Incremental sales and production have the obvious benefit of spreading all overhead costs, from research and development to rent and utilities. This can favorably affect product costs, margins and pricing.

3. *Smooth seasonal fluctuations.* Export sales often have longer lead times or operate on different seasonal patterns than in the U.S. market. This permits filling in slack periods in production with products for export.

4. *Create new markets, repeat orders.* As new markets are opened and distribution is arranged, repeat orders begin to appear month after month and year after year.

5. *Cushion declines in the U.S. market.* Exports offer some natural hedge against the possible ups and downs in your U.S. market.

6. *Increase productivity.* More sales tend to lower per unit fixed costs and more fully utilize company personnel.

7. *Increase your competitiveness.* As you become more aware of competition and competitive products in other markets, you will become more aware of opportunities for modifications and new products. Competing overseas also helps you become stronger when competing against foreign firms entering the U.S. market.

8. *Offer tax advantages.* The U.S. government encourages exports through the formation of what is called Foreign International Sales Corporations or FISCs. These will be described in a later chapter dealing with laws in international trade and exporting.

9. *Extend product life cycles.* Exports to new markets often allow you to prolong the life of your current models and even help dispose of obsolescent models.

10. *Timing.* This list should be sufficient evidence that exporting is advantageous at *any* time. But the opportunity is more timely now than at any juncture in recent history. The reason is dollar exchange rates. During 1985–1987, the dollar declined about 40 percent against other currencies. In exporting, that is directly comparable to offering your customers a 40 percent reduction in your price but without you suffering one dollar loss in revenue. This has made more American products fall within the reach and purchasing power of more people around the world than ever before.

This last factor, timing, makes international trade and exporting more attractive and more exciting than ever before. Yes, current conditions will change. Yes, the cyclical nature of our economies will bring changes to dollar exchange rates. But a solid assault on new markets for export *now* might be the wisest strategic decision a company can make for the future growth of that company.

SUMMARY

You have entered the theater of international trade. In this chapter, we have provided the setting, described the arena. The storyline of this business drama is about to commence. We will proceed slowly and carefully—right foot, left foot, right foot, and so on. Succeeding chapters will tell you how to start, where to go for help, how to make the first trip overseas, what laws apply and how to be aware of cultural differences so your path is free of potholes or foot-in-mouth problems. You will learn the essentials of shipping, documentation, and insurance; you will learn about how to look at pricing in international trade; and how to make absolutely certain you get paid properly. You will learn how to manage and motivate distributors and how to be an effective communicator whether you are in Calgary or Katmandu. All of this should make you feel more comfortable about dealing with foreign trade, foreigners themselves, and some of the tricks and techniques involved in both situations. Confidence is the key, and this book should be a useful confidence-builder.

Finally, we will examine some specialized situations: the tantalizing but mysterious Japanese market, and the new but ancient art of barter and countertrade. At the end of the book, you will find a collection of helpful resource lists.

Welcome to the wonderful world of trade and exports. You travel an ancient road and are part of an unfolding drama that began with the Phoenicians, Marco Polo, and countless other explorers and entrepreneurs who sought new worlds and new markets. It is said "there are good ideas, and there is good timing for good ideas." The decade ahead is surely the right time to expand into international trade. Be warned: If you believe we can live and work and prosper entirely within our own nation and our own marketplace, then you also believe the world is flat.

Economic interdependence is reality. Only a fraction of U.S. businesses are engaged in world trade, yet world trade has entered everyone's life. If you don't believe that, turn around and look at the label in your shirt or blouse collar; look at the "country of origin" of most any electronic device. The dollar is an added incentive to sell your product or service overseas. Our nation needs exports. The U.S. government—as you will see in the next chapter—has a basketfull of services to ease your journey.

Bon voyage!

2

How and Where to Start

America was outer space to
Christopher Columbus.

Anonymous

Columbus set out to find a passage to the Indies for trade and failed; he found America instead. This chapter will launch you on your private exploration of the world of trade. It will offer suggestions on exactly what to do at the beginning, and more importantly, where to go for help. Like Columbus, you may be in for some surprises, but they can be rewarding surprises.

We will assume that you presently have a good base of U.S. operations. Maybe you have even had an occasional inquiry or order from overseas. Or, perhaps you have simply decided to examine exporting as a business venture by itself. Maybe you are driven by one of the "reasons for exporting" detailed in Chapter 1, such as to smooth seasonal fluctuations, to use up extra capacity and spread overhead costs, or that most common motive of all, to seek new markets for more growth and profit.

Typically, one person in an organization becomes the "agent of change." You might be the CEO or owner of a business, or a far-sighted marketing manager, or the person charged with new market development. Or, you might have had your mental light-bulb lit by a seminar, article, or casual conversation with a colleague. Maybe your motivation is simply the itch to travel.

29

Whatever, the first step in this flowchart of exploration is the following question:

> Am I ready and willing to spend a few months doing desktop research, traveling to government offices, learning the fundamentals of the game, and generally schooling myself on what's involved and who is out there to help me?

You can plan on two to three months time for this plus some out-of pocket expense for mileage, phone calls, and maybe overnight accommodations. Additional costs might be incurred if you choose to buy some of the market research reports offered by the U.S. Department of Commerce.

At the end of this first stage, you will then face another crossroad with the question "Does this still look attractive?" If the answer is "yes," then a more serious decision is required, one centering on commitment: "Am I, or my management, willing to draft a marketing plan, commit some time, money, and other resources to have a whirl at this new venture?" As we will see later in this chapter, this matter of management commitment is *crucial* to everything else you may do thereafter. More about that later.

HOW INTERNATIONAL TRADE IS DIFFERENT

Is it different? The quick answer is that in many ways it is no different than expanding into a new region of the United States. It takes time, research, planning, travel, adapting to new conditions, finding new customers or distributors, and—as always—some risk.

It is different, however, in these ways:

▶ New needs and new tastes are likely.
▶ There are new and different forms of distribution duties, quotas, licenses; other new burdens are added.
▶ Distances are greater and therefore shipping, documentation, and insurance are more complicated and more costly.
▶ Financing and payment terms and methods are often different; even pricing can be different.
▶ Cultural peculiarities pop up.
▶ Time zones are an early nuisance (but quickly overcome).

These differences are what this book is all about. An open mind and a willingness to adapt are two qualities that will pay handsome rewards. The worst attitude is one that says "American methods and marketing techniques are the most advanced in the world. All I have to do is export my methods along with my product." Wrong! Here is a classic example:

> The American pharmaceutical industry is known as one of the most sophisticated marketing machines in the world. The reason is that their market—the medical profession—is, at the same time, the most clearly defined, best educated, highest paid target audience ever assembled. Consequently, advertising and promotional material for new drugs are presented in slick, four-color presentations filled with artistic quality and content.
>
> One of these pharmaceutical firms introduced a new drug for curing intestinal worms in humans. It was an immediate success in the United States and so the firm decided to market the product overseas, especially in certain African markets where they were certain the problem of intestinal worms was highly prevalent. They used the U.S. advertising-promotion campaign but nothing happened. No demand occurred even though they were absolutely certain the product was needed.
>
> A local advertising agency in Africa approached them saying "We think we know what the problem is. Your fancy American advertising approach is too indirect, too delicate. Let us have a try." They were told to proceed.
>
> The new agency produced an ad showing a pile of human excrement with worms crawling in it. The results were almost instantaneous; victims said "That's what I have." And the sales curve began climbing.

As crude as that true story may seem, the message is clear. What was crude to Americans was clear communication in another culture. American ways are not always effective in new markets. (More about this in Chapters 10 and 11.) Among your research tools, insert a mental reminder saying, "Remember—open mind, willingness to adapt."

U.S. GOVERNMENT SERVICES

Good news for the first step forward in your odyssey. There is probably universal agreement that the best single place to begin is at the nearest office of the U.S. Department of Commerce. Within DoC, as it is referred to, resides a group called the International Trade Administration (ITA), and so closely a part of the ITA as to be almost one-in-the-same is the United States and Foreign Commercial Service (US&FCS). This is the place to begin. This is the starting line, the first tee, and homeplate all wrapped into one.

In early 1988, the U.S. Department of Commerce, under the stewardship of Commerce Secretary C. William Verity Jr., made exporting the number one priority for the entire department. In February, Verity launched a national program called "Export Now," a campaign designed to help smaller companies capitalize on the highly competitive dollar-exchange rate to penetrate foreign markets. The drive was designed to "recapture the spirit of the Yankee trader," according to Verity. "Export Now" is like a "full court press" according to one Commerce department head, where every Commerce field office must create and implement new seminars and workshops to bring attention to exporting and help newcomers get started. Another Commerce Department official explained that regardless of which political party occupies the White House, the drive for exports will continue unabated because the trade deficit is a long-term problem. You can call "Export Now" at their toll-free 800 number, 1-800-88T-RADE.

The best single piece of advice for the new-to-export researcher is: Run, don't walk, to the nearest Department of Commerce District Office. Make an appointment to meet one of the trade specialists there, or, ask him or her to visit you in your own office. These trade specialists spend a great portion of their time on the road. However, you will probably want to personally visit the DoC office in order to become acquainted first-hand with the multitude of services offered to businesses interested in all forms of international trade.

Some who made that journey complain "Yes, I went to the local Commerce office and I ran into a snowstorm of paper." You have to realize that the trade specialists can hardly be expected to provide immediate and detailed data on your specific product— whether it be pool pumps or pool cues. First, it is essential to review the full menu of services offered by the US&FCS, as we will do shortly in this chapter. Then, it is essential to determine the precise category that your product fits within the huge government classification system. For example:

A manufacturer of navigational equipment had the Commerce office do a computer search on which countries were manufacturing certain navigational devices. The answer turned up: Canada. From practical knowledge, the firm thought this was wrong. Further digging discovered that the proper terminology for the search was "electronic radio directional instruments." The computer was looking in the wrong cubbyhole. The right answer turned out to be Japan.

Although it may seem that you have been hit by a deluge of paper, but remember, DoC is like a large haystack full of information and, with their help, you are searching for your particular needle.

DoC advertises that it has 1300 trade professionals to help your company export around the world. These specialists are located in 67 cities across America and in 127 cities overseas. (See the Appendix for exact addresses and phone numbers of the U.S. offices.) The full-time responsibility of these trade specialists in each district office of DoC is to reach out to businesses interested in international trade. The Commerce Department reports that over 100,000 one-on-one counseling sessions are held each year with U.S. companies. These home-based technicians are supplemented by commercial offices attached to U.S. embassies and consulates overseas who collect foreign market data, search for sales leads, identify qualified buyers and government officials, and counsel firms frustrated by trade barriers.

One of the first steps taken by the trade specialist in your district office will be to pinpoint your SIC number. This stands for Standard Industrial Classification, which is a standard numerical code system used by the U.S. government to classify products and services. Memorizing your particular SIC number is as useful as knowing your own telephone number, because it will help you again and again in your research.

When you make your first visit to the ITA office in your region, after discussing the preliminaries, the first important acronym you will learn is CIMS which stands for Commercial Information Management System. This new automated system electronically links the information resources of all ITA offices worldwide. It was installed in 1988. Prior to this you would have had to apply for market information which would arrive later in the form of leaflets, printouts, printed reports, spread sheets, and pamphlets.

CIMS allows your trade specialist to sit down at a computer information terminal, insert floppy discs that are supplied and replenished periodically from Washington, and immediately access the information you need about your product category and about the geographic regions that interest you. Furthermore, where previous printed materials often dealt with general information on industrial segments, the information supplied by CIMS can be more tailored to your situation, whether in manufactured goods or the service industry.

The cost for CIMS, at the time of this writing, is $10 for the first 10 pages of printed material plus 50 cents for each additional program. However, the Office of Management and Budget is assessing the actual cost to the government for this service and these costs may be increased.

A synopsis of some of the valuable information services offered by CIMS and the DoC/ITA/US&FCS follows. It is a rich platter of services—presented in condensed form here—fully deserving close examination and understanding. Your Commerce office has leaflets describing CIMS and the other services described here but for best results, visit the office and carefully review each one. The services are divided into three categories:

1. Identification and assessment of markets for your product
2. Contact services—ways to put you in touch with specific markets
3. Promotion—ways to help promote your product overseas

IDENTIFICATION AND ASSESSMENT

Export statistics are available that tell you the U.S. exports for a *single* basic industry, product-by-product and country-by-country, over each of the last five years. Data are often ranked in order of dollar value to quickly identify the leading products and industries. This information was originally called Export Statistics Profile (ESP) before the CIMS program but the same basic information can now be accessed automatically from computer diskettes virtually as you sit in the ITA office. This information consists of tables showing the sales of each generic product in the industry in each country, as well as competitive information, growth, and future trends. Also included is an *Export Market Brief*—a narrative analysis highlighting the industry's prospects, performance, and leading products. These export statistics have been prepared by Commerce for several dozen basic industry classifications, with more being added each year.

When you want to zero in on *U.S. exports to a particular country*, CIMS provides five-year trends of U.S. manufacturing and agricultural exports to a particular country. You can also obtain a comparison of U.S. and world growth rates for that category over five-year periods. When combined with the export statistics described above, your can begin measuring the export potential of your product country by country.

One possible early frustration will be that these statistics will deal with, say, medical instrumentation and your product pertains to only one thin slice, let's say it electronically monitors heart performance. Be patient. The early research process is one of sorting and sifting. Stick with it.

International market research is also stored in CIMS and you can receive reports that are in-depth analyses for one industry in one country. Reports include information such as market size and outlook, end-user analysis, distribution channels, cultural characteristics, business customs and practices, competitive situation, trade barriers, and trade contacts.

Market research is also available for 50 key industry groups such as agricultural machinery/equipment, communications equipment, computers and peripherals, electric power systems, electronic components, equipment and materials for electronic components production, food processing and packaging equipment, graphic industries equipment, industrial process controls, laboratory instruments, machine tools, medical equipment, and sporting goods and recreational equipment.

Unique marketing opportunities, such as the construction of a new hydroelectric plant or an entire cement factory, are collected and made available through CIMS. You can inquire where new cement factory opportunities exist or, instead, about any new major marketing opportunities in a specific country.

Overseas Business Reports (OBR) are still available in printed form by subscription or via CIMS. OBRs provide basic background data for business people who are evaluating the general panorama of export markets. These reports discuss pertinent market factors in individual countries, present economic and commercial profiles of countries and regions, and issue semiannual outlooks for U.S. trade with specific countries. These reports also provide marketing data on best channels of distribution, tariff structures, investment rules, and trade regulations.

Foreign Economic Trends (FET) are country specific reports, available either through CIMS or in a separate printed and bound form, that provide an in-depth review of business conditions and current prospects as well as a marketing outlook for U.S. products. From personal experience, these are helpful to take along on overseas business trips because they provide insight into a specific market and allow you to ask sound, intelligent questions about the history, geography, demographics, and economics in that country.

Industry specific statistical profiles are available via CIMS that include an export market brief with an overview of world demand for the industry and the prospects for U.S. exports. Also included is an export potential rating chart and product coverage guide.

A comparison shopping service, or a custom research service, is available for the following countries: Brazil, Canada, Colombia, France, West Germany, India, Indonesia, Italy, South Korea, Mexico, Philippines, Saudi Arabia, Singapore, and the United Kingdom. Selected key marketing facts about a specific product will be researched in the particular country. Several basic questions will be answered including overall marketability; names of key competitors; comparative prices; customary entry, distribution, competitive and promotion practices; relevant trade barriers; leads to local firms for representation, licensing or joint venture. The fee for this service is $500 per country surveyed.

CONTRACT SERVICES

The Agent Distributor Service (ADS) helps you locate interested and qualified overseas agents or distributors for your products or service. The ADS report contains information on up to six qualified representatives with interest in your company's sales proposal, including the name and address of the firm and brief comments about the suitability of the firm as a trade contact. The charge for this service is $90 per country or Canadian province. The ADS is available for most countries and usually takes 30 to 60 days for processing.

The *World Traders Data Report* (WTDR) prepared by US&FCS officers abroad, provides information on a foreign company with which it plans to do business. This report contains information on that foreign company's organization, year established, size, number of employees, general reputation, language preferred, product lines handled, principle owners, and financial and trade references. Reports are not available for the United Kingdom. The cost is $75 per report.

Information on foreign firms that have traded with the United States is a service tailored to fit individual requests on specific products, companies, and markets. These lists provide information such as the name and address of the firm, name and title of the chief executive, year established, relative size of the company, telephone/telex, products of service information, and type of business (e.g., manufacturer, wholesaler, distributor, etc.) Included in this program is a listing called the *Foreign Traders Index*. This index is designed to assist U.S. exporters by identifying key trade contacts abroad. It consists of compilations of potential agent/distributor prospects, major potential end-users, and publications and associations specifically elected in conjunction with each industry category. You can even order pre-printed mailing labels for these contacts. The fee for this service is $25 for set up and 25 cents for each name.

A continual access to timely sales leads from overseas firms seeking to buy or represent American products and services was originally called Trade Opportunities Program (TOP) and offered by the ITA. But as of 1988, this information was turned over to *The Journal of Commerce*, a daily newspaper, that is available by subscription for $195 for one year.

Commercial News USA is a monthly magazine that provides worldwide publicity for U.S. products and services available for immediate export. It is sent to over 240 U.S. embassies and consulates, 50 American Chambers of Commerce abroad, and Commerce Department district offices, reaching approximately 200,000 key business and governmental leaders worldwide. *Commercial News USA* offers the following advertising services for U.S. firms:

▶ *New Product Information Service (NPIS)*—A company may place a short, promotional description of its product and photo in the magazine. To qualify, products must not have been sold on the U.S. market for more than two years and must be currently exporting to no more than three countries. NPIS information on selected products is also broadcast by Voice of America. The charge is $150 per product and is subject to change without prior notice.

▶ *International Market Search (IMS)*—Products which do not
qualify for the NPIS may be eligible for publication in special issues of this magazine which promotes products and
technology of a single industry only. Several industries a
year are selected for promotion through this program. To
qualify, products must conform to the industry being promoted and must currently be exported to no more than 15
countries on a regular basis. The charge for the IMS is also
$150, which is subject to change.

PROMOTION

An overseas export promotion calendar is available via the CIMS
computer system. This calendar is designed to assist U.S. business
firms take advantage of various promotional opportunities. It provides a 12-month schedule of U.S. Trade Center Exhibitions, International Trade Fairs, plus Catalog Shows and Trade Missions
organized by DoC. The information can be retrieved either for all
overseas promotions or for industry-specific events.

The Matchmakers Service is not only the newest service offered by the ITA but is best-suited for small to medium-sized
businesses who are new to export. This is what Commerce officials describe as a "high-visibility trade event" designed to introduce companies to new marketing opportunities abroad. These
events are four- and five-day meetings or exhibitions, in specific
major cities and concentrate on specific industry categories. For
example, in 1988 Matchmaker events were held in Riyadh, Saudi
Arabia for agribusiness equipment, in Toronto and Montreal,
Canada for telecommunications, computers, and peripherals and
process controls, and in Brussels, Amsterdam and Luxembourg for
health care products and services. This program brings your company face-to-face with potential agents and distributors who
might make a good "match" for your marketing objectives. These
events are limited to 20 to 25 U.S. companies and fees are charged
for participation. The fee includes embassy briefings, on-the-spot
counseling by legal, financial, and industry specialists during the
event; and one-on-one business appointments with potential licensees and joint venture partners. This Matchmaker program is
co-sponsored by the Small Business Administration (SBA) that
provides some financial support to a limited number of qualified
businesses participating.

There are now only four permanent *U.S. Trade Centers* located around the world operated by DoC to provide U.S. firms with exhibition of their products to potential buyers. Located in Tokyo, Mexico City, Seoul, and London, these Trade Centers provide year-round facilities for display and demonstration of U.S. products. An American firm with products that fit a particular show product theme may exhibit for a participation fee. The Trade Center staff conducts a widespread market promotion campaign, special trade showings, conferences, and press reviews to attract importers, distributors, agents buyers and users to the exhibition. In addition, when major exhibitions are desired in other major world cities, ITA will contract for that space when needed.

In addition to exhibitions at the Trade Centers, U.S. pavilions at *International Trade Fairs* offer manufacturers and representatives opportunities to display their products at trade fairs around the globe. If there are no trade fairs in a particular market, the U.S. Department of Commerce may arrange a solo exhibition of American products. These exhibitions at trade fairs provide American firms with highly attractive, inviting, and functional exhibit areas at costs which vary from exhibition to exhibition, but which are far less than it would cost firms to exhibit on their own.

DoC sponsors two types of *Trade Missions*—U.S. Specialized and Industry-Organized Government-Approved (IOGA). The objectives are sales and the establishment of agencies and representation overseas. *Specialized* missions group American companies with related products within given U.S. industry sectors to which Commerce provides both an Advance Officer and Mission Director, and arranges an overseas itinerary, business appointments, and receptions. *IOGA* missions are organized and led by private export promotion organizations and receive substantial staff support from Commerce in the United States and abroad.

U.S. Catalog Exhibitions feature displays of U.S. product catalogs, sales brochures, and other graphic sales aids at U.S. embassies and consulates or in conjunction with trade shows.

Video Catalog Exhibitions are videotape presentations which take the place of live product demonstrations. A U.S. industry technical representative is on hand to talk with potential buyers and answer questions.

U.S. Trade Centers have occasional periods when the exhibit floor is not in use. U.S. companies, or their agents, may use the facilities at these times for *between-show promotions*. Technical sales seminars are another form of promotion which fit into between-show promotions.

MISCELLANEOUS SERVICES

The *Office of Major Projects* provides assistance to U.S. firms in identifying foreign capital projects with major export potential. Firms are informed of these projects and may receive assistance in competing for the contracts. The service is free.

The US&FCS sponsors the *Foreign Buyer Program* special trade shows for U.S. industries with high export potential targeted at foreign buyers, agents and distributors, potential licensees or joint venture partners.

If your head is swimming from this long catalog of DoC services, consider this. When you visit with your trade specialist, review each of these programs and ask to see examples of each form and data sheet. This will help you not only become acquainted with each service, but decide if the information is specific enough and useful for your purposes. Then you can decide which ones you may want to purchase.

Common sense will also assist. You already know that no one can sell vodka to the Russians or snowmobiles to the Sahara. But you *do* already know your product, your industry, your competitors—both national and foreign—and you may even have a rough idea which geographic areas are your most likely end markets. For example, it makes good sense to look at America's leading trading partner, Canada. In January, 1989 the United States and Canada signed an historic trade agreement that within the next decade will create the world's largest free-trade zone. You might begin your search exercise with Canada.

At the outset of this chapter, we talked about Columbus and about rewarding surprises. Working with government agencies can have both. Let me relate a personal experience:

> In preparation for the 1976 round of GATT (General Agreement on Tariffs & Trade) negotiations, the Department of Commerce formed what were termed Industry Sector Advisory Committees or ISACs. The purpose of these advisory committees was to tell the government negotiators what concessions they should seek from our trading partners.
>
> The writing instrument industry was invited to participate and, since I represented The Parker Pen Co. in our industry association

and headed the international trade subcommittee, I was asked to represent our industry interests.

Twenty-six ISACs were formed and we were placed in Number 26, gloriously categorized and titled *Miscellaneous*. Our pens and pencils were lumped in with musical instruments, sporting goods, and buttons, which caused me to immediately assume we would be lost in the crowd.

Undaunted, our industry formulated a trade position which simply said: We are in favor of freer trade and will agree to reductions in tariff and nontariff barriers on the importation of pens into the U.S. if to our trading partners will grant comparable and equivalent concessions in their markets.

To our great surprise, at one stage during the negotiating process, Commerce officials encouraged us to visit Geneva, Switzerland where the actual trade talks were being held. With the executive secretary of our association, I flew to Geneva and sat down with our negotiators.

"What does your industry want?" they asked. I told them and, impressively, they produced spread sheets showing all the tariff and nontariff barriers on pens for each major trading country. We systematically went through the list and developed our desired "comparable and equivalent concessions."

Months later, our industry learned that we had received exactly what we had proposed in Geneva. We had offered concessions amounting to 60 percent reductions, spread over eight years, on tariffs levied on writing instruments coming in to the United States if our major trading partners did the same. The other nations not only agreed but, as it turned out in succeeding years, the Japanese government actually accelerated the reductions and installed them in less than six years. The system had worked.

BOOKS TO OBTAIN

Early in your desktop research, you should obtain several valuable books from the government:

▸ The first is titled *A Basic Guide To Exporting*, published by the U.S. Department of Commerce. Your district office can help you obtain a copy, or you can write the Superintendent of Documents, U.S. Government Printing Office, Washington, DC 20402-9325. The cost is $8.50, ISBN (stock number) is 003-009-00487-0. Another place to look for this booklet is your local library. This is, perhaps, the best single booklet on exporting and will serve you just as the title states, as a basic guide.

▸ The second is called the *Exporters Guide to Federal Resources for Small Business,* a 1988 publication (127 pages) of the Interagency Task Force on Trade, again available at your DoC district office or by writing the Superintendent of Documents (see the first entry). The cost is $4.50 and ISBN is S/N 045-000-00250-1. This book informs you of all the other government agencies who support trade, exactly what they do, and the names and phone numbers for contacts.

▸ *Government Periodicals and Subscription Services* is a booklet also available from the Superintendent of Documents. This is an index of all publications offered to the public by all agencies of government. Under the Department of Commerce, some 40 different publications are listed. For the Department of Agriculture, which we will examine next, there are no less than 66 different publications offered. This index can be a good basic resource for your library.

▸ A bimonthly magazine that is a nongovernment publication called *Export Today* contains many timely and helpful articles on exporting and will help you keep abreast of changes and new ideas. For information on subscribing, write to *Export Today,* P.O. Box 28189, Washington, DC 20038.

U.S. DEPARTMENT OF AGRICULTURE: A CASE STUDY

I decided to test my own advice in these pages and play the role of neophyte exporter. I had worked with Department of Commerce officials for more than 25 years, but had scant experience in agriculture. I was aware that the United States was the world's largest exporter of agricultural products and that our farms were among the most productive and efficient in the world. But I was curious to see how the system worked if I simply picked up the telephone, called the nearest government agricultural agency and said "I am interested in exporting agricultural products, can you help me?" The answer arrived in the mail three days later—six inches high and eight pounds of it. I received three hefty packets of leaflets, reprints, booklets, and guides. The accompanying letter explained that each packet pertained to a special category of exporting including forestry products, food, and cattle—the three most common agricultural exports.

If your state has a state department of agriculture, begin there. They will outline state services and quickly acquaint you with the variety of aids provided by the U.S. Department of Agriculture or, more specifically, the Foreign Agricultural Services (FAS) which is a part of the U.S. Department of Agriculture (USDA). Unlike the Commerce Department, USDA does not have field offices. Most states have a cooperative agreement with Washington, and so the agency within state government responsible for agriculture will be your key linkage to all state and federal services.

"We try to offer one-stop shopping services," David Hammer, my local state official, explained. "When someone contacts us for help with exporting, we provide information on state services, federal services, and any specialized services for unusual agricultural exports—leather hides, for instance."

The FAS is responsible for four areas: market intelligence, market access, market development, and is the lead unit in administering the USDA's export credit programs and foreign assistance.

Providing information is the job of about 100 professional U.S. agriculturalists who are posted in about 70 American embassies around the world. They provide information on more than 100 different countries: foreign government agricultural policies, analysis of supply and demand conditions, commercial trade relationships and market opportunities.

This intelligence is digested and issued in periodic reports on a commodity-by-commodity basis. FAS publications include:

▶ *Foreign Agriculture*, a monthly magazine on foreign agricultural conditions, market development, and trade

▶ *FAS Circulars*, specialized commodity reports covering global production and trade for many commodities

▶ *Weekly Roundup of World Production and Trade*, highlights of current developments in international agriculture

▶ *World Crop Production Report*, a monthly report of USDA production estimates for grain, cotton, and oilseeds in major countries and selected regions of the world

Of special interest is the *Agricultural Information and Marketing Services* (AIMS), a computerized system to handle trade inquiries from foreign importers for specific products. To subscribe to any of these publications, contact the FAS Information Division, Room 5918-S, USDA, Washington, DC 20250.

If you are part of a commodity trade association, the FAS is probably already working with your association through its "cooperator program." These market development projects involve some 75 trade associations, from grains and soybeans to leather and logs.

Other marketing services offered by FAS include:

▶ *Export Briefs* is a weekly trade letter containing all inquiries received each week. The FAS advises that this is more appropriate for exporters and trade associations dealing with a range of products.

▶ *Contacts* is a monthly newsletter with information from U.S. agricultural firms interested in exporting. This is particularly useful, the FAS says, for new-to-market firms or for new products.

▶ *Trade exhibits* help introduce and promote agricultural products overseas.

Risk protection against nonpayment by foreign banks is offered U.S. exporters through the USDA's Export Credit Guarantee Program.

After becoming acquainted with all of these federal services, the next step is to meet with a representative of your state agricultural agency. At that meeting, they will run an assessment of your exporting capability: management commitment, capital resources, and product suitability. "We then arrive at a 'red light/green light' decision point," my state official explained. "If signs do not point to exporting, we turn them over to our domestic service which may help them find new markets within the United States."

Farm equipment and machinery products are the responsibility of the Department of Commerce, where commodities or processed foods or value-added products (e.g., leather, forestry products) and biotechnology related products are the responsibility of agricultural trade specialists.

The FAS has developed a list of 10 steps to marketing success which concisely enumerate the exporting process regardless of product. Here they are:

1. Seek out potential customers overseas.
2. Determine product tastes and preferences.
3. Encourage removal of import barriers where necessary.
4. Introduce product offerings to potential customers.
5. Provide quality products that meet customer needs.
6. Price products competitively.
7. Take advantage of USDA credit programs.
8. Follow up sales to ensure satisfaction of buyers.
9. Demonstrate commitment to export market sales.
10. Be attuned to business etiquette.

Succeeding chapters deal with many of this proper and sensible set of steps.

OTHER GOVERNMENT AGENCIES

Aside from the Departments of Commerce and Agriculture, there are several other agencies that may eventually prove useful to firms expanding into overseas markets.

The *Export-Import Bank* aids with export financing and helps U.S. exporters compete against foreign government subsidized financing. More on this important agency in Chapter 8.

The *U.S. Small Business Administration* (SBA) offers various types of assistance to small or minority exporters through two programs: business development assistance and financial assistance. The SBA also supervises SCORE, an acronym for a corps of senior retired executives who are available for counseling in all facets of business. If you are fortunate to have a SCORE group in your area, and if you can be paired with the right executive, the years of experience and knowledge available to you, at no charge, can be extremely valuable. Field offices of the SBA are located throughout the country. (Addresses are listed in the Appendix.)

In both of these cases, and for other government services, it is probably best to confer with the trade specialist at your district DoC office to learn if, how, when, and where these other agencies could be helpful to you.

Another service group you should know about is the *District Export Council* (DEC) in your area. There are 51 DECs in the

country comprised of 1500 experienced business people—
experienced, that is, in international trade, many of them from
small businesses. These mentors donate their time to help stimulate exports and trade from the United States. They work in conjunction with the local DoC district office and provide a variety of
services—seminars, counseling, training, workshops—for the
neophyte to international trade.

STATE-SPONSORED ASSISTANCE

Individual states are becoming increasingly active in encouraging,
stimulating, and servicing medium and small businesses that
wish to explore and expand into exporting. In fact, each US&FCS
office has signed a partnership agreement with its corresponding
state.

Just one manifestation of this growing state-sponsored activity is that the Japanese have become accustomed to seeing, not one,
but several state governors in Tokyo at the same time, heading
trade missions, and courting both exports to Japan and Japanese
investment in their states. In fact, 28 states have trade offices located in Japan for both those objectives.

The National Association of State Development Agencies
(NASDA) reports that at last count at least 30 states were operating
a total of 67 offices in 15 countries overseas. Further, this same
association reports that states now spend almost $40 million a year
on export promotion and attracting foreign direct investment (often
called "reverse investment"). This is an increase of nearly $12 mil-
lion in the past two years, with the average state expenditure on
trade promotion now $980,000.

After your visit to the U.S. Department of Commerce district
office, you would be wise to also contact the agency in your state
designated to promote trade. (See listing of members of NASDA,
complete with addresses and phone numbers, in the Appendix.)

Another agency to contact is called the *Small Business Development Center* (SBDC). This is often a joint service funded by both
federal and state funds. There are between 400 and 500 of these
centers around the United States, but there is not one in every state.
For a listing of SBDC headquarters state-by-state, see the list in the
Appendix. Certain states have developed their SBDCs into extremely valuable resources for small businesses, assisting with

everything from start-up to technology development to patent evaluation to exporting.

The most active support area for states appears to be in financing. Some 23 states have passed legislation to create export finance assistance. This assistance ranges from seed money at low interest rates to pre-shipment loans for labor, material and other expenses, to post-export loans (or loan guarantees) to permit an exporter to provide more flexible terms for the foreign buyer. Until states began to take some of this burden, the only alternative for businesses that were unable to get commercial loans was with the Export-Import Bank.

As we will see in Chapter 8 on Financing and Payments, financing for export is extremely important. In order to export, businesses often need guarantees to protect their bankers from loss in case the businesses fail to deliver their products abroad, and they need insurance in case they cannot collect when they do deliver. Small businesses have the hardest time, according to L. Fargo Wells, director of California's Export Financing Authority. "They're too small for the big banks, and the smaller banks don't want to touch deals with foreign receivables" because of the difficulties of putting together an international transaction and the risk of not being able to collect. As a result, many states now offer financing programs and five states have even joined to form the Mid-South Regional Trade Council (Arkansas, Alabama, Louisiana, Mississippi, and Tennessee).

Here is a cross-section of states and a sampling of their individual programs designed to stimulate trade:

▶ Montana's Governor Ted Schwinden was the guest of honor at a large beef fair in Tokyo and his state now exports 90 tons of beef to beef-starved Japan.

▶ Both Alaska and Wisconsin have established a special relationship with Heilongjiang Province in the People's Republic of China to which Alaska now sends $40 million a year in exports of timber, fertilizer, and oil-related products.

▶ Wisconsin's Governor Tommy G. Thompson, in his first two years of office, led five trade missions abroad and helped create a World Trade Center in Milwaukee. In addition, his Advisory Council on International Trade has created mentor programs, established honorary attachés in seven countries, briefed all state legislators on trade issues, entertained 65 Consul Generals from the Chicago area, and generally raised the level of awareness and interest throughout the state which records $4.5 billion each year in exports.

▶ Oklahoma found a market for its oil-drilling equipment by opening the first state trade office in India.

▶ Maryland offers matching grants to counties that join together and come up with innovative ideas for exporting. Director Harold Zassenhaus calls his work with medium- and small-sized businesses "hand-holding" but has helped market abroad soft-shell crabs, wooden toys, medical equipment, and dredges. His office even helped a Maryland firm that manufactures wave-making machines for amusement park wave pools sell its product to a French boat designer for use in stress-testing of sailboat hulls.

▶ New York got an early start with export promotion when Governor Nelson A. Rockefeller launched his program in the early 1960s. Today, they rely on developing "trade leads" for state businesses and have established working relationships with 11,000 businesses in New York State. Further, New York has established trade offices in London, Wiesbaden, Tokyo, Montreal, Toronto, Dublin, and Milan.

Even at city and county levels support for international trade is springing up. The Community Development Trading Group is a cooperative made up of cities from around the United States. With headquarters in Providence, RI, director Mark Tigan explains why small businesses need help: "They need to know who the actors are, who does what at what stage of the game and where to go to get things done."

Fifty-two cities have named official protocol officers to assure that relationships with overseas visitors are handled with diplomacy and tact. St. Paul, MN has a trade director for the city itself and helps sell locally made products via video films sent to overseas trade shows.

Port cities are especially active. Cities like Miami, New Orleans, Seattle, and Los Angeles—all have burgeoning export promotion programs.

From 1983 to 1985, Madison County, AL sold $1 billion worth of goods to buyers overseas, probably qualifying it for the largest and most ambitious county trade program in the country.

The list of city, county, and state initiatives grows each year. Your trade specialist at DoC will know who, what, when, and where activities are available to assist you. This is further affirmation that the timing is right for international trade. One US&FCS official put it this way, "In the 1960s, it was the environment; in the 1970s, it was energy; and in the 1980s, it's trade. Trade is the area into which you can put money and resources and get public approval."

FOREIGN TRADE ZONES

If you are currently importing any parts or subassemblies for your product, or if you are considering this for the future, you should acquaint yourself with the possible advantages offered by Foreign Trade Zones (FTZs).

These zones are permitted by the U.S. government and growth and activity within them are booming. At this writing, there are a total of 247 FTZs scattered among 47 states and Puerto Rico. In 1975, there were only 27. About $40 billion of goods moved through them in 1986. All three major U.S. auto makers use them along with many of America's largest companies.

An FTZ is defined by law as an "isolated, enclosed, and policed area, operated as a public utility, in or adjacent to a port of entry, furnished with facilities for lading, unlading, handling, storing, manipulating, manufacturing, and exhibiting goods, and for reshipping them by land, water, or air."

The purpose is to encourage final processing in the United States of a variety of imported goods rather than having that processing take place in the country of origin. This special concession by the government may reduce the value of imports, thus, improving the U.S. balance of trade. It may also create jobs by employing people in the zones and by causing increased production of U.S.-made components that are incorporated into imported goods.

The National Association of Foreign Trade Zones explains them this way:

A Foreign Trade Zone is a site within the United States, at or near a U.S. customs port of entry, where foreign and domestic merchandise is generally considered to be in international commerce. Foreign or domestic merchandise may enter this enclave without a formal customs entry or the payment of custom duties or government excise taxes.

Merchandise entering a zone may be:

Stored	Mixed
Tested	Cleaned
Sampled	Assembled
Relabeled	Manufactured
Repackaged	Salvaged
Displayed	Destroyed
Repaired	Processed
Manipulated	

If the final product is exported from the United States, no U.S. custom duty or excise tax is levied. If, however, the final product is imported into the United States, customs duty and excise taxes are due only at the time of transfer from the Foreign Trade Zone and formal entry in the United States. The duty paid is the lower of that applicable to the product itself or its component parts. Thus, zones provide opportunities to realize customs duty savings by zone users. In addition, zone procedures provide one of the most flexible methods of handling domestic and imported merchandise.

As we have learned, FTZs are useful to exporters if and when they bring imported parts or subassemblies into the United States, combine them with a U.S.-made product, and then export the final product. Thus, the benefits include savings on customs duty, indefinite storage time of goods to allow an exporter to ship goods out of the zone at the most favorable time, and side-benefits such as local quality control and local employment.

While in this area of importing parts, combining them with U.S.-made components and then exporting them, you should probably be aware of the term duty drawback. The U.S. government allows you to import certain parts *without* paying duty on them at the time if they are ultimately intended for export. The rationale is to encourage American commerce or manufacturing to compete in foreign markets without the handicap of additional cost from duties paid to import materials, parts, or components that are eventually exported. You must either pay the duty and request repayment later (called a drawback), or the government will allow you to post a bond which insures those duty payments. In the case of posting the bond, you import the parts and then export them at a later date while keeping meticulous records to verify that they were, indeed, exported. You recover 99 percent of the import duty, the remaining 1 percent going to the U.S. government to help defray its costs. To obtain a drawback, your must first prepare a proposal and file it with a Regional Commissioner of Customs for 1313(a) drawback.

You have three to five years to export the imported item, and payment of the drawback can, under certain conditions, be paid to you within two months, but, in this case, you must file for an *accelerated payment.*

The availability of Foreign Trade Zones and features like duty drawback may be superfluous to a company just starting to look at the export process, but these are services made available by federal law and it may be useful to at least be acquainted with them. They could prove valuable at a later time.

SUMMARY

At this point, you are well and truly launched on your journey of exploring international trade. You have learned that exporting is different from doing business within the United States, but not drastically so. The common sense and logic that caused you to develop a solid U.S. base will serve you equally well as you look at the horizon of trade overseas.

Your desktop research has already begun. You have been introduced to the diverse services offered by the U.S. government, and paid for by you, the taxpayer. Likewise, your state government probably also provides advice, counsel, and maybe even financial incentives.

The next chapter will explain and describe other organizations that you should investigate as part of your preliminary research. At the end of that chapter, you should be about ready to draft a marketing plan outline. If you believe more market research is required before making the all-important commitment, some ideas and sources for aid are listed at the end of that chapter.

3

Additional Help

The back-up bench in international trade reads like an All-Star game.

Trade Consultant

While the U.S. government is both first base and the starting lineup for assistance, it is by no means the only source of help. World Trade Centers, local trade associations, clubs, universities, chambers of commerce, private consultants, export management companies, private trading firms, market research services, and even vocational school systems are part of the support team.

In this chapter, we will examine these resources so you have a nodding acquaintanceship with each. Again, your helpful trade specialist in the U.S. Department of Commerce district office should already be aware of this reservoir of assistance and be able to advise what portions might be most suitable to you in your particular case and in your particular region.

Finally, at the end of this chapter we will suggest an outline for a first draft of a marketing plan that will then bring you to that critical crossroads we called *commitment*.

WORLD TRADE CENTERS

While there are currently 70 World Trade Centers (WTCs) around the world, with another 19 in the planning stages, the idea in America first materialized in Houston as far back as 1927. There the objective was to encourage foreign commerce and the growth of the Port of Houston and other Texas ports. New Orleans was another of the earlier North American world trade centers, established in 1943 to "promote world peace, trade, and understanding." This Center is very important to Louisiana because the state lacks a manufacturing base but has an excellent year-round port. The New York World Trade Center was created in 1962 by the New York and New Jersey legislatures. The Port Authority there financed and built the World Trade Center which now serves as the headquarters for the Association of World Trade Centers around the world.

While these WTCs provide a locus, or gathering point, for people interested in trade, probably the most attractive, visible feature is an electronic *network*. This allows members (you must pay a membership fee to belong to a WTC) to quickly and economically relay information to all or to selective members of other WTCs around the world. The WTC Association claims this network service is capable of reaching 1.7 million readers at more than 400,000 international trading firms from Abidjan in the Ivory Coast to Xian in the People's Republic of China.

In reality, the network is nothing more than a high-tech bulletin board or messaging system that provides trade leads and a data base with others who have subscribed to the system.

You, as a WTC member, subscribe to the service by paying for the right to print a short message on the electronic system. Here are some examples:

▸ Under the heading "To Sell," you might find varied messages (abbreviated here) such as "bearings from China" or "world famous Bar-B-Que mesquite charcoal for export" or "960 cases Marlboro cigarets" or "Military footwear, steel toes, below wholesale."

▸ Under the heading "To Buy," you might find: "1 million glass jars" or "3000 turkeys per month for a customer in Brazil" or "50 tons of shrimp a month for a customer in Switzerland" or "47,000 tons of seed potatoes" or "50,000 underwater speakers."

Member-subscribers tap into the international bulletin board by ordinary telephone lines and a personal computer in their office, home, or even a hotel room. They also have access to a data base that will list addresses, lines of business, and banking relationships of other members. Using the network, an exporter can obtain names and addresses of all importers of underwater speakers, seed potatoes, shrimp, or whatever.

World Trade Centers commonly offer other services. Depending on the sophistication of the WTC nearest you, they can usually be counted on to provide some combination of the following services:

1. *Education.* In cooperation with local universities, government organizations, and private consultants, WTCs will sponsor, stage, or host programs on trade with specific countries or on new developments in international trade.

2. *Club services.* Private dining and meeting room facilities are often provided. This may be a private club within the WTC for members only or an arrangement with another restaurant or club for use of a portion of their facilities.

3. *Information services.* These may include a data bank that may be tied into government, associations of commerce, or university facilities. It also often contains a directory of all available sources of specialized industry and population data for the area. A library and newsletter are two additional information services often offered.

4. *Hosting.* These centers are usually an excellent first stop for foreign visitors. The center staff will often arrange meetings with specific individuals in the business community and receptions where appropriate.

5. *Trade missions.* These are often coordinated with other agencies interested in encouraging international trade and directed at markets with strong trade potential.

6. *Exhibit space.* Centers often have exhibit space available. Some even have complete convention facilities such as in Boston, New Orleans, London, Singapore, Amsterdam, Tokyo, and Seoul. They may also offer simultaneous translation capabilities.

7. *Temporary office space.* The traveling business person can usually obtain temporary office space with access to telex, facsimile, PC computer, and word processing. These are usually available on a cost-for-service basis.

8. *Hotel discounts.* Hotel discounts are usually available in a nearby first class hotel. Discounts generally range from 20

to 30 percent off list prices. Some WTCs also offer hotel or sleeping room accommodations as part of the complex such as in New York, London, Vancouver, and Amsterdam.

A list of existing World Trade Centers can be found in the Appendix.

LOCAL TRADE ASSOCIATIONS

Many metropolitan areas have associations formed to represent and promote international trade. Size may range from less than 50 members to as many as 600. Like any industry or trade association, these groups meet periodically for dinners and programs, or stage seminars or workshops on timely trade matters.

Qualifications for membership vary from group to group but you will usually find them open, friendly, and anxious to admit anyone interested and involved in international trade. Many of the members, as you might expect, are from the service side of the field—that means they represent companies that offer insurance, shipping, financing, customs brokerage, and other services related to trade. The remainder will be from industry, agriculture, education, or government.

These association meetings offer an excellent common ground on which to become personally acquainted with professionals in international trade. Unfortunately, there is no common term or name for these groups, but your DoC trade specialist will undoubtedly be acquainted with the one closest to you.

UNIVERSITIES AND COLLEGES

More and more state and private educational institutions are becoming involved in international trade. While this usually consists of undergraduate classes and, in some cases, graduate degree programs in international business, the activity that you should explore is the outreach program. This refers to classes, programs, seminars, and even trade missions offered to business people in the area. For example, a common service is to provide a course in export shipping and documentation.

Local universities and colleges also are good sources for reference materials, translators, faculty who may serve as consultants, and even graduate students who—under faculty supervision—are sometimes available for outside research projects.

Like trade associations, there is no single, commonly agreed on designation for this resource within colleges and universities but you will usually find them associated with either business schools or foreign language departments. In other schools, they may be a part of those departments offering continuing education classes.

CHAMBERS OF COMMERCE

Local or state chambers of commerce may have special sections or subcommittees that concentrate on international trade. They may even be the host organization for the local trade association or club. Local chambers also often sponsor seminars and "how to" sessions on exporting that are valuable to attend. In the area of "reverse" investment, your local chamber might be among the first to learn if and when a foreign investor is examining your city as a site for a factory, distribution center, or some other major investment. In these cases, the chamber becomes an important part of the selling team and also helps welcome new executives to the community. Whatever the case, you will probably find some complementary relationship between these local chambers and your exploration of international trade. Therefore, it is worth inquiring at these chambers about the types of services and activities they offer.

PRIVATE CONSULTANTS AND EXPORT MANAGEMENT COMPANIES

As you realize that international trade is complex yet filled with opportunities, it will be no great surprise to learn that a thriving and helpful cadre of private consulting and service firms is available. A list of these is probably as close as your nearest telephone book. Alternatively, your DoC trade specialist probably has a list already prepared. As is wise in choosing any specialist for help, ask to speak to some previous clients to obtain references for the firm or individual you choose.

In the private consultant category, size ranges from large national consulting firms such as Arthur Young International in Washington, DC, to one-man firms operating out of their homes. Depending on the size, experience, and specialization, these consultants offer services such as helping select the right entry markets, helping determine how best to enter a market and when, identifying possible product modifications, advising on pricing and marketing strategies, and generally providing advice of all kinds as you prepare to participate in foreign trade. Whether you choose a private consultant is a purely personal decision based on timeliness, cost, experience of the consultant, and your own personal comfort level with the firm or individual.

On the other hand, Export Management Companies (EMCs) are exactly what the name implies. An earlier title and designation was CEMs which stood for Combined Export Managers, but that has given way in recent years to EMCs.

An EMC will offer to "act as your export department," selling your products overseas along with other, usually allied but noncompetitive product lines. People who head EMCs have usually come from the export departments of larger firms and ventured out for themselves. There are well over 1000 EMCs throughout the country. You can learn the names of the ones in your region from the DoC trade specialist, or, if you want a free national listing, write to: Superintendent of Documents, U.S. Government Printing Office, Washington, DC 20402.

Just exactly what does an EMC do? Here is a list of services offered by most EMCs:

- Does market research to help determine where you have the best opportunities to sell your product
- Travels overseas on your behalf to examine markets and contact potential customers
- Appoints overseas distributors or commission sales agents
- Exhibits your products in international trade shows
- Handles routine steps in getting your product to the overseas customer, such as export documentation, shipping, insurance, banking, etc.
- Arranges finance terms and assures payment to you
- Prepares correspondence in the required foreign language
- Advises on patent and trademark protection

▶ Ships merchandise from several manufacturers together at lower, negotiated rates

In summary, your EMC will advertise that it "can be your entire export department," providing experience while handling all the necessary details of selling and shipping overseas.

EMCs operate on either a buy-and-sell arrangement, or on a straight commission basis. In the former, the EMC places the order with you, takes title to the merchandise and then turns around and sells it to the end customer. Under a commission arrangement, the EMC acts as your exclusive sales representative for certain markets or regions or even the whole world and simply charges a sales commission for its services. Commissions vary from 7.5 to 20 percent of the wholesale distributor price.

Most EMCs insist on a contract for at least 3 to 5 years. The reason for this is that it sometimes takes a full year or longer to develop customers overseas. Without this measure of protection, the EMC could establish the sales chain and, once in place, you could eliminate the EMC as the middleman.

When considering an EMC, it is important to select the right type of firm for your product. Many EMCs are specialists. One may specialize in air-conditioning equipment, another in enzymes, and still another in farm machinery. As in selecting any private consultant or service agency, it is important to interview them carefully, check on references, and generally assure yourself of the competency and proven performance of that firm.

If, in this examination of international trade and what is right for your company, you decide you do not have the time, personnel, or money to develop foreign markets but you still see opportunities, then hiring an EMC may be the right decision.

There are, however, some limitations of EMCs such as:

▶ EMCs are usually small and may have limited financial resources. If they operate on a buy-sell arrangement, they will probably only buy from you when they have a firm order from a customer. Thus, they may not stock your product which then slows the supply line and may result in lost sales.

▶ EMCs are like other wholesalers who focus their efforts on the most profitable business. New lines, or those with limited potential, may be overlooked.

▶ By using EMCs, you lose some control over sales. You must assume that the EMC is giving you your fair share of energy, but that is often difficult to judge.

▶ Some foreign buyers may resist buying from EMCs, preferring to deal directly with the manufacturer.

▶ Your product is usually one among many that the EMC is selling.

The EMC has many advantages but some disadvantages as well. It may be a quick and easy method to enter the world of export, but as a middleman the EMC adds to the cost that may make your product less competitive overseas.

EXPORT TRADING COMPANIES

In a general way, Export Trading Companies (ETCs) act in the same manner as EMCs. Both provide services on behalf of a variety of clients and either may take title to some or all of the merchandise it exports. EMCs tend to concentrate on exporting, while ETCs engage in import and export between different countries. In addition, ETCs may engage directly in production, transportation, distribution, financing, and even resource development. EMCs, as we have learned, act as a wholesaler or intermediary between you and export customers abroad.

Export Trading Companies are not abundant in the United States, however, your DoC trade specialist will know where the nearest one is and if and how it specializes.

A distinction should be made between private Export Trading Companies and those permitted by the Trade Act of 1982 which are called government certified ETCs. The latter was a long-considered and innovative step by the federal government which allows firms in a common industry to form specialized trading companies, also called ETCs, for the purpose of international trade. At this writing, 91 of these have been formed since the law was passed. The chief advantage is that after the somewhat complex task of achieving government sanction, these ETCs can consist of firms normally in competition with one another. Further, they are exempt from anti-trust enforcement in the United States if they consult one another on pricing. (This must be pricing for export only.) Note that these government certified ETCs are exempt from anti-trust enforcement in the United States; this does not exempt them from anti-trust regulations in other countries, if such regulations exist.

The largest general (noncertified) ETC in the United States is Mitsui Trading Co. This Japanese-owned firm also happens to be the fourth largest exporter in the United States.

As you explore alternative ways to sell your product overseas, be certain to take time to become knowledgeable about EMCs, private consultants, and ETCs. They just might offer the right solution in your particular situation.

THE MARKETING PLAN

When your desktop research has been completed, you should consider drafting a marketing plan. It's very likely that one has been forming in your head or among your many notes and files, but here are some of the key points this plan should cover. The following outline will help you organize your thoughts:

I.   Objectives

What am I trying to achieve?

What advantages will international trade bring in my unique situation?

II. Self-Assessment

What indications do I have that my product can be sold overseas?

What have I learned from my research about the potential for my product in overseas markets? Does there appear to be an opportunity? What are the obstacles?

III. Resources

Do we have the capacity for extra sales?

Am I prepared to modify my product for overseas markets if the rewards are attractive enough?

Do I have the time to devote to the next steps? Who will manage this new activity?

IV. Financial Pro Forma

How much has this investigation cost so far?

How much do I estimate it will cost to proceed to the next steps, namely trips overseas?

What additional costs might be involved if new orders come in? Example: Will we have to add people in the shipping department?

Will there be additional expense in tying up inventory for export?

What is a reasonable expectation for revenue in the first year? In the second, third and fourth years?

V. Next Steps

What is my flow chart of activities if I am given approval to proceed? Which markets look most promising? What sequence of steps will I follow?

How long will it take and how much will it cost?

When and how will I evaluate results?

Whatever marketing plan outline you adopt, the whole purpose should be to lay out the facts as known at this stage in order to present a proposal to your management which will lead to either a decision to stop, or to modify the plan, or to proceed. *If you decide to proceed, it is essential at this stage to obtain a firm commitment from management.* Every experienced person in international trade, every consultant, every seminar will stress this point.

A commitment is necessary because, for example, you may be asking for $50,000 and one year to launch the company into exporting, with meager returns in the first year, breakeven in the second, and substantial net profit in the third. In order to stay the course, it is critical to have a commitment. Without that pledge, your international trade initiative will be considered a step-child or poor relative who gets second class treatment when it comes to financing, service, product allocations, and general backing. It is not uncommon to see a company with a part-time export manager who is told "Sell and ship only when we have the product available, and don't give them any special terms or selling arrangements. Use our domestic sales materials and pricing and above all remember that our domestic business has top priority in every circumstance." That attitude is comparable to saying "If we must change any of our procedures, we don't want the business." Or, "Sell to all the other states in the United States, but when business comes in from the West Coast, we're just not that interested."

The more positive attitude is seen in medium- and small-sized businesses where the CEO himself or herself is the agent of change. In these cases, the CEO goes on a trade mission, or attends an overseas trade exhibition, or merely decides now is the time for the company to launch itself into the rest of the world. These are usually where the success stories are born, because the CEO automatically provides that quintessential ingredient, *commitment.*

SUMMARY

There are two teams available to support you in your quest for ways to enter international trade. The first is government-sponsored and the second is in the private sector. Both squads are growing larger and gaining strength each year.

On the public side, there is little or no opposition in either Congress or past administrations, whichever the political party, for exporting. The first line of debate in government over international trade argues over how little or how much protectionism is proper. The pendulum of protectionism swung to the far right, or conservative side, in 1933 with the Smoot-Hawley Bill. That bill intended to protect American manufacturers during the onset of the Depression by raising high tariff barriers around the perimeter of the United States, effectively cutting off imports. Instead, it had just the opposite effect. Trading partners retaliated and our export customers disappeared and jobs were lost. Instead of healing the growing wounds caused by the Depression, it exacerbated it. From this lesson in history, Congress has generally worked toward the carefully crafted phrase *freer trade.* Notice this does not say *free* trade, which suggests a totally open market. Instead, it represents the view that trading interdependence is solidly established and we must keep the trading lanes open . . . but there will be violations of trade pacts and individual situations where the administration and Congress must thump the table and demand fairness and equality and enact, or threaten to enact, retaliatory legislation. A policy of *freer trade* has generally prevailed through several administrations with the result that services and support from Washington, DC have improved and grown dramatically.

In the private sector there is an expanding roster of clubs, centers, campuses, and consultants available to assist you. It is significant that 10 years ago, any one person well-versed in international trade could probably enumerate most of the aids and agencies at work to support exporting and other facets of international trade. Today, because of the rising levels of concern, interest, and activity, there are so many that no one person can possibly know all of the public and private services. The result is that for any planned journey overseas, the individual business person, no matter the product or the size or the resources, has a cadre of professional assistance available.

Now it is time to plan that first trip. This can be an enjoyable and challenging time. It is time to carefully examine the different methods of entering world trade, establishing the objectives and, most important, avoiding mistakes wherever possible. Chapter 4 should help you with each of those challenges.

4

Planning the First Trip

You gotta know the territory!

In Meredith Willson's classic musical, *The Music Man,* the opening scene takes place aboard a 1920s train crossing the flatlands of Iowa. The first musical number is sung by a group of traveling salesmen, called *drummers* in those days. Their musical message is that to be a truly successful salesman, "You gotta know the territory!" The lead singer is a salesman of anvils. Imagine, if you will, a more challenging assignment than selling anvils.

Selling in the overseas market is, assuredly, easier than selling anvils across the Middle West in the 1920s, but the admonition, "you gotta know the territory," still applies. If there is one cardinal rule that all experienced international managers agree upon it is this: There is no substitute for getting out into the marketplace. One veteran calls it "foot-slogging," a British term that means "to trudge like an infantryman" implying that in sales there is no alternative to slogging through the mud, water and wastelands in search of sales.

Some beginners to world trade will view world travel as both a blessing and a reward—a dream fulfilled to travel to faraway lands. And so it is . . . especially for the first few trips. But just like feasting on a steady diet of chocolate sundaes, the glamor and sweetness can wear off. Richard Brewer, a 20-year veteran of sales in the Pacific Basin quipped that he considered petitioning his management to go off salary and on to mileage, figuring he would earn far more money on the basis of miles traveled. Further, he said his wife was becoming so accustomed to sleeping alone that when he did return home, she would wake up screaming that there was a strange man in her bed. Still another experienced world marketer, working on his sixth filled passport, noted that "Anyone who thinks constant world travel is all glamor must be part of a front organization for Pepto-Bismol."

Upset stomachs aside, there are ways to mix business with pleasure in international travel and ease some of the discomfort. For example, frequent flyer awards permit taking a spouse on a combination vacation and business trip overseas. There is also usually time for some sightseeing, and can include some of the truly great wonders of the world. There may also be unexpected rewards. After traveling to Hong Kong four times a year for several years, I finally managed to take my wife along ostensibly for a vacation; it resulted in her setting up her own business importing Chinese antique wood temple carvings to the United States.

First, travel is essential to success in international trade, and second, it involves equal parts of new fairylands and numbing fatigue. So, be forewarned.

HOW TO BEGIN

Your homework done, your marketing plan outlined, it is now time to consider the first venture abroad. It could take many forms, for example:

▶ Attend an overseas trade show featuring your industry; this is probably the most common way to test the waters.

▶ Join in on a trade mission, organized by your industry or your state or some other group; this is especially attractive because much of the hassle of travel arrangements and accommodations is handled by the organizer, and if your mission leader is a high-placed official, this facilitates meeting important counterpart officials in the country you are visiting.

▶ Participate in the Department of Commerce's *Matchmaker* program, described in Chapter 2. These are special events scheduled in major cities around the world especially designed for new-to-export medium- and small-sized companies. Commerce will take 20 to 25 such firms in a common industry, like agribusiness or computer-related products, and arrange for one-on-one meetings with prescreened candidates who might serve as distributors or licensees. This is a new program inaugurated by DoC in 1988.

▸ Employ an EMC or other consultant to show you the ropes, save time, and beam in on the highest potential markets and customers.

▸ Fly off to the markets you have identified with the highest potential.

Whichever the mode, the next critical step is to plan and implement a trip, samples in hand, to "get to know the territory."

Before embarking, there are two nuggets of information you will want to refine and store in your mental briefcase. First, you should understand that there are several different ways of gaining distribution in a foreign country—using U.S.-based agents, appointing exclusive distributors, licensing, and joint ventures, just to name four. Second, the exportation of some products is regulated by the U.S. government and these products must be approved or licensed before they can be shipped. Let's examine each of these.

Types of Distribution

There are two basic categories—*direct* and *indirect*—and the terms are almost self-explanatory. The difference between them is that with indirect you employ a middleman usually located in the United States and that intermediary develops and handles your sales to overseas markets. With the direct form of distribution, obviously, you deal directly with your sales channels in overseas markets.

Whether you use direct or indirect forms will depend on several factors including amount of time and capital you are willing to invest in your campaign, previous export experience, complexity of target markets, availability of competent intermediaries, whether you can remain competitive in the end market with the additional expense of middlemen, and so on.

Indirect distribution can take several forms:

▶ *The export jobber, wholesaler, or broker.* Here you sell to an independent firm in the United States who finds an overseas customer for your product. You have the least control but also the least risk since it is usually a sale on U.S. domestic soil.

▶ *Commission house or manufacturer's representative.* These firms usually seek out overseas customers for your product or service and take a commission on the sale. Most often, these deal in engineered industrial products or highly technical products and involve negotiated sales contracts, installation engineering and after-sales service.

▶ *Export agent or Export Management Company (EMC) described in Chapter 3.* The word agent is highly important and often misused, even by experienced world traders. Attorneys experienced in international trade will advise care and caution in talking about sales agents or, indeed, any type of agent. The reason is that according to most legal interpretations, an agent is empowered to act on your behalf. Therefore, be wary of talking about appointing agents unless you are willing to entrust them to make commitments on your behalf and, in that case, have a clear written agreement covering that relationship.

To review the function of a EMC, it does the following: finds customers, handles other noncompeting lines, is often a specialist in your product category, operates on a commission, may or may not take title to the goods being sold, helps in financing and shipping, assists in general marketing chores, and most often requires an exclusive contract covering specific territories and over a specified period of time.

▶ *Export trading companies.* These were explained in Chapter 3. They operate much like EMCs but are usually larger, have firm distribution channels or even subsidiary selling companies overseas, normally buy the product from you and resell to a market or customer it has cultivated overseas, and so on.

All indirect forms of distribution have certain common pros and cons: they reduce your risk and save your energy and capital, but they add cost to the end user which may make your product less competitive and, as with any middleman, you lose control and must battle for their time and attention.

Direct distribution takes longer to establish and more management time to administer, but those drawbacks are offset by shorter, more efficient pathways to your end user.

By far the most common form of direct distribution is a *distributor*. They may be called overseas or foreign distributors or, depending on your arrangement, an exclusive distributor. Whatever the variation, this is a firm in a foreign country who is experienced in importing your type of product and selling it in that market. Such a distributor customarily has exclusiveness for your product in that market and, in return, should not carry directly competitive lines. They expect to buy from you at the lowest possible discounted price. Precisely what range of services you can expect from this type of distributor and what support it can expect from you is detailed more fully in Chapter 10. As explained, this is the most popular and common form of foreign representation and, consequently, much of the language in this book will deal with appointing, managing, and motivating distributors. There are, of course, other means of direct foreign distribution and these will be explained next and many of the management methods described in this book apply equally to them. Here are some other variations on the basic distributor.

▸ *Sell to foreign retailers.* There is nothing to prevent you from selling your product directly to foreign retailers. A subform is the exclusive retailer for a given market, but this usually occurs in a very small trading area.

▸ *Direct sales to end-users.* It is common, of course, to be a supplier directly to a manufacturer or processer in any given foreign market. In this case, you deal directly with the purchasing department. Other direct buyers can be banks, hospitals, and other institutions as well as foreign governments.

▸ *Establish your own sales office in a foreign country.* This form of direct distribution is used only when either the potential or actual demand for your product warrants the cost of part-time or full-time employees, rent, and other expenses associated with a branch sales office. Opening a branch office in Japan, for instance, can be extremely expensive. One Midwestern company calculated that placing three

U.S. executives in a small sales office in Tokyo cost them in excess of one million dollars per year.

▶ *Appoint commissioned representatives.* A variation on having your own branch sales office is to appoint commissioned sales representatives or manufacturers representatives within a foreign market. This can be very effective especially if and when local warehousing is required. Another variation is local franchising using either independent franchises, company-owned franchises, or a combination of both.

▶ *License, assemble, and manufacture.* These are considered as giant steps forward in comparison to simply appointing overseas sales reps and distributors because it usually involves assignment of patents or unpatented know-how. Licensing becomes more complex because of the legal implications and the sometimes problematic area of receiving royalties or equity or both. You can either grant the right to others to assemble or manufacture your product, or you can invest in local assembly or manufacturing yourself, or arrange joint ventures. There are dozens of permutations within this general category: cross-licensing, consortiums, purchasing an equity interest in an existing local operation, using free trade zones, join a third-country partner, and so on.

The licensing of technology is described by the U.S. Department of Commerce as "a contractual arrangement in which the licensor's patents, trademarks, service marks, copyrights, or know-how may be sold or otherwise made available to a licensee for compensation negotiated in advance between the parties." The compensation is usually in the form of royalties. The advantages of this type of licensing are as follows: allows quick entry to a market, reduces investment risks, overcomes many tariff and nontariff barriers, and uses local expertise to market your product.

Another form of technology licensing is franchising. Most common among service companies, the licensor is called the *franchisor* and the licensee is the *franchisee*. The franchisor usually supports the franchisee with counseling on how to run the business plus advertising and accounting help. The franchisor will also often provide training plus materials and sometimes even products. An excellent example of a service industry succeeding overseas is Manpower Inc., the largest supplier of temporary help services in the United States. Over 60 percent of Manpower's total revenues comes from its foreign operations. Manpower either has its own wholly-owned subsidiary in a foreign market or establishes franchises.

Technology licensing also has its drawbacks. First, royalties from licensing are usually much less than profits generated from direct exporting. Second, the licensor has less control over the product, in this case licensed technology, than it would have over direct exportation. Third, in certain countries, it may be difficult to protect the licensed technology from unauthorized use by others. Fourth, the licensee may find ways to use your technology to produce products or services that are used in other markets, thereby competing directly with you in those markets. This latter problem can be overcome by specific conditions in the license agreement concerning geographic territory and by careful registration and enforcement of foreign patent, trademark, and copyright laws.

Here are some checkpoints regarding technology licensing: research the licensor carefully, just as you would a distributor; determine if you must obtain prior approval from the host country's government for a licensing agreement and for the remittance of royalties; make certain your technology licensing does not run afoul of the U.S. or foreign antitrust laws; and, finally, be certain to obtain legal advice in both the United States and the host country before embarking on any technology licensing compact.

▶ Joint ventures would probably appear next on the ladder of sophistication of different forms of direct distribution in international trade. This term has the same connotation and implications as in U.S. domestic business with the same advantages and disadvantages. However, in some foreign markets you will find that host governments will require that local nationals own 51 percent of the co-venture. Mexico is a good example of this restriction. The attraction of this option is that you gain the knowledge and perhaps influence of your local partner while also spreading your risk, but the disadvantage is sharing control and encountering possible disagreements with your partner over policies and practices. As with technology licensing, you would be well advised to obtain experienced legal counsel both in the United States and in the foreign market before proceeding with any form of joint venture agreement.

▸ Wholly owned subsidiaries are the major league form of attaining direct distribution overseas. The principle advantage is 100 percent control and undiluted profits while the major disadvantage is the risk taken by investing your capital in a foreign country. In the area of control, you can transfer your technology safely and securely, knowing that it will be guarded carefully by your own employees. Host countries also frequently offer attractive incentives to encourage this type of major investment. Federal and local governments customarily have economic development specialists available to help you in many ways including applying for incentives, obtaining permits, pointing out attractive sites, advising on local contractors, informing you on local labor laws, explaining tax requirements, plus other services. These are usually provided on a free and yet confidential basis. When considering building an operation in a foreign country, the best place to start is with these economic development offices in each country and then within each state or province of that country.

As for the disadvantages in a wholly owned subsidiary operation in a foreign country, your investment there will depend to a large extent on the political and economic stability of that country. Also, while those host markets may offer tax and other incentives to locate there, many have strict registration procedures and requirements. Furthermore, in many countries you can only withdraw profits, usually in the form of dividends, according to fixed percentages of your registered invested capital. This is done to prevent draining a successful operation of all its revenues and profits, going deeply into debt, and then simply closing that operation and moving on to another country.

If you are new to export, each of these different forms of distribution to foreign markets should be considered. Most likely, in your desktop research with the DoC trade specialist, you have already decided on the most suitable forms. Now, as you pack for your trip, these varied modes of distribution should be periodically reviewed as you examine opportunities in a specific market or region.

EXPORT LICENSE REGULATIONS

It will surprise even some veteran exporters to learn that *all* exports from the United States are controlled by the government through two types of licenses: *general* and *validated*. Most products fall under the "general" category where no application need be submitted to the Department of Commerce and where no documentation is issued by them. A general license is, therefore, a blanket license granted automatically to a host of product categories for shipment to almost all destinations. There are managers who have been involved in international trade for decades who never realized they were actually operating under a government license.

The validated license category is, however, an entirely different matter. You fall into this category if your product is one or more of the following: a "strategic" commodity, a "short supply" commodity, "unpublished" technical data, and if the destination is one where the United States has foreign policy concerns or even embargoes, such as in Cuba, North Korea, Cambodia, and Vietnam. This category also applies to high technology parts or products destined for the Soviet Union and other Eastern European countries. Before becoming unduly concerned about all this, if you have followed the advice in Chapter 2, your trade specialist at DoC has probably already advised if you require validated licenses.

A validated license is loaded with specifics. It allows a specific exporter to export a particular product to a certain destination. Validated licenses are granted on a case-by-case basis for a single transaction and normally have a two-year validity. For those wishing to become thoroughly acquainted with this topic, obtain a copy of the complete "Export Administration Regulations" from your trade specialist.

For many years, exporters requiring validation complained that the lengthy processing time for validated licenses often put them at a competitive disadvantage. Competitors from other countries were able to make quotations and assure shipment and delivery faster than a U.S. exporter, they argued. Late in 1987, the DoC took steps to hasten the license processing times. Among other efficiencies, new electronic systems were installed to speed up the system.

One department within DoC is responsible for the administration of these export controls. It is called the Bureau of Export Administration (BXA). Instructional courses explaining how these regulations apply are offered by DoC at various locations across the United States. You can obtain the course schedule from your trade specialist.

OBJECTIVES FOR THE FIRST TRIP

Having filed away this information on the different types of distribution and government licenses, it is time to plan your first trip. Let's examine some objectives:

▶ To examine first-hand the markets you have selected. To verify and amplify the information you have collected in your desktop research. To study the competition, the conditions, the attitudes, the burdens—in a word, the potential.

▶ If there is potential, to determine which type of distribution may be best for your product: direct sales to end user, appointment of a distributor, appointment of a commissioned salesperson or manufacturer's representative, etc.

▶ To establish contacts for more information: bankers, embassy commercial attachés, American Chambers of Commerce in that country, trade associations, interpreters and other local consultants, airlines and other transporters, import brokerage houses; in short, anyone who might contribute to your store of information.

▶ To determine if more formal market research is required to pinpoint competitive marketshare and potential for your product. You should also be sensitive to if and which modifications might be required to make your product not just acceptable but attractive to that market.

▶ To acquire a "feel" for the people, the culture and the methods of doing business. Most successful international traders are good chameleons—they are able to acquire new visages and habits to fit more comfortably into diverse environments.

Don't expect to come back with orders in hand. There may be a few sample or trial orders, but it is unlikely that any substantial business will result from the first trip. A period of months will probably be required to create the pipeline and get it properly installed at both ends.

Here is a general checklist to help you assure a pleasant and productive trip:

1. Check the national calendar of the country you will be visiting to assure you will not be there during important national or religious holidays. In some countries, the same applies to important national elections because very often they interrupt the normal flow of business. As just one example of holidays, in Hong Kong and other Chinese countries, the New Year holidays are probably the most important of the year. They fall in either January or February, varying because they are based on the lunar calendar. Visiting at that time would almost be comparable to having your non-Christian customer notify you that he was coming to the United States to have meetings with you on December 24th. The whole month of August in Europe is a very bad time to try to conduct business because it is the custom there to schedule summer business vacations at that time. A Miami executive relates that his biggest single personal faux pas on scheduling was to instruct the manager of his factory in Argentina, where soccer is the national sport, to come to the United States for meetings at precisely the date Argentina was confronting its arch-rival Brasil in the World Cup Soccer finals. He salvaged this monumental gaffe only by sending the Argentine to the closest U.S. large-screen, closed circuit television broadcast where he probably saw the match better than if he had actually been in the Buenos Aires stadium.

2. Check normal work day schedules. For example, in most Middle Eastern nations, Friday is the day of rest; and in most Latin countries, lengthy lunch hours of two to even four hours are customary.

3. Make as many appointments in advance with key contacts yet keep your schedule flexible enough to permit forays into subjects or areas that arise during your visit. Confirm, and re-confirm

if necessary, all travel arrangements, hotel accommodations, and business appointments.

4. Review every step of the trip with your travel agent including required visas, currency restrictions (if any), ground transportation facilities (especially from airport to hotel), and vaccination requirements (if any).

5. Your passport, money (in traveler's checks), and confirmed airline reservations are as important as air, water, and food so take every possible measure to carry all three as close to your body at all times as possible. There are many other neat tricks advocated by travel experts—for example, throw an old passport in your suitcase in case your current passport is lost or stolen. Reason: It makes issuance of a new passport faster by the local U.S. embassy or consulate. Many of these special tricks can be found in travel tip columns in newspapers and magazines or in popular books on travel.

6. Order and pack a plentiful supply of business cards—you will be passing them out like handbills. If you are going to countries where English is uncommon—Japan, for example—have the information translated into the local language and printed on the opposite side of your card in the same quality printing lest you imply their language is not as important as yours.

7. Check seasonal weather conditions in the countries you are visiting. Most travel agencies have charts showing climatic conditions around the world. Carry appropriate clothing for the weather.

8. As for safety and health, a useful guidebook is entitled *Safety and Health Abroad* (Datafax Corporation, Minneapolis, MN) 1985. It offers advice on such diverse maladies as stomach distress, jet lag, stress, drugs, terrorism, and even espionage.

9. Another useful small booklet to consult or carry along is *Key Officers of Foreign Service Posts*, a compilation of addresses, phone numbers, and names of U.S. economic and commercial officers in U.S. embassies and consulates. It can be obtained from the Superintendent of Documents, U.S. Government Printing Office, Washington, DC 20402. Telephone: (202) 783-3238. Cost is $10 for one year and includes three updates.

10. Ask your travel agent about customs regulations—namely, what you can bring into your destination country duty free, and

also U.S. customs regulations on what you can bring back into the United States duty free.

11. In some countries, the U.S. Foreign Commercial Service operates Export Development Offices and can provide, for a nominal fee, an office with local telephone service, audiovisual equipment, a market briefing, and general assistance. Help in obtaining both secretarial and interpreter services may also be offered.

12. The World Trade Centers, described in Chapter 3, also may offer some of these same services as well as telex, facsimile, and even discounts at hotels for accommodations. Check to see if there is an active chapter of the American Chamber of Commerce (Amcham) in the market you are visiting. These Amchams are particularly active and useful in Latin American markets.

13. If you are planning to carry along commercial samples, tools of the trade, advertising material, audiovisual material, medical or scientific equipment, it is wise to investigate the ATA Carnet system. The United States is a member of this system that permits business travelers to carry these materials into a country for temporary periods without paying duties, taxes, or posting a bond. Contact the U.S. Council of the International Business, 1212 Avenue of the Americas, New York, NY 10036, (212) 354-4480 for a list of member countries of this Carnet system and the schedule of fees required.

14. After meeting you and examining descriptive materials on your product, the single most important piece of information a distributor will want is your price list. Chapter 7 deals with pricing and it would be wise to study that before revealing prices prematurely. A shortcut would be to provide your current price list for U.S. customers, just to give an indication of prevailing prices. But, as you will learn in Chapter 7, we strongly advocate building a price structure exclusively for export, and not just duplicating U.S. prices.

15. Finally, it would be wise to pack a book or two on varying cultural idiosyncrasies to help you avoid "foot-in-mouth" disease while traveling. Several recommended handbooks are as follows:

> ▶ *The Economist Business Traveller's Guides,* Prentice Hall Press, New York, 1987. Separate handbooks for Britain, Japan, and the Arabian Peninsula are available, with more countries to be added. These not only provide maps of key

cities plus lists of hotels and restaurants in each, but essential background on the economy, politics, business structure, major industries, and the underlying social factors that influence business and the economy.

▶ *Do's and Taboo's Around the World*, John Wiley & Sons, New York, 1986. This is a guide to international behavior with separate chapters on protocol, behavior, customs, and etiquette; American jargon and baffling idioms; gift giving and receiving; hand gestures and body language. A handy reference guide also tells what you should know about punctuality, conversational taboos, names, and greetings, and general protocol arranged country-by-country. All this is presented in a light, informal style with plenty of anecdotes.

A CASE STUDY

George S. Parker, the founder of the Parker Pen Co. appointed his company's first foreign distributor in 1902. That resulted when a Danish stationer saw an advertisement for Parker pens in *The Saturday Evening Post* magazine. In 1911, Parker appointed his second importer-distributor, this time in Thailand. Both of these appointments were made by mail. Recognizing the value of these overseas sales outlets, the penmaker started after World War I to make a series of trips to overseas markets where he systematically appointed distributors. By the 1950s, according to trade surveys, the Parker brand name had become one of the best-known American brand names in the world marketplace. By the 1980s, over 80 percent of Parker's total worldwide sales came from 153 distributors outside the United States.

How did Parker locate and appoint distributors? He would select a market, do his preparation, and then plan to spend two or three weeks there. He would tour the streets, visiting retail stores unannounced and generally soaking up the commercial environment. He would, of course, carefully examine competitive pens, their prices, and how they were boxed and sold. After this, he would begin making inquiries of store owners about which pens sold well, and why, and how they obtained them. Slowly, he would build a mental portrait of how pens were sold in that market, each with its special characteristics and favoritisms. He would compile a list of the key wholesalers of products akin to pens and—more importantly—the key importers. Then he would visit the American consulate or embassy, plus several banks, to verify names of candidates for his pen distributorship. Soon, a short list of nominees would develop and then—and only then—he would start calling on the prospective distributors themselves.

With painstaking care, Parker would interview each one. He would cautiously check bank references, plus their reputation among the trade. Later, when he returned to the United States, he would contact the other firms here who sold their lines through each distributor candidate and ask for evaluations. (Even today, U.S. exporters are often cooperative in providing these types of references, both good and bad.) He did this exhaustive research, he reported in later years, because he realized that appointing a distributor was like a marriage. He wanted a long-term commitment, with rising mutual benefits, someone he could trust and who would value his product as he did himself. He realized that the distributor would, in effect, be The Parker Pen Company in that market. His reputation would depend on the performance of the distributor. In turn, he would depend on that distributor to counsel him on what variations might be required in the product, how to best advertise quality pens in that market, how to accommodate quirks in sales and promotion methods, and a host of details that would determine their joint future.

Throughout the decade of the 1920s, Parker appointed dozens of distributors in this manner, many of whom are still with the company. Last year, for example, a young fourth generation family member from that very first distributor appointed in 1902 spent a six-month training program at the U.S. headquarters of Parker. Distributor appointments can, indeed, last a considerable time.

THE TEN MOST COMMON MISTAKES OF POTENTIAL EXPORTERS

The first trip abroad can be extremely significant. Life-long relationships can develop from this first sortie overseas. Steady, growing sales can result or, if the distributor selection was ill-advised, a steady stream of headaches and problems can result. It is worth very careful preparation and planning.

Here, as compiled by the U.S. Department of Commerce, are the ten most common general mistakes of potential exporters. You will quickly spot some of them from reading earlier portions of this book. The other mistakes listed next deal with topics that will be discussed in succeeding chapters.

1. *Failure to obtain qualified export counseling and to develop a master international marketing plan before starting an export business.* To be successful, you must first clearly define your goals, objectives, and the problems you face. Secondly, you must develop a definitive plan to accomplish your objectives despite the problems involved. Unless you are fortunate enough to possess a staff with considerable export expertise, you will not be able to take this crucial first step without qualified outside guidance.

2. *Insufficient commitment by top management to overcome the initial difficulties and financial requirements of exporting.* It may take more time and effort to establish yourself in a foreign market than in domestic ones. Although the early delays and costs involved in exporting may seem difficult to justify when compared to your established domestic trade, you should take a long-range view of this process and shepherd your international marketing efforts through these early difficulties. If you have laid a good foundation for your export business, the benefits derived should eventually outweigh your investment.

3. *Insufficient care in selecting foreign distributors.* The selection of each foreign distributor is crucial. The complications involved in overseas communications and transportation require international distributors to act with greater independence than their domestic counterparts. Also, since a new exporter's history, trademarks, and reputation are usually unknown in the foreign market, the foreign customers will buy on the strength of the distributor's reputation. You should therefore conduct a personal evaluation of the personnel handling your account, the distributor's facilities, and the management methods employed.

4. *Chasing orders from around the world instead of establishing a basis for profitable operations and orderly growth.* If you expect distributors to actively promote your account, they must be trained, assisted, and their performance must be continually monitored. This requires a company marketing executive to either visit the distributor often or, at a later stage, perhaps even be permanently located in the distributor's geographical region. Therefore, new exporters should concentrate their efforts in one or two geographical areas until there is sufficient business to support an

assigned representative. Then, while this initial core area is expanded, the exporter can move into the next selected geographical area.

5. *Neglecting export business when the U.S. market booms.* Too many companies turn to exporting when business falls off in the United States. When domestic business starts to boom again, they neglect their export trade or relegate it to a secondary place. Such neglect can seriously harm the business and motivation of their overseas representatives, strangling their own export trade and leaving them without recourse when domestic business falls off once more. Even if domestic business remains strong, they may eventually realize that they have only succeeded in shutting off a valuable source of additional profits.

6. *Failure to treat international distributors on an equal basis with domestic counterparts.* Often, companies carry out institutional advertising campaigns, special discount offers, sales incentive programs, special credit term programs, warranty offers, etc., in the U.S. market but fail to make similar assistance available to their international distributors. This is a mistake that can destroy the vitality of your overseas marketing efforts.

7. *Unwillingness to modify products to meet regulations or cultural preferences of other countries.* Local safety and security codes, as well as import restrictions, cannot be ignored by foreign distributors. If necessary modifications are not made at the factory, the distributor must do them—usually at greater cost and, perhaps, not as well. It should also be noted that the resulting smaller profit margin makes the account less attractive to the distributor.

8. *Failure to print services, sales, and warranty messages in locally understood languages.* Although your distributor's top management may speak English, it is unlikely that all sales personnel (let alone service personnel) will have this capability. Without a clear understanding of sales messages or service instructions, these personnel will be less effective in performing their functions. For common languages like Spanish, French, and German, good translation services are readily available in the United States; for less common ones, like Thai or Finnish or Dutch, your distributor can provide that extra service.

9. *Failure to consider use of an export management company.* If a firm decides it cannot afford its own export department (or has

tried one unsuccessfully), it should consider the possibility of appointing an appropriate Export Management Company (EMC).

10. *Failure to consider licensing or joint-venture agreements.* Import restrictions in some countries, insufficient personnel and financial resources, or a too limited product line cause many companies to dismiss international marketing as simply not feasible. Yet, nearly any product that can compete on a national basis in the United States can be successfully marketed in most markets of the world. A licensing or joint venture arrangement may be the simple, profitable answer to your reservations. In general, all that is needed for success is flexibility in using the proper combination of marketing techniques.

5

The First Handshake

Look 'em straight in the eye.

When I was a teenager, whenever I was introduced to someone, my father would consistently growl at me to "Give 'em a good, firm handshake and look 'em straight in the eye." He would warn that "No one likes a limp hand, and if you avoid their eyes, they'll think you are shifty and untrustworthy." That fatherly advice has undoubtedly been repeated millions of times in America to countless sons and daughters.

What my father failed to tell me, because he didn't know it, was that millions of other fathers in dozens of other countries were schooling their children quite differently. In Japan, for example, the bow is the customary greeting. Hand-shaking is an occidental custom and focusing straight into the eyes of another person in Japan is an intimidating gesture—one to be avoided. In the Middle East, young men follow the advice and example of their fathers and offer a limp handshake, and the eyes more often than not are hooded, even languid. And in Latin countries, handshaking is a bit more exuberant and might even include a grasping of the wrist or elbow with the free lefthand.

Even within Western Europe, where social customs are more like our own, there are variations on this seemingly simple act of protocol. Germans and Scandinavians tend toward a firm, one-pump handshake. The French and Italians adopt a softer grip. And throughout Europe, women shake hands when introduced much more than here in the United States. And if you are interested in the exotic, the Maori tribe in New Zealand greet one another by rubbing noses.

As you travel abroad, perhaps for the first time, differences will abound, even with everyday customs like shaking hands. One of the most eminent observers in cross-cultural communication is Edward T. Hall who writes that "the single greatest barrier to business success is the one erected by culture." And he also tells us that some 80 to 90 percent of a culture is found in its nonverbal messages, which means behavior, protocol, gestures, and other body language.

This chapter will deal with how to anticipate some of these strange encounters. For example, we all carry with us stereotypes of other nationalities, and these will be laid out for careful and critical examination. Differences in business protocol from region to region will be explained. If you will be working through interpreters, this chapter will also provide some useful tips on making that unique experience more comfortable and more effective. If your first venture abroad involves exhibiting at a trade show, a concise checklist is provided to smooth the way. A likely encounter will involve the question "must I modify my product to make it suitable for the foreign marketplace?" Answers to that question will be reviewed and, finally, you will be ready to consider appointing a distributor and begin developing a pipeline for foreign sales.

Cultural Stereotypes

When presenting seminars across the country on doing business with people outside the United States, I often begin with a group participation exercise which demonstrates our built-in perceptions of other nationalities. Here are some results from one of those seminars:

Question: In one-word responses, give me your basic impression or image of the English.
Answers: Conservative. Reserved. Polite. Proper. Formal.
Question: What about the French? What one-word perceptions do you have of them?
Answers: Arrogant. Rude. Chauvinistic. Romantics. Gourmets. Cultural. Artistic.

Question: Here's an easy one—Italians. What images do you have
of Italians?
Answers: Demonstrative. Talkative. Emotional. Romantic. Bold.
Artistic.
Question: O.K. Now let's do all Latins. This isn't fair, incidentally,
because there are many different types of Latins, but what charac-
teristics pop into your mind when I say Latins?
Answers: Manana attitude. Macho. Musical. Lovers. Hot food.
Touching.
Question: Now let's go to the Orient.
Answers: Inscrutable. Intelligent. Xenophobic. Golfers. Group
oriented. Polite. Soft-spoken.
Question: Now let's do the payoff one—Americans. What is the
world's stereotype of Americans?
Answers: Arrogant. Loud. Friendly. Impatient. Monolingual.
Generous. Hard-working. (And at one of these seminars someone
shouted: "All of the above!")

These are common stereotypes. These are perceptions about nationalities and groups of people, and the psychologists teach us
that "perceptions are reality." These are the images we Americans
carry in our baggage when we travel to other countries. We unpack
them and look for these separate national characteristics in each
country we visit.

Are they accurate? Not, really. All French are not rude; all
Americans are not loud; all Latins are not macho. But unfortunately, these built-in images are what we expect to find and, consequently they are "reality" and often distort and disrupt smooth
business transactions.

For many years, the image of *The Ugly American* was projected on the international scene by the 1958 book with that title
written by William J. Lederer and Eugene Burdick. It portrayed
Americans as insensitive and uncaring about other cultures and
other beliefs. The book's title became a catchword for years after-
ward. Was it accurate? Not really. Today, Americans are more often
pictured by other cultures as friendly, out-going, hard-working,
impatient, and sometimes a bit loud. Ian Kerr, a respected British
public relations executive who has worked in the United States for
over 30 years, protests with this explanation: "I think the 'Ugly
American' label is totally wrong. It is more accurate, I think, to say
the 'Uninformed American.'"

Americans have a tendency toward carrying and using stereotypes about other cultures because most of us must travel thousands of miles before bumping into a distinctly different culture. In Europe, traveling on a train for just one hour will find you in the midst of a totally different culture.

Cultural stereotypes should be used with great caution. Americans, especially, should not be encumbered with them when doing business in foreign countries. Americans should be more openminded and should take the time to study other cultures rather than relying on dusty, prepackaged stereotypes. Yes, there are certain customs, practices, and rules of behavior in each country or region, but it is dangerous to automatically conclude that all people of any one nationality have certain, innate characteristics or manners of behavior. Ian Kerr advises: "When dealing with national stereotypes and characteristics, there is only one safe generalization and that is 'Don't generalize.'"

Test yourself with this one: Canada. What preconceived notions do many Americans have about Canada? (Immediately we run into trouble with the word "Americans" which technically refers to all North Americans.) Until the 1988 Winter Olympics, the standard reaction would have been "Eskimos and mounted policemen." While the Olympics did much to show the true Canada, Americans are still guilty of lumping all Canadians as "just like us" instead of respecting their separate culture and history. How well do we know Canadian history? Ask an American to name four historic Canadian figures. I do that in my seminars. After an embarrassed silence, someone once ventured "How about Michael J. Fox and Anne Murray?" How many of us are aware that the term Eskimo is now considered rather rude and the proper term is Inuit?

Americans, it is said, have a "benevolent ignorance" about Canada and so our nearest neighbor serves as a good example of how we must school ourselves before venturing outside our borders. We should avoid sounding like Al Capone who was once asked where Canada was located and he answered, "I don't even know what street it's on."

While there are few superficial differences between Americans and Canadians, in business relationships it is essential to know and respect those differences. For example, Canadians are proud of their history and heritage, their clean cities and their industrious multi-ethnic society. It is a misuse, but common and accepted, to refer to those who speak French in Canada, about 25 percent of the population, as French-Canadians. More properly, they are French-speaking Canadians. Most, if not all, government employees there are bilingual. If one must resort to stereotypes and generalizations about the Canadians, it might be correct to say they are more subdued, more conservative, and, as one TV commentator put it, "their national color is tweed." But lest you think Canada is nothing but icebergs and wastelands, you should know that the lower part of Hudson Bay is at the same latitude as London, England and as for the wastelands, as one U.S. State Department official stated, "Canada is about as underdeveloped as Brigitte Nielson."

Canada is one close-to-home illustration of the fickleness of stereotypes and how they should be treated.

BUSINESS PROTOCOL

If you arm yourself with one, and only one, important piece of knowledge about business protocol it should be this: Be patient.

Americans are taught that time is money. We are proud of our practice of jamming a lot of work into a short time and wasting no time getting right down to business. It is a business virtue in the United States to spend little time socializing and we expect the same from others. But our sense of time is not necessarily shared in other cultures. Others march to varying tempos, often slower tempos than ours. Americans tend to find this frustrating, and so they attempt to hurry the process along and, instead, it tends to break down. That's when the phrase "time is money" could convert to "haste makes waste."

Japan is a notable example. It is said that Americans think and act in terms of days, weeks, and months, and the Japanese think and act in terms of months and years. Chapter 12 deals exclusively with this so-called mystique. It can take years before relationships develop to a point that fellow Americans reach in weeks or months. Roy Benjamin, head of Benjamin Inc. of Elmsford, NY, has been doing business in Japan for 11 years. It was not until a recent trip there, he reported, that his Japanese business colleagues intimated he was now (after 11 years!) truly a close business associate and friend.

European business relationships, on the other hand, are more similar to ours. They develop faster but, still, a good dose of patience is required. In England, for example, a specific protocol should be followed with routine business appointments. Never expect a meeting to be held on the spur of the moment. Instead, they are invariably fixed, or booked, days and even weeks in advance. The same is true for social engagements. To Americans, it seems every Britisher walks around with a diary or appointment book in his pocket which dictates his every move.

The Middle East is another test of American patience in business. In Baghdad, it once took me days of waiting and posturing before serious business was discussed. Moreover, business meetings throughout the Middle East are commonly conducted in large rooms with several other visitors clustered in small groups around the room. Your host may visit with each group in turn. This is not being impolite, but simply the practice. Rounds of tea will be served, and then seemingly without notice your host may also disappear for 20 minutes or more. The reason: daily prayers.

One explanation for this slower pace, other than pure cultural difference, is that business people in other countries are more interested in you as an individual and therefore wish to take the time to get to know you. They do this by socializing more. A good rule to practice is this: Continue the socializing and general conversations until *they* initiate the business discussion. Or, if you can't wait, broach the business at hand very cautiously.

Punctuality is a business practice that varies from country to country. The Northern Europeans (Scandinavia, West Germany, Netherlands, etc.) tend to be very punctual. Farther south in Europe, it is less important. Latin America is known for what Americans consider a mañana attitude. It is considered ordinary for Latins to appear a half hour or hour after the appointed hour. In fact, seasoned American visitors, when discussing a time for a business or social appointment, will pointedly but pleasantly ask "The Spanish hour or the English hour?" the Spanish hour meaning "late" and the English hour meaning "punctually." The books on customs and behavior listed in Chapter 4 provide guidelines, country-by-country, on this question of punctuality.

Next on any list of general business protocol would be such things as handshaking, business cards, smoking, dining, drinking, entertaining, attitudes toward women, gift-giving, lingo, gestures, body language, and even offering a toast at the dinner table. Each can be complex and inconsistent; furthermore, separate chapters could be written about each. Here is some basic information in each category.

HANDSHAKING

Limp handshakes, firm handshakes, pumping handshakes, elbow-grasping handshakes—you will encounter all forms. One thing is certain: You will do it often, more often, than in the United States. In France, for example, there is the handshake at the beginning of the meeting and at the conclusion, and close associates will even shake hands at the beginning of each day. Remember, too, that women will offer their hand in both business and social settings more often than in the United States. Faced with these new customs, it is easy to go overboard. A French business executive once observed an American friend at a formal party in England working his way down a reception line greeting his hosts. When the American came to a woman host who offered her hand, the Frenchman could sense a flash of inspiration go through the American's head: the woman was offering her hand to be kissed, but the American decided to outdo the locals and so he took her proffered hand and instead of shaking it, he kissed it, but instead of kissing it on the back of the hand, he turned it over and kissed the palm. The American bobbed up with a triumphant look that said: "There! Now I've shown all these folks some real Continental manners." He may have been the first American and, indeed, the first person in all of Europe, to ever display such a unique bit of protocol.

In Southeast Asia, the handshake is replaced by the *wai*, or *namaste* as it is called in India. This involves putting the palms together in front of the chest, as in praying. In Japan, most everyone knows that the bowing is the traditional form of greeting but few outsiders realize the complexity of the bow. Basically, the lower one bows the more humble one is, and it is important to display humility in Japan. In the Middle East, a limp handshake is more common than a firm handshake.

BUSINESS CARDS

Mentioned in an earlier chapter, the basic rules here are as follows: Carry an abundance because you will likely be passing them out frequently; have the information printed in the local language, especially if you are in a country with an uncommon language; avoid confusing American titles like "Deputy Assistant General Manager"; *read* the card before depositing it in your pocket; keep track of the cards for future reference, and write notes (later, in private) on each to help you remember the person, the occasion or the subject. Business cards can also have hidden symbolism. I once observed a Brazilian executive carefully bending one corner of his card before passing it over. When I asked why, he said "I do that as a personal code that I, personally, handed this card out. It helps in the case of bogus cards."

In England, recipients of royal honors from the Crown are entitled to put the initials of that honor following their name on business cards and in correspondence. Therefore, Mr. L. Jack King, O.B.E. signifies that Mr. King has been awarded the "Order of the British Empire." One unobservant American reportedly glanced at such a card handed out by Mr. John Lee, O.B.E. and proceeded to refer to him as "Mr. Obe" for the remainder of their visit. Moral: Business cards may carry more than just printed basic information.

SMOKING

Smoking has become a hotly contested national issue in the United States. One national news magazine summarized it as "where there's smoke, there's ire." In most other countries, smoking is a less divisive social practice. Two pieces of advice when traveling out of the country: First, the safest act of propriety would be to ask "Do you mind if I smoke?" before lighting up; the second piece of advice is if you do not smoke don't expect your overseas host or associate to ask for *your* permission to smoke, as might be done here. The United States has become polarized on this issue, moreso than other countries.

All you can do is be prepared with a few tips such as: do as your leader does, watch what others around you are doing, look for ashtrays or other signs, and as a last resort, ask what the local practices are concerning smoking. In England, for example, when taking out a cigarette, it is polite to offer one to others at your table or in your circle, an act of courtesy rarely practiced by Americans at home. At formal British dinners, an announcement is sometimes made, usually after the meal, "Ladies and gentlemen, you may smoke." The Japanese and Chinese are, by our standards, very heavy smokers and customarily light up in most any setting, without asking. Finally, in the People's Republic of China, you may be surprised to see what at first appear to be large round receptacles on the floor in offices and meeting rooms. A second look will confirm that they are spittoons. Expectorating is common there—in fact, it is viewed as hygienic because one is getting rid of a bodily waste. The practice continues out-of-doors and also includes nose-blowing, without benefit of a handkerchief. While the government is reportedly campaigning to discourage these practices because they realize it is offensive to visitors, don't be surprised to see more than just smoking in public.

DINING

Rule number one: You will probably have heavier meals at noon than customary. Rule number two: If you are the guest, you will probably be treated to a heavy meal at *both* noon and in the evening. Rule number three: You will very likely be faced with strange foods.

Let's start with breakfasts. In Europe, you will very likely be served coffee and hard rolls, or French *croissents,* along with jams and perhaps a small variety of cold meats and cheeses. Whether Westernized breakfasts are served will depend on your hotel.

Lunch overseas is rarely the "soup'n sandwich" so popular in the United States. (One Latin American sales manager said when he first came to the United States he heard that phrase so often he tried to find it, as a single word, in the dictionary.) What we call "lunch" at midday is customarily the main meal of the day in most other places in the world. Another source of confusion is the "entree." In Europe, it is what we would call the "appetizer"; in the United States, the entree is the main dish or main selection. If you dislike having large, heavy meals at noontime, here is a trick: order two appetizers, one to join your dining mates with during their appetizer, and one for the main course.

Be prepared for strange and exotic foods: haggis in Scotland, sushi in Japan, octopus in Latin America, and lots of lamb in the Middle East. Also, the guest of honor in the Middle East is served the sheep's eyeballs. One well-traveled executive offers this advice for such stomach-turning foods: slice it thin, swallow it quickly, pretend it is chicken, and don't refuse—after all, your hosts have probably been eating that food for centuries and it hasn't hurt them. Besides, he counsels, these are national delicacies and it would be like having a guest come to America and refuse apple pie.

Drinking

One member of the American Chamber of Commerce in Lima, Peru tells of this true incident involving an American businessman who imbibed too much of the potent local drink, Pisco Sour, at a formal Peruvian banquet. After the dinner, the American weaved his way into the nearby ballroom where the music had begun. Spotting a tall, grey-haired and distinguished Peruvian wearing a long red robe, he asked for the first dance. The reply was, "I'm terribly sorry. I must decline. First of all, they are playing the Peruvian National Anthem, and secondly, I am the Archbishop of Lima."

Socializing in business almost invariably involves drinking spirits except, of course, in the Middle East where alcohol is forbidden by strict practitioners of the Moslem faith. Each culture seems to have its special concoction of alcohol which can either be a delightful experience in sampling or, as in the case of the American in Peru, a disastrous exercise in foot-in-mouth disease. Among beers, there are lagers, pilsners, ales, porters, and stouts; in the clear vodka-like family, there is schnapps (Germany), genevre (Netherlands), ouzo (Greece), akvavite (Scandinavia), and mao-tai (People's Republic of China); in the whiskey family, bourbon, scotch, and rye; and among wines, a countless variety. Potency of some of these beverages is viewed differently, depending on your locale. In Italy, there is one liqueur labeled in English "Dangerous if consumed in large quantities" yet the Italian version of the message says "Consume until the desired effect is reached." In Japan, drinking after hours is a ritualistic way of shedding the formality of the rigid social and office structure and letting your hair down. One Western authority on Japan writes that the Japanese believe you really don't get to know a person until you get drunk together. Further, he advises to avoid trying to match your Japanese counterpart drink-for-drink, and, by the same token, don't refuse to drink together unless you have good medical or personal reasons for doing so.

The question is often asked "What if I don't drink alcohol? How do I handle that?" Drinking alcohol is not an absolute requirement, of course, and there are understandable alternatives. Politely explain in advance to your host that "for health and other personal reasons" you do not drink alcohol but that you certainly have no objection for others to do so. Ask for mineral water, or some other substitute, and have the bartender put a slice of lime or lemon in it so you won't feel conspicuous. When the wine is served, either quietly tip your glass upside down, or place your palm over the glass when the waiter approaches.

TOASTING

Americans seldom offer toasts when dining or drinking, except perhaps on New Year's Eve or if you are the best man at a wedding. In other countries, however, it is more common and therefore wise to be prepared. At a Chinese meal, for example, the apex of the multi-course meal is in the middle when the shark's fin soup is served. It is also the customary time to present toasts. Here are some guidelines for toasting wherever you are in the world. The host toasts first. If at a dinner, rise at your place. Keep the toast short. Avoid attempts at humor or, even more tasteless, anything even tinged with blue words or suggestiveness. Comment on the graciousness and hospitality of your hosts, the friendship between countries, and the value of good relations both personal and in business. It can be a moment when just the right sentiment can be expressed that will be both memorable and lasting. Therefore, a well-delivered toast is worth anticipating, even to the point of developing a small repertoire for different occasions.

Among smaller groups at less formal occasions, one-word toasts between individuals is also common. "Your good health" is almost a universal toast and a common sentiment in several languages: *salud* in Spanish, *santee* in French, "cheers" among the British, and *skoal* in Scandinavia. Be cautious in the Far East, however, where *kam-bye* and variations on that toast literally mean "bottoms up" and where you are expected to drain the glass and turn it upside down as proof. An opposite message is sent in Australia where draining a glass of, say, beer and turning it upside down on the bartop declares "I can lick anyone in the place!" The moral here is that even with the innocent and somewhat unaccustomed act of toasting, there are important messages being issued.

WOMEN TRAVELING IN FOREIGN COUNTRIES

Women have advanced in business in the United States farther and faster than in any other country. Businesspeople coming here from other countries and seeing the valuable roles of women helps to advance the role of women in those countries. In the People's

Republic of China, women already occupy important managerial positions. In Europe, the barriers have also been lowered substantially. In Latin America, it is still uncommon to see many women in key executive positions. Ingeborg Hegenbart, a highly respected and world-traveled senior bank executive with the Southern National Bank system in Charlotte, NC tells this story about Japan where she has been traveling and doing business for many years. On one occasion, after several visits, her male counterpart finally agreed to let her pay for lunch. When they departed the restaurant, though, he still preceded her by several steps, making her walk a few paces behind him in customary Japanese fashion. "It is still difficult for a Western woman to do business in Japan—possible, but difficult," Hegenbart says. "But I would never attempt to even try to visit certain Middle Eastern countries where women are still distinctly subservient to men."

Some general advice for American women traveling in other countries on business: dress conservatively, don't do anything that is considered even remotely flirtatious, be careful about dining alone lest it convey you are inviting company, don't give business gifts unless they are for the family of the business contact, and don't insist on picking up luncheon or dinner checks. A helpful book for women travelers is *The International Businesswoman*, by Marlene R. Rossman, Greenwood Press, Westport, CT, 1986.

GIFT GIVING

Business gift giving in the United States is a $4 billion business but largely restricted to calendars, imprinted pens, diaries, key rings, golf caps, and thousands of gadgets. Because of tax regulations, such gifts are also usually restricted to a value of $25 or less, which then qualifies them for a business expense deduction. Overseas, business gift giving is more common. Furthermore, in certain countries, there are specific customs and practices worth knowing.

Japan is one of those. There, gift giving is an ingrained part of the culture. If you are visiting Japan or receiving Japanese visitors in this country, be prepared to exchange gifts. And this important rule applies: It is not the substance of the gift that is so important as the style and thoughtfulness behind it. (More details on gift giving in Japan are provided in Chapter 12.)

The Middle East is known for its generosity in gift giving. Many Americans have returned with cumbersome packages among their baggage after admiring a picture on a Middle Eastern wall, or casually admiring a tea serving set, only to have the host insist that it become an instant gift. In the Middle East, if a guest admires something it is customary to make him a gift of it.

Gift-giving practices around the world are worth some special homework. To illustrate that point, here are some examples of specific "don'ts": Don't give a clock in China because that word in Chinese has a morbid, funereal connotation; don't gift handkerchiefs in the Middle East because it connotes the breaking of a relationship; don't give a set of knives in Latin American because it signals the cutting of a relationship; don't give four of anything in South Korea because the number four is unlucky, like our number thirteen; don't give white flowers in Japan, they are the flower of death; and, don't give red roses to a hostess in West Germany because in that country they suggest a romantic interest.

Here are some "do's" in this business of gift giving: anything connected with the old American West, such as cowboys and Indians, is usually well-received because it is unique to America; subscriptions to U.S. magazines are sometimes a good idea, especially if they are uncommon and difficult to receive in that country; edibles like Oreo cookies, peanut butter, Vermont maple syrup, and Wisconsin cheeses are often well-received, although there can be some pitfalls, as when Governor Lee Sherman Dreyfus of Wisconsin went to the People's Republic of China bearing gift cheeses, only to find that cheese is not a part of the Chinese diet and in fact is disliked. The lesson here, as in many parts of this book, is *do your homework.*

LINGO

A separate book could be written on this topic alone. This may seem strange since English and American/English have become the lingua franca for business around the world. But, be aware of two facts: First, American/English has become cluttered with slang, jargon, buzz words, colloquialisms, idioms, acronyms, military, and sports terminology. Second, there are often vast differences between American/English and English/English; therefore comprehension depends on which version your overseas listener is accustomed to.

As for the proliferation of American/English, the business community is among the worst offenders. The insurance department has more recently become known as risk management, and the personnel department is more likely called human resources. Americans have a penchant for expanding the language, often with two words instead of one. This makes it exceedingly difficult for our foreign business contacts who may have spent years trying to learn English only to find that it's a moving target.

Here are other examples of mixups and differences between the United States and the United Kingdom. Certain words that would be considered ordinary to American ears (fanny, bloody, bugger) are terribly rude in Britain. The glossary for automobile parts contains no less than 60 words that are different: An American windshield is a British windscreen, the trunk is the bonnet, the muffler is the silencer, the dashboard is the fascia, and so on. For more examples of these mixups, see Chapter 11 on Language and Communication, and specifically the section "American/English versus English/English."

Back here at home, our language is a constantly moving, shifting mass of words. In the dictionary department of bookstores, one can also find separate books with titles like *The Morrow Book of Words, 8,500 Words Not Yet in the Dictionary*. Pity the poor foreigner trying to communicate with us from a limited vocabulary learned back in school days and from even more outdated textbooks only to find that new and different words are constantly being added. The lesson here for the American embarking on trips abroad is to keep the conversation basic, avoid using buzz words and jargon, and stop for clarification if there is any indication whatsoever that the person across the table is having problems with comprehension. Speaking slowly, but not necessarily more loudly, is also recommended. It is said that one can tell veteran export executives by the slow, metered pace of their speech. As for loudness, many Americans seem to think that when overseas a higher volume will automatically create comprehension.

GESTURES AND BODY LANGUAGE

You have probably read that if two people were stranded on a desert island and neither spoke the other's language they could communicate via gestures. Wrong. They would very likely end up punching each other in the nose. Here is some evidence. The "O.K." sign, thumb and forefinger forming a circle with the other fingers fanned outward, is a terribly rude gesture in Brazil. Furthermore, in France it means "zero" or "worthless" and in Japan it signifies "money." The "V" for "Victory" sign, forefinger and middle finger pointed upward with palm facing outward, was made famous in World War II by Winston Churchill. It is shown in all the history books, and former President Richard Nixon made it something of a trademark with both arms raised and both hands forming this "victory" sign. It's perfectly O.K. to flash it in Britain—but, for goodness sakes, don't turn the hand around, with the palm *facing* you. In Britain, that version is just as ugly as the "O.K" sign in Brazil, and one guaranteed to get you a poke in the nose. The "thumbs up" signal, with hand in a fist and only the thumb sticking up, is recognized almost every place in the world . . . except in Australia and West Africa, where it is every bit as rude as the "O.K." in Brazil and the reverse "V" in Britain. The "fig" gesture—hand in a fist, thumb protruding upward through the crevasse, means "good luck" in Brazil, but in Turkey and certain other Middle Eastern countries it is comparable to the rudest hand signal here in the United States.

One can quickly see that innocent hand gestures can produce unwanted results, depending on where you might be visiting. It is, of course, impossible to learn all of these signals in advance, so the best advice is to be reserved in your gestures, just as you should be conservative in your use of slang and jargon. The second piece of advice is to be observant—watch how gestures are being used and diplomatically ask what they mean. Even the simple act of hailing a waiter has its variations around the world, and a restaurant is a wonderful place to practice your new powers of observation.

Body language also has its own set of rules. Let's start with spatial relationships. Americans and Central Europeans unconsciously stand, literally, an arm's length apart. That is the accepted spatial difference. Orientals will stand even farther apart and, as a general rule, Latins and Middle Easterners stand closer and are more touch oriented. Most veteran American travelers return from those two regions with stories of how uncomfortable it is to be in toe-to-toe social conversations, or how strange it is to have a male business associate gently hold your elbow when engaging in a social dialog.

Here are some other bits of body language to watch for. Throughout the Middle East, you should eat only with the right hand because the left hand is customarily reserved for purposes of bodily hygiene. This is important because some dining events in the Middle East consist of large banquets with a full roasted lamb that is divided and served by hand—but, the right hand only. So important is this dictum that the worst punishment meted out to a thief is to cut off the right hand, so that the offender is destined to go through life with one hand, the unclean hand, which effectively ostracizes that person from communal eating. Don't point with your toes in Thailand because that is considered rude. Don't show the sole of your shoe in the Middle East because that is an unkind gesture. In the Orient, when the mouth is opened widely as when laughing, it is considered unmannerly; that is why you will note that most Orientals cover the open mouth with the hand. In Japan, touching is just the opposite of Latin America and the Middle East—they refrain. Never clap a Japanese on the back or grab his forearm, or hug in any form. In Italy and other Romance countries, the hug is a desired form of body language. The *abrazo* is very common among people who have come to know one another even fairly well, but you needn't worry about it on the first, or even second, visit. Handkissing is best reserved for the French, who do it with special élan. And cheek-kissing is certainly more popular in parts of Europe and throughout Latin American than here in the United States but, again, it is done only after a friendship develops and blossoms, so don't worry about it on the first trip.

Many of these nuances of behavior—hand gestures and body language—will go unnoticed, but it is useful to be aware and to avoid being overly surprised when confronted with a rare, unexpected act or motion. Avoid inadvertently offending someone you are trying to do business with by using some gesture or action that is considered rude or offensive in that country.

WORKING THROUGH INTERPRETERS

When former President Jimmy Carter visited Poland in 1977 for the first time, his official translator mangled the official arrival message so that it came out "The President says he is pleased to be here in Poland grasping your secret parts." Translators are far from infallible, and it is helpful to know some tricks for working with and through interpreters. The tips and advice that follow will help even if your foreign associate has limited knowledge of English and assures you that a translator will not be necessary. Another option is that when language is a hurdle, your foreign contact may bring someone from his own firm into the meeting who is fluent in

English. Or, if that is not possible, an independent translator may have to be hired.

Incidentally, if you need translation help here in the United States, there are several places to seek help. First, the yellow pages of your phone directory will quickly show if there are commercial translators available in your city. Next, local colleges, universities, or even high schools might provide names of competent language experts who provide freelance services. Lastly, you can contact the American Translators Association, a trade group in Ossining, NY who have 2500 members. For written translations, payment is usually by the word and runs from 6 cents to 16 cents, depending on the technical nature of the material and the commonness of the language. For on-the-spot verbal translations, fees run from $25 to $35 per hour.

Here are some specific tips for working with interpreters, whether in the United States or in another country.

▶ *Get to know the interpreter in advance.* Your phrasing, your accent, your pace, your idioms—all are important to a good interpreter.

▶ *Review technical terms in advance.* An American steel company executive tells how he was describing a heat-treating process called "pickling" to his West German contact. The translator asked for a pause to research that term and decided on the German word "gurke." Throughout the rest of the conversation the West German listener was confounded, wondering what the heat-treating process had to do with "cucumbers."

▶ *Speak slowly and clearly.* Americans claim that foreigners speak "too quickly." Well, that's what foreigners complain about Americans, too. When working with translators, try to phrase your thoughts into single ideas or for not longer than, say, two sentences.

▶ *Don't be afraid to use gestures and show emotion.* Even though your words must be converted into the listener's language, your body language helps convey your thoughts. The translator will never be able to transmit your inflections and tone, so you must find other ways to underscore what you are trying to say.

▶ *Watch the eyes.* The eyes, it is said, are the key to comprehension. We can often detect if "the eyes disappear behind the mind," as one experienced Danish businessman described inattention. Obviously, the listener may not attend your words with rapt concentration, but watch to see if the translator's words are hitting the mark.

▶ *Insist that the interpreter translate in brief bursts, not wait until the end of a long statement.* If the translator must listen and analyze and then summarize, much could be lost. Two Illinois executives once hosted the president of a competitive Japanese firm who was accompanied by a hired translator. Over lunch, the Americans asked a blunt but appropriate question: When would Japan lower duties and other barriers so that their American product had the same free access to the Japanese market as the Japanese producer had to the American market. The Japanese executive launched into a long-winded reply that lasted through the soup and salad courses, and well into the main course. At long last, the Japanese visitor finished, and the translator looked at the Americans and simply said "He doesn't know."

▶ *Be careful of humor and jokes.* Everyone enjoys a good laugh, but it is difficult to export American humor. That is because much American humor depends on word plays or current events. Neither translates well. It is better, perhaps, to smile often and show a happy and pleasant disposition rather than try to "warm up" your listener with the latest in American humor.

▶ *Use visual aids where possible.* Professional communicators recommend using as many of the senses as possible for optimum results. Therefore, if you can combine the translator's words with visual messages as well, the chances of better communication are increased. Obviously, if the visual messages use the universal language of pictures, your job of communication will be much easier. This requires that you spend time in advance acquainting your interpreter with the visual material, but it is usually time well spent.

▶ *Be especially careful with numbers.* Write out critically important numbers to assure absolute understanding.

▶ *Confirm all important discussions in writing.* This is true of telephone calls as well as face-to-face discussions. It is simply a common sense, back-up act that can avoid much confusion and misunderstanding in the future.

EXHIBITING AT TRADE SHOWS

Probably the most common way to venture abroad in search of new business is to attend, or possibly exhibit at a trade show. This is an excellent way to survey a market, examine competition, and make fast contacts with potential customers or distributors in a broad region. Be aware, though, that there are significant differences to consider if you plan to exhibit overseas: Booths are usually called "stands"; dimensions are in metric; the pipe and drape configuration common in the United States is uncommon; and booths are usually constructed of hard walls built on site or assembled from modular components.

A checklist follows in a "countdown" format designed to help you prepare for and exhibit your products at an overseas trade show. It is drawn from material provided by James L. Arndt, International Consultant with the Bureau of International Trade in the Wisconsin Department of Development.

Nine Months in Advance

▶ Select the fair carefully. This is a significant investment in time and money. Some firms plan as far as two years in advance.

▶ Assign one person to coordinate everything connected with the trade fair.

▶ If you already have a distributor in the market where the exhibition is being held, arrange to work hand-in-hand on all basic decisions including the nature of the exhibit, sales literature and translations, prices, samples, staffing, and all major items on this checklist.

▶ Obtain logistical information from the organizer such as a map of booth locations, days and hours the exhibition will run, voltages, names of local booth designers, names of customs brokers and shippers at point of entry for equipment and materials, door and elevator dimensions, and then decide on space requirements.

▸ Begin a pro forma budget that includes the cost of exhibit space and booth, staffing, transportation, hotels and meals, literature, entertainment, samples, freight costs for any machinery exhibited, and final disposition of that equipment. A general rule-of-thumb is that our expenses will probably double or triple over a comparable U.S. exhibition.

▸ Contract for the space.

Six Months in Advance

▸ Communicate your ideas on layout and motif of the exhibit to the designer. Place heavy emphasis on moving demonstrations of your product and, if appropriate, take-away samples. Also, decide if small, private conference areas are necessary in order to talk in confidence with customers. If the booth is to be constructed in the United States, allow at least three months for shipping.

▸ Make plane reservations. Using economy fares booked well in advance can save significant money.

▸ Determine exactly what to ship, what to sell at the show, and what to bring back. Choose a freight forwarder to handle shipment of the display, sample products, and literature. Explore if and how the products exhibited at the display can be sold locally in order to keep samples in that market and also save on return freight costs.

▸ Decide on a hotel and make hotel reservations. Do the same with auto rentals. In major exhibition cities like Hanover and Frankfurt, West Germany, first-time exhibitors are amazed at how quickly available hotel rooms are gobbled up. At one of these fairs, I once had accommodations 25 miles away from the fair, and even then it was a boarding house and not a hotel.

▸ Begin preparing literature, especially if language translations are required. Develop an invitation list to prospective buyers, encouraging them to visit you.

▸ Work on staffing assignments. Assure that all U.S.-based staff planning to serve at the fair have valid passports, plus visas if they are required. Arrange for an international driver's license if you plan to drive.

▶ If food is to be transported for exhibit and use, contact your local Department of Agriculture or the Department of Commerce and the trade show organizer to find out if the products need special approval for importation and if there are any guidelines on the shipping process. Work with the freight forwarder on scheduling the shipping—timing, marking of crates, and special handling.

Four Months in Advance

▶ Finalize booth design. Decide if a separate hospitality room or hotel suite is required.

▶ Finalize shipping arrangements.

▶ Check on progress with literature, equipment, samples.

▶ Arrange for insurance coverage for staff and equipment.

▶ Determine if vaccinations or other health shots are required and make appointments for these shots.

▶ Notify and begin establishing appointments with key customers.

▶ Assure that staff assignments are made, that price lists are accurate and complete, and that delivery schedules, credit, and quantity discount terms are clear and available.

▶ Determine if local interpreters or demonstrators will be required at the exhibit and, if so, arrange for hiring.

▶ Determine if and how products will be disposed of after the fair.

Two Months in Advance

▶ Send a list of booth personnel to fair management in order to obtain entry passes and identifications.

▶ Re-confirm travel and hotel reservations, availability of sales literature, and gift giveaways.

▶ Prepare a tool kit for emergency repairs of display units and equipment.

▶ Assure that all staff traveling to the fair have travelers' checks for personal expenses. It is usually unnecessary to obtain foreign currency in advance, unless advised by the fair exhibitors. Learn from the exhibition organizers what union rules apply regarding setting up of displays, maintenance, and repairs, and how payment is customarily made.

One to Two Weeks in Advance

▶ Ship foodstuffs and perishables by air.

▶ Confirm with the freight forwarder that your shipment is safely at the trade show. Assure installation is arranged.

▶ Orient and train booth personnel on work schedules, sales policies, and literature available. Have them take some other proof of citizenship along—an old passport, or copy of their birth certificate—in the event their current passport is lost or stolen. Discuss local safety and health precautions.

▶ Assure that someone is at the booth at all times who will have the authority to make major decisions on sales points.

▶ Prepare a list of important telephone numbers: fair manager, decorator, freight handler, local American consulate or embassy, and number at the booth itself.

▶ Assure that you have quantities of business cards available, plus place them in everything: luggage, camera cases, equipment, and samples.

▶ Plan your wardrobe, establish methods of keeping track of daily expenses, assure personal medications are on hand, and take extra passport photos.

▶ Plan to register your camera and other expensive electronic equipment with U.S. Customs at the point of departure to assure easy re-entry into the United States.

When You Arrive

▶ Send a telex or cable home so the company and staff families know the name of the hotel, room number, and phone numbers. This can save valuable time in cases of emergency.

▶ Visit the trade show site to become familiar with the travel route, transportation, and travel time.

▶ Conduct a final check of booth and equipment.

▶ Obtain locations of nearest medical facilities, telexes, fax machines, secretarial services, and security.

▶ Survey other competitors at the fair and try to obtain prices and samples of sales literature.

▶ Meet with full staff and review sales methods and materials.

▶ Evaluate better booth sites for future exhibitions, and take advantage of attending seminars at the trade show.

After the Show

▶ Review all bills and charges, especially in terms of the prevailing exchange rates.

▶ Try to remain a few days to follow up on local contacts and visit the marketplace to note competitive products and prices.

▶ Review names and evaluations of all new prospects made at the exhibition and begin deciding on when and how next contact will be made.

▶ Assure that the exhibit will be repacked and shipped, or properly stored or disposed of. Dispose of all remaining samples, products, or machinery by either shipping them back to the United States, selling them locally, or turning them over to your representative in that market.

After Returning Home

▶ Write and send personal thank you letters to appropriate people.

▶ Determine final costs and weigh against actual and estimated results.

▶ Record your recommendations for making the next exhibition more efficient and less costly.

▶ Immediately consider a next trip to follow up on the best potential sales prospects.

MODIFYING YOUR PRODUCT

Purple is the color of death to people in Mexico and Brazil. White is bad in Japan, for the same reasons. People in Southeast Asia like bright, vibrant colors; so do people in the Southern markets of the European Common Market, while in the North—Scandinavia, West Germany—more somber colors are favored. In Japan, silver precious metals are preferred over gold, because gold is considered gaudy. Yet several thousand miles south, in Hong Kong, it is the opposite and gold is preferred as a precious substance over silver. Even *shadings* of gold make a difference and have different supporters. In the Middle East, a darker, more orange-tinged gold is the favorite, while in the United States a lighter "champagne" color is much preferred, something a Middle Easterner would reject because it looks "washed out and therefore cheaper."

The purpose of this hop-scotching around the color globe is to underscore the obvious: People's tastes vary, depending on the market. That means your product may have to be modified before it will be successful in other countries.

Many budding exporters resist this and, happily, with many products it is not necessary to modify a product for export. But this concern should rank high on your list for examination during this first exploration and discovery trip abroad. This subject—modifying your product to be more successful in a given market—is also where your soon-to-be appointed new distributor can advise and assist you. More about that later.

According to a 1983 Conference Board Report titled "Adapting Products for Export," there are nine good reasons why it might be necessary and wise to modify your product. It is highly unlikely that all of these will apply to your product, but one or several of them might apply. Only you will know. At Parker Pen, we were fortunate. "Our pens write in any language," founder George S. Parker was fond of saying. Even so, we learned over time that Orientals liked extra-fine writing points, while Germans favored heavy and flexible points. We learned that Northern Europeans judged a product mainly by function and performance, while Southern Europeans looked first at design and style. Experience, common sense, and research will help you decide if and how you might want to modify your product. As a checklist, here are the nine reasons as cited by the Conference Board research:

1. *Government regulations.* This will be an "old friend" to manufacturers already producing in the United States and it should be no surprise to learn that other governments have their own set of rules and regulations. A company making electrical power

tools, for example, may find that a certain government requires a hand-held electrical tool to pass a submersible test before being acceptable.

2. *Tariffs and taxes.* A minor modification to a product, such as removing a gold decoration or embellishment, might cause the product to be significantly reclassified, saving substantial amounts on tariffs and taxes.

3. *Nontariff barriers.* Other governments may impose testing procedures, certifications, inspections, quota limitations, and other such nontariff barriers. Often, these are set to help protect local manufacturers from outside competition. Happily, the GATT negotiations steadily peck away at these nontariff barriers, but nonetheless they can be a factor and may require some form of modification to your product.

4. *Regional trade associations.* Almost everyone has heard of the European Economic Community (EEC), also called the common market. But there are a handful of other such regional trade associations, one for Central America, one for Southeast Asia, one for Latin America, and so on. Often, these regional trade associations will have separate regulations, motivated mainly to protect manufacturers or sources within their geographic group.

5. *Competitive offerings.* This means, simply, that a competitive product in a given foreign market may be offering a feature that you do not offer. Obviously, it is your responsibility to determine if you must modify your product to compete successfully in that market.

6. *Culture.* No matter how special your product, in most cases it will have difficulty bucking ingrained cultural habits and preferences. Hot dogs cannot be marketed in the Middle East because according to religious codes a follower of Islam cannot eat any pork or pork derivatives. Cheese will not find a ready market in the People's Republic of China because cheese is not known or produced there and therefore disliked.

7. *Economic development.* Mercedes Benz has great difficulty selling many automobiles in Haiti, the world's poorest nation. The economy has to be able to support your product.

8. *Purchase and distribution patterns.* Direct mail sales may not be as common, door-to-door selling may be unheard of, and attempting to bypass wholesalers may be suicide—each of

these may affect how and what you sell in a selected market overseas.

9. *Climate and geography.* Engines may have to be modified for humidity and altitude, metal finishes may have to be protected from saltwater spray and breezes, and anti-freeze chemicals may have to be injected into liquids headed for cold climates.

Among all of these reasons to modify your product, the common-sense ones will probably pop up first: electrical requirements, such as differing phases, cycles, and voltages; packaging preferences or requirements for labeling; language requirements, such as the bilingual requirement in nearby Canada; and basic government requirements such as in West Germany where most everything must conform to DIN standards, a complex set of prescribed standards that apply to everything from the size of stationery to ski bindings.

Here is another example of common-sense product modification. A U.S. Midwestern manufacturer of front-end loaders soon learned that it was inefficient to ship their product with the heavy metal bucket attached to their machine because of the excessive weight and size. Furthermore, since there was nothing special about their bucket, they quickly decided to modify their product by exporting them without the front end attached and buying that part overseas. The savings in the end market were substantial. As you can see, there are many ways to consider modifying your product.

At this stage, a neophyte exporter might not be blamed for a shake of the head and the question "Is it all worth it?"

The answer is yes and the best support for that answer is that your foreign competitors are quickly and readily modifying their products in order to compete in the U.S. market. Just imagine the changes that the foreign car manufacturers must undergo when shipping automobiles into the United States; imagine the clothing manufacturers who must conform not only to American tastes but to our system of sizes (e.g., if you wear a size 10 shoe, your European shoe size is 43). Furthermore, as one of the last holdouts against the metric system, any product shipped to the United States has probably had to be measured, specified, and registered in inches, feet, and pounds rather than in the metric system.

Incidentally, The U.S. Omnibus Trade and Competitiveness Act of 1988 has an obscure section that designates the metric system as the preferred method of measure for trade and commerce and requires U.S. government agencies to start buying metric whenever possible.

Modifying a product should not be a shock to most any U.S. manufacturer. Henry Ford got away with making one model in one color—black—but competition quickly revolutionized the auto industry so that today, with all the permutations available through sizes and colors and options, it is said that General Motors could run its production lines night and day for a year and never produce exactly the same car twice. Whether we like it or not, the days of fragmented and segmented marketing are here and, therefore, modifying a product for export should not be a surprise.

It is entirely possible to *not* have to modify your product. Tobacco companies, tire producers, chemical manufacturers, paper companies, and many others report that they can still export their basic products without modification. But the message here is "Be alert. Do your homework. Be prepared to modify, within economic boundaries, in order to compete successfully in foreign markets."

Whether you should modify your product should be high on your survey list on the first trip abroad. Advance preparation with your trade counselors will help, and first-hand examination of both products and regulations in your target market will complete the picture. Also, one of the tasks and responsibilities of any distributor you might appoint will be to determine if and how your product must be modified to either conform to regulations, to compete with rivals, or to capture fresh customer interest.

MORE ITEMS TO INVESTIGATE

Installation, warranties, and *after-sales service* are three more critical areas for you to be examining on this first prospecting trip.

The U.S. Department of Commerce offers this advice on the ease of *installation* a product may require: "If technicians or engineers are needed overseas to assist in installation, the company should minimize their time in the field if possible. To achieve this, the company may wish to pre-assemble or pre-test the product before shipping. Disassembly of a product for shipment and reassembly abroad may be considered by the company. This can save the firm shipping costs, but it may add to delay in payment if the sale is contingent on an assembled product. Even if sending trained personnel is not required, the company should be careful to give training manuals, installation instructions, parts lists, etc., that have been carefully translated into local languages."

Warranties and the expectations involving warranties may vary from market to market. This should be investigated and discussed with your candidates for distributors. After all, they are the ones that will most likely have to honor any obligations under the warranty, with your help of course. The type of warranty you offer may also depend on what your competitors in that market offer, and a strong, well-advertised warranty may be just one way to break into a new market. Examine competitive warranties carefully, and discuss this important part of the sale with your prospective distributor.

It is said that good after-sales service can turn negatives into positives. The extra distances involved when selling products in other countries make servicing especially important. Again, your appointed distributor will usually have the first line of responsibility for service after the sale. This means training of service personnel, purchase of proper tools, and maintaining local inventories of spare parts. You can also assist your distributor with advice and counsel on costing and pricing this service. Depending on competitive practices, one policy to consider is that pricing of after-sales service should be on a breakeven basis. That way, neither you nor the distributor must add to your margin and you can offer the end customer this service at an economical cost.

There are several other options when considering after-sales service. For example, you could franchise this work to an outside, independent organization within the market or region. However, this adds to the cost. Another option is to locate your own service facility in the market or region. With some products, notably large machinery, the supplier can even provide service from the United States on a case-by-case basis by sending service personnel directly into the market when the need arises. Finally, another option would be to join with other manufacturers in your field and provide a joint cooperative-type service.

Whichever option you choose, it is important to collect data on quality and service problems, just as you most likely do in the United States. This feedback can be obtained through customers, wholesalers, distributors, sales personnel, or through direct mail research programs.

SUMMARY

It should be obvious that your first trip, the "first handshake," can be exciting, challenging, productive, busy, and tiring all in one. However, to make it productive, it is worth careful planning and execution.

We began with a discussion on cultural differences and business protocol around the world. This was certainly a proper place to begin because it is—literally—the first thing you will bump into when traveling abroad. Successful business in other countries is difficult without an appreciation and awareness of culture and protocol. Next, we dealt with talking through interpreters. Heeding a few of the tips presented here could avoid problems, even a gross misunderstanding, at a later time. If your first trip involves exhibiting at a trade fair, the checklist earlier in this chapter should serve to help you prepare thoroughly and carefully. Finally, we listed the reasons why it is important to consider if your product should be modified to be more successful overseas.

At the conclusion of this first trip, you should have a bundle of valuable information under your arm, ready to spread out, examine, digest, and discuss with colleagues. You should have a list of solid candidates for your distributorship, you should have a first-hand knowledge and examination of the market and your competitors, and you should have preliminary ideas on modifying your product and how you are going to handle warranties, installation, and after-sales service. It is now time to consider some laws and legal aspects: What type of legal agreement to have with a distributor, laws affecting exporting and importing, and finally, a U.S. law that can help you defer taxes on export sales.

6

The Law and
Exporting

. . . be brave, clean and reverent.

Laws governing exports and international trade are frighteningly complex, vary significantly from country to country and are constantly changing. For example, as recently as January, 1988, major changes in the law governing international contracts were implemented when the "United Nations Convention on Contracts for the International Sale of Goods" came into being after 50 years or more of ongoing study.

Faced with this, I must admit to some personal apprehension about presenting a definitive chapter on laws governing exporting and trade. Where does one start? All those laws muddy up the marketing waters and make it difficult to see the targets. Yet the lawyers do come to your rescue, as one by the name of Robert E. Collins, General Counsel for the Parker Pen Co. did for me when, during one period, I was being sued for no less than $5 million by several different distributors for what they considered improper terminations.

In compiling this chapter, the question that bedeviled me was: "What advice can I give to prospective international traders about the laws governing trade that will not scare the living daylights out of them?"

I decided to turn to another expert on the laws of international trade, Eugene Theroux from the law firm of Baker & McKenzie, one of the best known law firms in the United States in international business.

Theroux also is an expert on the legal aspects of doing business with the People's Republic of China and shares his time between Beijing and Washington, DC.

When I asked him the question: "What do I tell my readers about the law and international trade?" Theroux replied as follows: "My usual advice to exporters, at meetings I address, and concerning *all* jurisdictions, not just China, is that they should be trustworthy, loyal, helpful, friendly, courteous, kind, obedient, cheerful, thrifty, brave, clean, and reverent. That, of course, is the Boy Scout oath, and, really, is all most exporters need to follow if they want to be successful."

There is your first and most basic guideline for dealing with the law.

Now let us turn to some fundamentals in the law and international trade. None of this will make you a lawyer, but what follows will equip you to ask the important questions of any lawyers you consult and also be aware of some of the legal bear traps as you weave your way through the thickets of laws governing trade around the world.

It is interesting to observe that in China, with its one billion or more population, there are very few lawyers. American attorneys like Theroux advise Americans what to do, not the Chinese. When I was first there in 1976 as part of a group to examine the Chinese market, I remember being told an old Chinese proverb: "It is better to be vexed to death than enter into a lawsuit." That, it seems, is why there are so few lawyers in China. Perhaps that would be good advice for us here in the United States where we seem to have developed, as described by former Chief Justice of the Supreme Court William Burger, our "over-litigious society."

Based on the likelihood that you will first enter international trade by shipping finished goods to a distributor, we will begin this chapter by presenting probably the single most important legal document you will require in exporting and international trade: a distributor agreement. This agreement is essential because it lays out the rules for this highly important new and, hopefully, long relationship. In this document, you will want clear agreements on what each party expects from the other in terms of territory, payment, marketing expectations, as well as some understanding on the length of the agreement and how it can be terminated. You will learn that there are distributor agreements that can be as short and simple as a single one-page letter, or there can be distributor agreements covering dozens of pages. Whichever you and your lawyer prefer, in this chapter, you will find a checklist of items that should be discussed and agreed upon by you and your distributor in advance.

We will also discuss licensing agreements because you may find it necessary to allow your distributor or another foreign manufacturer to use your patents, trademarks, technology, and knowhow in return for a royalty.

Next, we will turn to several important U.S. government laws dealing with exporting and international trade. For example, two important areas are the *antiboycott regulations* and the *Foreign Corrupt Practices Act*. Both will be explained so that you will know if and how they affect you and how to abide by them.

We will review how U.S. law permits Export Trading Companies to be formed allowing the association of U.S. competitors in joint export activities without running afoul of the Sherman antitrust laws.

Under U.S. tax laws, you can—and probably should—establish a Foreign Sales Corporation (FSC), called FISC for short. When your export sales reach a certain dollar volume, it may be worthwhile to establish a FISC in order to obtain certain tax benefits. This provision in the tax laws was created to be an incentive to exporting, so it is important and useful to understand.

Finally, the matters of patents, trademarks, and product liability in foreign countries will be summarized as well as how to obtain legal help on personal matters when traveling and doing business outside the United States.

DISTRIBUTOR AGREEMENTS

C. Edward Boggs spent four decades helping U.S. consumer goods firms establish hundreds of distributorships all over the world. He helped such companies as Fabregé (men's toiletries), Oneida (silverplate flatware), and Parker Pen obtain distribution in not only the largest but some of the remotest markets in the world. Says Boggs,

> A distributor relationship and agreement is just like getting married. It can be mutually delightful, supportive, and rewarding . . . or it can be a living hell, resulting in pain, anger, and the loss of lots of money. Yes, even more than alimony.

This good advice serves to underscore earlier counsel given in this book: Search out, examine, and evaluate distributors with extreme care. Use long and careful consideration to make sure your choice is a good one. Then craft an agreement that both parties can agree upon with confidence and comfort.

The U.S. Department of Commerce, in its 1985 booklet titled "Foreign Business Practices," subtitled "Materials on Practical Aspects of Exporting, International Licensing and Investing," offers this basic advice on distributor agreements:

▸ The agreement should be in writing. Failure to do this may subject the agreement to the arbitrary whim of local law.

▸ The agreement should set forth the benefits to both parties. Well-balanced agreements should not place an excessive or profitless burden on only one of the parties.

▸ A clear definition and meaning must be given to all contract terms. Many English words have the same or similar spelling as foreign words but with different meanings.

▸ The rights and obligations of the parties should be expressly stated. For example, it may be prudent to expressly waive provisions of certain foreign laws, assuming that is permissible in that country.

▸ A jurisdictional clause should be included. Many countries insist that any adjudication of disputes must be referred to local courts, but if local laws allow it may be advisable to specify another jurisdiction to handle any legal disputes.

▸ A clause should provide that disputes are to be settled by arbitration and would identify the arbitration body or forum. This could be useful in avoiding litigation in foreign countries.

▸ The impact of foreign laws on the contract should be carefully considered. What is legally valid in the United States may be invalid in the foreign country and vice versa.

Most disagreements about distributor relationships arise first over payments and then over poor performance, which then leads to termination. Therefore, one of the very first pieces of information you should acquire is: What are the local laws governing and protecting distributors from improper termination?

> *Example:* Puerto Rico is infamous among export managers for its "Law 75." This is the law protecting dealers and distributors in Puerto Rico. In summary, under this law, if a manufacturer-supplier terminates or refuses to renew a Puerto Rican distributorship without "just cause" (and in Puerto Rican courts it has been found very difficult to prove "just cause"), the manufacturer-supplier is required to compensate the distributor for expenses in setting up the distributorship, the value of the distributor's inventories and stock, the value of his goodwill, and an amount equal to his profits for the past five years. All this can amount to a healthy settlement, even more, as Boggs would say, than alimony.

Puerto Rico's Law 75 is considered perhaps the most onerous of all laws around the world regarding the termination of a distributor. The functional word here is "indemnification." That is what the distributor is paid for unjust termination. As a general rule, the laws requiring substantial indemnifications are more harsh and more complex throughout the Latin American markets than in other parts of the world. In fairness, it should be explained that these indemnification laws were developed to protect local importing businesses who devote time, energy, and money in establishing a new market for a foreign producer. Without some legal protection, a local importer-distributor could establish a new market only to have the sourcing company turn around and drop him and install its own, private distribution company in that market.

Therefore, one of the first provisions of any distributor agreement form will be: How long will this agreement be in force, and what do we do if either side wishes to terminate it before that term expires or does not wish to renew it when it expires? In considering these two points, you must, as we have emphasized here, be certain to take into account local laws pertaining to distributor agreements in each country. A digest of these laws, listed market-by-market, can be found in the booklet titled "Foreign Business Practices" that can be obtained at your nearest U.S. Department of Commerce International Trade Administration office.

CHECKLIST OF IMPORTANT PROVISIONS

The following is a long, general checklist of items to consider when discussing provisions of a distributorship and, ultimately, when drawing up a distributor agreement. Like most legal matters, this list covers many contingencies, but is not exhaustive. Rather than get bogged down carefully considering each and every point, consider this an unabridged checklist and read it more for general effect. Following this list, you will find a discussion on the relative pros and cons of long-form agreements versus short-form agreements.

1. Time period the agreement will be in effect
2. Options when that time period is finished
3. Termination by either party *before* that time period
4. Jurisdiction
5. Arbitration
6. Geographic designation of the territory involved
7. Exclusivity or will certain other parties be permitted to import the product; if so, explain
8. Definitions of the products involved
9. Sales quotas
10. Responsibility for importation: duty, freight, and insurance
11. Responsibility for warehousing, order-filling, payments, and collections
12. Reporting responsibility, e.g., monthly sales figures to the sourcing company
13. Currency in which payments will be made to the source
14. Payment terms for the goods
15. Secrecy provisions

16. Can competitive products be handled or not

17. Warranty claims and after-sales repair service responsibilities

18. Advertising, merchandising, and public relations support—whose responsibility, who pays, who approves materials, etc.

19. Patent and trademark protection (i.e., who does what)

20. Appointment of subdistributors (e.g., is drop-shipping permitted and expected)

21. Commissions, bonuses, or other payments

22. Taxes—who is responsible for which taxes

23. Indemnifications

24. Translations

25. Other legal considerations: assignment, waivers, force majeure, notices, severability, Foreign Corrupt Practices Act

26. Prices—subject to change without notice, or fixed for certain time periods

27. If the distributor sends "indent" orders (orders to be shipped to a second party directly from the source), who has final responsibility for collection of payment, called "del credere" responsibility

When drawing up a distributor agreement, whether long form or short form, it obviously makes good sense to obtain the assistance of a law firm within that market. They should know local laws and their responsibility to you is to protect your interests. The U.S. embassy or consulate in each market can provide a list of recommended local law firms, and further, it might be wise to select one with strong U.S. connections or affiliations. In that way, if and when questions or disagreements arise, you can work through the U.S. affiliate of the firm rather than having to travel to or communicate with the law firm in the market itself.

From the checklist, one can easily see how a distributor contract could cover pages and pages of legal provisions, clauses, and conditions. According to experienced international attorneys, there are two schools of thought on the size and content of a distributor agreement:

▶ Your industry, or your product, may customarily require a very comprehensive agreement between seller and distributor. Or, you just may feel more comfortable operating under specific and complete provisions governing your relationship. In these cases, it is likely that your distributor agreement form will be quite long and involved. Under this practice, you "live and die by the contract" so to speak, because theoretically you try to anticipate every possible contingency and cover it in writing in the contract.

▶ The alternate view is "make the contract cover the basic provisions of the relationship in simple and uncomplex form, without a lot of detail to quibble over, and hope that you can settle any differences by discussion and compromise."

This latter philosophy is more common and actually preferred in Japan. There, *context* of an agreement is more important than literal meanings of specific words. That is also why the Japanese may not feel obliged to obey every letter of a contract. More about that in a Chapter 12. This short form, of course, has its own set of risks but has the advantage of not constraining either party to a strict literal interpretation of a long document.

The letter on page 119 is an example of this second view—that is, a simple one-page distributor appointment and agreement form. This form, reprinted with the permission of the Parker Pen Company, was used regularly over a span of 60 years and applied to well over 100 distributors around the world.

When disagreements occur, they are likely to occur over pricing practices, compensation changes, advertising and promotion support, return of goods, after-sales servicing, maintenance of inventories, sourcing from different plants in different countries, and modification of the product. It is common for export managers to return from arduous trips, angry with a distributor, ready to cancel the agreement. But, as we pointed out earlier, changing a distributor can be exceedingly costly in money and time. To avoid hasty decisions, some companies require the executive recommending the cancellation to submit detailed reports outlining the exact problems, as well as general information about the market, how it could be improved, and the prospects for finding a better distributor. The best preventive medicine is, of course, to try to work harmoniously with the distributor. The best motivation to work together is that you

---

Sample Distributor Agreement Letter Form

Dear _____

This is to advise you of our decision to appoint you the PARKER distributor throughout (name of market), effective when we receive your letter accepting the distributorship on the terms stated herein.

Each of your orders will be subject to acceptance by the Parker Company to which it is directed before it shall become a binding order. We shall make shipments direct to you, or to third parties in your territory approved by you.

While this arrangement is in effect, we shall not enter a similar agreement covering PARKER products with anyone else in the territory mentioned. You, in turn, will not handle writing instruments or inks manufactured or distributed by others.

We shall support the sale of our products by the appropriation of funds for advertising and the provision of promotional materials.

You, in turn, will do all possible to meet the demand for PARKER products, expanding distribution and providing and maintaining repair service facilities.

This distributorship may be terminated by either party giving three months written notice to the other.

When we receive your letter of acceptance, we will forward details of the PARKER products available, the current prices and terms. We shall keep you informed as to any changes in our products or prices from time to time in the future.

Very truly yours,

---

both want the same objective: sales and long-term, solid growth. If the distributor succeeds, you succeed. Each party needs the other.

In Chapter 10, you will find more information on how to work successfully with a distributor. That chapter covers the working relationship between you and the distributor—what you can expect from a distributor, what he can expect from you, and how to motivate that distributor to do the best possible job. But, that whole relationship begins with a mutual understanding about who does what for whom, and that relationship is expressed in this vital legal document called the distributor agreement.

LICENSING AGREEMENTS

When direct export of your product is not possible, because of tariff or other barriers, you may want to consider authorizing a local company to manufacture or assemble your product. In that case, you will want a licensing agreement. Under the licensing process, what is "sold" are such things as rights under patents or trademarks, know-how or technical expertise, and architectural and engineering designs. With technology on the rise all over the world, licensing becomes a popular vehicle to "sell" technological know-how. So specialized is licensing that there is a new profession—licensing executive—and a new trade association, Licensing Executives Society (1444 W. 10th St., Cleveland, OH 44113).

The Department of Commerce booklet titled "Foreign Business Practices" spells out the implications of licensing. For example, it lists these pros and cons of licensing in lieu of direct foreign investment:

Pros

1. Licensing permits entry into foreign markets without large capital outlays. It is, therefore, a favorite device for small- and medium-sized companies.

2. Returns are apt to be more rapidly realized than in the case of manufacturing ventures.

3. The income from foreign licensing helps to underwrite costly research programs.

4. Licensing enables a firm to retain markets otherwise lost by import restrictions or because it is being outpriced.

5. Licensing can be used to test a foreign market and then to service it without costly additions to production or detracting from the supply available for local customers.

6. Licensing permits a company to develop outlets for components or other products and to build goodwill for other company products.

7. Licensing enables a company to establish an operation in countries that will not permit the establishment of a local subsidiary controlled by foreigners.

8. Licensing is a two-way street that may permit the American company to get access to a foreign company's technology

and even acquire a whole new product line without the delay and expense of development.

Cons

1. Every licensee is a potential competitor. If the arrangement continues over time to be of mutual benefit, both parties will want to perpetuate it and continue to exchange know-how and product improvements. However, once a licensee has acquired technical proficiency and a good market, pressure can build up to terminate the license or at least revise it to the licensor's detriment.

2. Licensor control over the licensee's manufacturing and marketing operations is rarely completely satisfactory. This can result in damage to trademarks and company reputation. The technique for averting this problem lies in careful investigation before selecting a licensee and maintaining quality control whenever a trademark or trade name is licensed.

3. Licensing is probably the least profitable way of exploiting a foreign market. On the other hand, the risks and headaches are usually less than those experienced with investing, at least in the short run, although perhaps more than those experienced with exporting. Moreover, licensing may represent the only way to enter certain markets.

The U.S. Department of Commerce recommends that licensing agreements should include consideration of the elements listed next. It may seem a complicated and lengthy list, but licensing is a complex business. At Parker Pen, for example, we licensed selected distributors to make and bottle fluid ink for fountain pens. This could be done in a facility not much larger than a one-car garage and involved the seemingly simple act of mixing dyes with water and putting it into bottles. Nonetheless, Parker licensing agreements for bottled ink covered most of these points, so they are worth considering. With high technology, the agreements might be considerably more complex. Here are some key considerations:

▸ The products covered
▸ The rights licensed under the contract—patents, trademarks, know-how, and copyright

▶ Territorial coverage

▶ Tenure or term of the contract

▶ Extension and renewal clauses

▶ Protection of rights subject to license

▶ Future rights and options

▶ Merchandising and management assistance

▶ Quality control

▶ Grantback and cross licensing

▶ Royalty rate and structure

▶ Service charges

▶ Royalty-free licenses

▶ Terms and conditions of payment

▶ Reporting and auditing requirements

▶ Equity participations

▶ Currency control

▶ Choice of law

▶ Know-how and trade secret protection

▶ Plant visits

▶ Commercial arbitration

▶ Taxes

▶ Termination provisions

▶ Terminal rights and obligations

Keep in mind that each foreign government has its own set of laws governing licensing and it is important to explore these before signing any type of licensing agreement.

Closely related to licensing is the large, complex matter of *joint ventures*. As pointed out earlier in Chapter 2, the possibilities and permutations within the field of joint ventures are immense and cannot possibly be covered here. However, joint business ventures often evolve from licensing agreements when, for example, the licensor takes an equity in the licensee company in return for rights to patents or know-how. The precaution is the same here as it is for licensing: Obtain the help of competent and reputable lawyers who know the specific laws governing joint ventures in the market you are considering.

ANTIDIVERSION, ANTIBOYCOTT AND ANTITRUST REQUIREMENTS

There are three important U.S. government requirements that you should be aware of in order to comply with the existing laws.

The first of these is the antidiversion clause which deals with the subject of U.S. government licenses to export. Earlier we explained that all exports from the United States fall into two categories: either under General License, where no specific application or action is required, or under a Validated License, where specific applications must be made and approvals must be received before shipment. If your product falls under the General License provision, there is still a qualifier about *destination.* It is U.S. policy to either impose embargoes or restrictions on trade with certain countries such as Cuba. Under the Antidiversion Requirement, the commercial invoice and bill of lading (or air waybill) for nearly all commercial shipments leaving the United States must display a statement notifying the carrier and all others that the U.S. material has been licensed for export only to certain destinations and may not be diverted contrary to U.S. law. More simply stated, this requirement says "you musn't say you are sending a shipment to one country and then divert it to a country the U.S. government has designated restricted."

The antiboycott regulations are designed to prohibit U.S. firms or individuals to be a party to foreign boycotts. This is largely an outgrowth of the turmoil in the Middle East and, in practice, most often arises when, for example, a Middle Eastern customer directs that you must not ship his order on an Israeli-owned vessel, or use an Israeli-owned insurance company. In government language, "The United States has an established policy of opposing restrictive trade practices or boycotts fostered or imposed by foreign countries against other countries friendly to the United States."

In general, under this antiboycott regulation, U.S. firms and individuals are prohibited from refusing to do business with friendly countries, or from discriminating against other U.S. persons on the basis of race, religion, sex, or national origin in order to comply with a foreign boycott, or further, from furnishing information about their business relationships with either friendly foreign countries or blacklisted companies in response to boycott requirements.

Furthermore, U.S. firms or individuals must report any requests for any of these actions to the Office of Antiboycott Compliance (OAC), which is part of the Department of Commerce. As a newcomer to international trade, it is easy to dismiss the likelihood of this ever happening and forgetting about this national legal requirement. However, you may be surprised as your export trade grows to suddenly be confronted with an innocent-appearing request on a routine order than could easily constitute aiding a foreign boycott. If you proceed without notifying the OAC, you can be subject to very large fines for complying with an antiboycott request or for failing to report the receipt of the request.

The antitrust laws are designed to ensure fair competition and low prices to all U.S. consumers. Among the practices prohibited by these laws are price-fixing agreements and conspiracies, divisions of markets by competitors, and certain group boycotts and tying arrangements.

Where the antitrust laws are especially significant to exporters, however, are in the areas of overseas distribution arrangements; overseas joint ventures for research, manufacturing, construction, and distribution; patent, trademark, copyright, and know-how licenses; mergers and acquisitions involving foreign firms; and raw material procurement agreements and concessions. Suffice it to say, if you have any questions or concerns about antitrust violations involving any of these eventualities, you should consult with your own antitrust counsel.

Somewhat related to this issue is the Foreign Corrupt Practices Act (FCPA) of 1977, now known as the Business Practices and Records Act. Quoting the U.S. Department of Commerce "Basic Guide to Exporting," this act ". . . makes (among other things) certain payments, offers of payments and gifts to foreign officials, foreign political parties, or foreign political candidates illegal if made corruptly for the purpose of obtaining, retaining, or directing business to any person. It also establishes record keeping and internal accounting control requirements for all publicly held corporations, whether or not these corporations are engaged in international business. The U.S. Department of Justice and Securities and Exchange Commission (SEC) share responsibility for enforcing this law." In a word, bribery is forbidden.

One way to recall and respect the purpose of this law is to remember when and why it was originated. During the mid-1970s, numerous scandals occurred involving huge cash payoffs to middlemen, some of them connected with foreign governments, for the sale of everything from airplanes to commodities.

This whole subject of morality in exporting has been a lively issue for the past decade. It is a polemic consisting of one side that argues "we must not impose our morality on other nations" and at the other pole which argues "we must not allow U.S. business firms to use graft and payola as an accepted and tax-deductible business expense." Interestingly, one footnote to this whole question of bribes and payoffs is that the U.S. government does accept and permit the payment of what are variously called "grease" or "facilitating payments." These refer to modest sums of money that are paid to foreign government officials to influence and persuade them to hasten what would be their normal official duties. The best example would be a customs inspector at a foreign port. This, it seems, is recognition that such practices are, indeed, more common and accepted in other countries.

A Latin businessman, commenting on the U.S. attitude toward morality in international business, once confronted me with this rather different perspective.

> Take the word "contraband," he said. Here in the United States it is a very bad word. It suggests breaking the law by smuggling. However, in my country, the Spanish word is *contrabando*. It comes from the word *contrabandido*, which means literally "against the bandits." When I was a child in the villages of my country, we were taught that the *bandidos*, the bandits, were the land and shop owners. I remember that even candy was illegally brought into our village and we were taught to favor that contraband candy because it was a way of fighting back against the *bandidos*. So, you see my culture was raised to view contraband as a good thing. That may help explain why there are differing values and differing perceptions of morality between our continents.

While this anecdote may give reason to pause over such differing perceptions, and while it may be a good cocktail party story, the fact remains that U.S. laws must be observed and respected. They are not that forbidding. Some experienced international trade executives in this country have spent an entire career doing business overseas and never once have been confronted with an attempted bribe or questionable payment or outright blackmail. Many others have, indeed, run abruptly into them but have quickly recognized the hidden dangers and known what to do. Therefore it is important to, first, be aware and prepared, and secondly to know about U.S. laws and abide by them.

In addition to these laws, it is important to know about certain rules and regulations involving the Federal Drug Administration (FDA) and the Environmental Protection Agency (EPA).

Here is how the Department of Commerce explains the role of the FDA in exporting:

> If the (food or drug) item is intended for export only, meets the specifications of the foreign purchaser, is not in conflict with the laws of the country to which it is to be shipped, and is properly labeled, it is exempt from the adulteration and misbranding provisions of the Act. This exemption does not apply to "new drugs" or "new animal drugs" that have not been approved as safe and effective, and certain devices. If the exporter thinks the export product may be covered by the FDA, it is important to contact the nearest FDA field office.

The involvement of the Environmental Protection Agency has to do with the exportation of hazardous wastes. In this case, the exporter must notify the EPA before shipment, and shipment cannot proceed without approval.

All of these regulations come under the heading of *Export Administration Regulations*. A subscription, which consists of a loose-leaf binder with the basic manual and periodic updates, can be obtained for $86 by writing the Superintendent of Documents, U.S. Government Printing Office, Washington, DC 20402.

EXPORT TRADING COMPANIES

President Reagan, in October 1982, signed a law that permitted two basic innovations for U.S. exporters which were heralded as signaling a new era for international businesses. The changes were significant, but the results have been less than spectacular.

The law was the Export Trading Company (ETC) Act that provided two new benefits to exporters. First, it allowed competitors that normally would be prohibited from associating because of antitrust regulations to join together in a business endeavor. Second, it allowed bank holding companies to own and operate export trading companies.

The objective of this legislation was to encourage and allow U.S. companies of all sizes to band together in trading companies similar to the famous British, Dutch, and Japanese trading companies. By allowing banking institutions to invest for the first time in commercial ventures outside banking, it was thought that the two essential ingredients—money and a desire to trade—would boost exporting. This protection results from a process performed by the Office of Export Trading Company Affairs, a department within the U.S. Department of Commerce, with concurrence from the U.S. Department of Justice, called *certificate of review.* This legal instrument provides antitrust protection for specific activities. Users of this process have been *trade associations* (e.g., the Industrial Safety Equipment Association, Millers' National Federation, and the American Film Marketing Association), *shippers' associations* (e.g., the International Shippers Association which negotiates transportation contracts for export for 14 suppliers of fish and agricultural products), *agribusiness* (rice, prunes, raisins, Alaskan lumber, and pecans from four states in the Sunbelt), *technology-licensing agreements* (very few so far), and *banks* (up to mid-1988, 42 bank holding companies have invested $85 million in export trading companies).

In addition, local and state governments are slowly showing interest in developing their own export trading entities under this act. Several port authorities have started or are considering export trading companies and individual states are attempting to serve companies within their boundaries by forming state-owned or operated ETCs. Your Commerce trade specialist will know if either of these forms of ETCs is available in your region.

The Office of Export Trading Company Affairs also facilitates contacts between producers of goods and services and organizations offering export trade services. A directory, called the Contact Facilitations Service (CFS) directory provides information on banks, ETCs, export management companies, manufacturers, exporters of services, and freight forwarders. Inclusion in the directory is free. A revised and updated version of this directory, *Partners in Export Trade* (PET) is an expansion of this directory. Finally, *The ETC Guidebook* explains the ETC Act in full detail. All of these publications are sold through the Government Printing Office. To obtain copies, information about price and order number may be obtained by writing the Office of Export Trading Company Affairs, Room 1222, U.S. Department of Commerce, Washington,

DC 20230. Seminars and regional conferences on the ETC Act are also offered by DoC, and dates and locations can be obtained at your nearest district office.

FOREIGN SALES CORPORATIONS

As mentioned earlier, the Foreign Sales Corporation Act was passed to serve as an inducement to engage in exporting in the form of income tax deferral. Here is the background as well as an explanation of how it works, and what is required to form one.

The Foreign Sales Corporation Act of 1984 was passed by Congress as a replacement for the Domestic International Sales Corporation Act (DISC Act) which had been in effect since 1971. The purpose of the DISC Act had also been to provide incentives for U.S. companies to export. However, the General Agreement on Tariffs and Trade (GATT) treaty signatories argued that DISCs were a partial subsidy to U.S. exports which was a violation of GATT agreements. As a result, in 1984 Congress replaced the DISC legislation with the FSC Act.

The FSC Act contains more technical compliance requirements and provides less of a tax incentive than did the DISC Act. First, to qualify for these benefits, a FSC must meet certain incorporation and other requirements, and then the FSC must show that the income it derives from exporting qualifies as foreign trade income as defined by the law. The tax exemption will depend on pricing and special pricing rules as specified within the law. Here are the incorporation requirements:

1. The FSC must be created or organized under the laws of a foreign country or of a possession of the United States.
2. The FSC must not have more than 25 shareholders at any time during the taxable year.
3. The FSC must have no preferred stock outstanding at any time during the taxable year.
4. The FSC must maintain an office located outside the United States in a foreign country or possession of the United States.
5. The FSC must maintain a set of its permanent books of account, including invoices, at the foreign office.

6. The FSC must maintain certain corporate records at a location within the United States.

7. The FSC's Board of Directors must contain at least one individual who is not a resident of the United States.

8. The FSC must not be a member, at any time during the taxable year, of any controlled group of corporations in which a DISC is a member.

9. The FSC must have made an election, in effect for the taxable year, to be treated as a FSC.

There are also requirements regarding the following: foreign trade income, foreign management, and what is called foreign economic process. Foreign trade income merely means that gross receipts must come from exporting property or from services performed outside the United States. The foreign management requirements are that Board of Director and shareholder meetings must be held outside the United States, the principal bank account must be outside the United States, and all dividends, fees, and salaries of officers and board members must be disbursed out of corporate bank accounts maintained outside the United States. Foreign economic process requirements means that the solicitation, negotiation, or contracting of the export transaction must have occurred outside the United States and that a certain portion of the direct costs of an export transaction must have been incurred outside the United States. What is a "certain portion of the direct costs"? Two methods are allowed. The first is 50 percent of the costs for the following eligible activities: advertising and sales promotion, processing and delivery of orders, transaction time, time between final invoice and receipt of payment, and assumption of credit risk by the FSC. The other method is that the FSC incurred foreign direct costs of 85 percent or greater in at least two of the five categories above.

As for pricing rules, it would be best to review your special circumstances with an accountant or attorney who is familiar with the FSC Act and who can then provide a pro forma showing where and when your export sales volume would justify incurring the costs of creating a FSC. One rule-of-thumb is that the maintenance costs of a FSC run from $1500 to $3000 annually, and that a firm would need from $27,000 to $45,000 of taxable income from the foreign rules to justify the expense of establishing a FSC. Almost all firms engaged in any significant volume of exporting have taken the time and trouble to form FSCs because the resulting tax benefits become worthwhile.

As a special aid and incentive to smaller firms, the FSC Act permits a firm to declare itself a "small FSC" which has two advantages and one limitation. The advantages are that a small FSC need not meet the foreign management and foreign economic process requirement, but the limitation is that not more than $5 million in foreign trade gross receipts may be taken into account.

Several individual states have formed, or are considering, what is being called a state shared FSC. This means that a state government is taking on the job of forming the corporation, with not more than 25 shareholders, to bring the benefits of a FSC to very small companies who might not be able to bear the costs of incorporation. The idea is that the state performs all the administrative work and then apportions the costs and the benefits among the shareholders.

PATENTS, TRADEMARKS, AND PRODUCT LIABILITY

These three areas are, quite obviously, as important as they are complex to a neophyte exporter. The U.S. Department of Commerce booklet titled *Foreign Business Practices* provides helpful information on each subject. Also, the obvious course of action would be to review the recommended measures for protection in each case with attorneys who serve you in each area within the United States.

In the area of patents and trademarks, you begin in the United States where the U.S. government provides a wide range of protection for intellectual property. To acquire similar protection in each foreign country, you should consult with a competent international patent and trademark attorney. Your trade specialist at the U.S. Department of Commerce can refer you to these experts in your area. Applications for protection must be filed, country-by-country, and renewed after certain periods of time. Many famous trademarks—Levi jeans, Rolex watches, Johnson Wax, just to name a few—have been pirated in certain foreign markets. Without registered trademark protection, these companies would be helpless to retaliate. Therefore, if you have what you consider valuable patents and trademarks, it is worthwhile to contact an attorney who specializes in this field for advice.

As for product liability, as a general rule other markets around the world are not as zealous as we are in the United States. Furthermore, the laws of product liability differ from country to country. Foreign markets are, however, starting to impose higher standards of liability on manufacturers, sellers, and others involved in the commercial transaction. The U.S. Department of Commerce predicts that within a few years, the markets of Western Europe will probably have rules nearly as strict as those of the United States. If product liability claims have been a problem for you and your product in the United States, it would be well to review this, first, with your DoC trade specialist, your attorney, and your insurance company.

GETTING OUT OF LEGAL TROUBLE IN OTHER COUNTRIES

In 25 years of traveling abroad, and after talking with scores of seasoned international business travelers, I have not encountered one serious case of running afoul of the law. Anecdotes about brushes with the law and with foreign officialdom are common. For example, a Company Internal Auditor made the mistake of abbreviating that occupation on her passport. When entering countries, she soon found herself being whisked to the desk of immigration officials and being asked about her profession with the CIA.

In my own experience, on a trip to Iraq, I took special care to reconfirm my departure flight not once but several times, the last time at the airport itself several days before the flight. When I arrived at the airline registration desk on the day of the flight I was told I had not reconfirmed and therefore my reservation had been canceled. When I protested, they literally threw my ticket and passport back at me. I was stranded. My visa had expired, hotels were completely filled, and no other outbound flights were available. I literally had no place to go and yet could not stay in Iraq. At the very last moment, the ticket agent brusquely called me over, gave me a ticket and I raced up the ramp as the last passenger to board. I never learned the full story, but associates speculated my seat was merely being saved in the event some government official came along and needed a seat on that outbound flight.

These experiences are, indeed, minor incidents. But they turn young men into old men if repeated often enough. Here are some tips for avoiding problems with the law and, when they are encountered, what to do about them:

1. Register with the U.S. embassy or consulate. This is especially important if you plan to stay a long time, are in Eastern Europe, are traveling or hiking in a remote part of that country, or are anywhere near civil unrest or an unstable political climate.

2. Turn to American Consuls for advice and help, especially if you encounter trouble. They are experienced in handling serious legal, medical, or financial problems. (This is where I would have turned for help in that airport in Iraq.) They also provide help on more mundane matters, such as absentee voting, Selective Service registration, travel advisories, lost passports, and U.S. citizenship. They can also be helpful with U.S. tax forms, social security forms, serving warrants or subpoenas on foreign defendants, and a host of other legal actions.

3. If you are arrested, the American Consul can normally visit you in jail, give you a list of local attorneys, notify your family and friends, and protest mistreatment or abuse. The Consul *cannot* demand your release or get you out of jail, represent you at trial or give you legal counsel, or pay legal fees, bonds, or fines. In some cases, emergency loans can be arranged, however.

4. Remember—when you are in any foreign country, you are subject to the laws of that land.

5. In some countries, when you expect to stay for long periods, you may be required to register with local authorities. In addition, in some countries when you register at a hotel, it is customary to have your passport taken overnight in order for local authorities to note personal data, or you may be asked to complete a card for the hotel indicating your passport number, destination, and other personal information.

6. Use caution when cashing checks and buying airline tickets. Use only authorized outlets for both. Avoid black market or "street" money changers.

7. Be cautious about taking photographs. In some countries, there are restrictions about photographing airports or anything

connected with military installations. In other countries, there may be religious or cultural limitations.

8. Notary Publics in many foreign countries perform different duties and have broader powers than here in the United States. For example, I once needed a notary to verify my absentee voting ballot, and ended up paying $25 for the right to vote.

9. The most common nondrug related arrests overseas are customs violations, immigration violations, drunk and disorderly conduct, and business fraud. Taking historic artifacts or antiquities out of a country without specific approval is a serious offense everywhere.

10. For driving an automobile, obtain an international driver's license (your travel agent will assist), but you usually will also need your U.S. license as well. In addition, in some countries you may need proof of insurance coverage while driving.

11. One serious offense in *all* countries is dealing in drugs. Penalties can be unbelievably harsh. In Iran, Turkey, Malaysia, and Thailand, the penalty is often death. There is usually no distinction between "hard" and "soft" drugs, and you are not covered by U.S. laws or constitutional rights if you are arrested.

12. Lost credit cards should be reported to the firm issuing the card. Keep records of card numbers and traveler's check numbers in a safe place and also back at your home office.

13. Obtain a copy of *Know Before You Go* and *Customs Hints for Returning U.S. Residents* from the U.S. Customs Office, P.O. Box 7118, Washington, DC 20044. For foreign country customs information, ask for copies of *Country Information Notices* from the Office of Passport Services, Department of State, Washington, DC 20514.

Finally, here are some telephone numbers for U.S. citizens arrested abroad:

▶ *The U.S. State Department,* Washington, DC (202) 635-5225

A citizens' emergency center operates from 8 A.M. to 10 P.M. Eastern Time weekdays and 9 A.M. to 3 P.M. Saturdays. For late nights, weekends, and holidays, the on-call duty officer number is (202) 632-1512. Better yet, carry with you at all times a copy of *Key Officers of Foreign Service Posts,* a publication available from the Superintendent of Documents,

U.S. Government Printing Office, Washington, DC 20402.
Cost is $10 for 1 year and includes 3 updates.

▶ *Amnesty International,* New York (212) 807-8400

For human rights and political rights violations.

▶ *International Legal Defense Counsel,* 1420 Walnut St., Suite
315, Philadelphia, PA 19102 (215) 545-2428

For misdemeanor and criminal violations.

SUMMARY

Many exporting firms proceed comfortably without need for legal
counsel, but when they do need counsel, it probably begins with
the appointment of the first overseas distributor. Next on any priority list where counsel is important would probably be the protection and safeguard of patents and trademarks. Licensing, as
explained, is a specialized field in itself. The U.S. government can
become involved in various ways, and there are at least two acts
involving Export Trading Companies and Foreign Sales Corporations that are intended to encourage exporting. For both of these
you will need help from experienced legal counsel.

An excellent text for practicing attorneys and law students is
Foreign Trade and Investment, a Legal Guide, by Thomas F. Clasen,
published by Callaghan & Co., 3201 Old Glenview Rd., Wilmette,
IL 60091. This book explains all types of business transactions (but
not tax issues). There are separate sections on import regulations,
customs laws, unfair trade practices, import relief, export transactions, selecting distributors, sales agreements, licensing, patents,
trademarks, technology transfer, direct foreign investment, and
join ventures. For the serious student of the law in international
trade, this can be a most valuable resource.

However deeply you investigate the law in trade, throughout
every aspect and especially in regard to personal conduct abroad, it
will pay to abide by the 12 words of wisdom offered at the beginning of this chapter: be trustworthy, loyal, helpful, friendly, courteous, kind, obedient, cheerful, thrifty, brave, clean, and reverent.

If the research, foot-slogging, and legal labyrinth have been
successfully traversed, now is the time for *action.* The time has come
for that all-important act in exporting—pricing. In the next chapter,
you will find ideas and information on how to price your product

for export. Following that is a basic primer on the critical category of exporting called freight forwarding, shipping, and insurance. That, then, leads into managing and motivating distributors.

At this stage, you are well along on your journey into exporting with the rewards close at hand. Price the sale correctly, receive your payment, ship it efficiently and the circle has been established. Then it is a matter of motivating your distributor to repeat the cycle over and over again. That is where the next few chapters will lead us.

7

Pricing

. . . the world's oldest game.

Before the disastrous civil war that has ravaged Lebanon over the past decade, Beirut was known as the "Geneva of the Middle East." Beirut was a glamorous, vibrant city where one could literally snorkel in the Mediterranean on one day and ski the slopes of nearby mountains on the next. It was also the commercial and trading capital of the Middle East where rich sheiks stored their money and bargain seekers shopped the bazaars. It was the most popular marketplace of the Middle East where, if you did not pause to haggle, the merchants became visibly disappointed. Moreover, the Lebanese are descendants of the Phoenicians, perhaps the world's first great international traders. Consequently, the merchants of pre-war Beirut believed they bore a legacy for trade stretching back before the time of Christ.

Mr. Halim Kurban was one of those twentieth-century Phoenicians. He was a major account for my distributor in Lebanon and during a visit to his store in 1968 I decided this was my opportunity to learn the wisdom of over 2000 years of trade. "What is your pricing policy, Mr. Kurban? How do you price your products?" His reply was as memorable as it was succinct: "My pricing policy begins the moment the customer walks in the door. It is the world's oldest game."

Game it is, but like any contest there are also certain fundamental rules that must be considered. That is the purpose of this chapter. Here we will examine why in this new "game" of exporting and trade it just may be appropriate to throw out your domestic pricing structure and build a new one based on the reduction of certain traditional costs and the addition of unfamiliar costs.

We will begin by, once again, reviewing your objectives in entering an overseas market because those objectives will determine some of export pricing decisions. In addition, knowing the glossary of export pricing terminology is essential, so key terms and phrases will be explained here. A detailed review of traditional and unfamiliar costs will be presented, which will lead you to drafting comparative domestic and export prices. There will also be a section on providing price quotations and pro forma invoices for export.

Finally, a troublesome and somewhat exotic manifestation of pricing will be described: "pirating" or trans-shipping. This does not come into play, fortunately, until you have a well-constructed sales pipeline abroad where demand for your product then creates new, unauthorized channels commonly called pirating. More about this later.

For firms who negotiate single-sale export contracts or for firms selling occasional export orders direct to single customers, pricing is a somewhat less problematic matter. Single-sale contracts can be developed in much the same manner as for the domestic market. But this chapter will still be helpful by providing a list of unexpected or unfamiliar costs. As for firms selling a single or occasional export order, it is a common and certainly acceptable practice to simply use a prevailing domestic price list. However, the whole purpose of this book is to encourage and create a conduit for a steady stream of sales overseas. That requires a distributor, or some form of permanent system to generate demand. And pricing to a distributor network is a special skill requiring a new outlook, as we will see.

Perhaps the *worst* attitude toward export pricing is one that, unfortunately, is common among many American businesses. That attitude has been expressed innumerable times when a sales manager says "You say more inquiries have come in for export? Just send them our domestic price list. I'm not going to make any deviations just because of some overseas market." Such a policy could be the end of the beginning of a beautiful friendship.

PRICING OBJECTIVES

The first and most obvious question in your plan for pricing must be "What is my primary goal for this new marketplace?" The most likely answer is "long-term sales." However, you might also be trying to wedge into a new market where competition is fierce and that might indicate sacrificing short-term profit for long-term marketshare. Another strategy might be to gain incremental sales, thereby spreading existing overheads or smoothing out seasonal fluctuations. Still another tactic might be to dispose of obsolescent inventory. Finally, your pricing might also be determined by the economic status of the end market, where, for example, for an impoverished market you would purposely sell stripped-down models and shave profits knowing that was the only way to build a foothold.

Whatever your objective, the three traditional ingredients of pricing—cost, market demand, competition—remain dominant and each must be carefully considered in exporting, but from a different viewpoint. Philip R. Cateora, in his textbook *International Marketing* (Fifth Edition, Richard D. Irwin, Homewood, IL, 1983) describes the differences this way: "Firms unfamiliar with overseas marketing and many firms producing industrial goods orient their pricing solely on a cost basis. Firms which employ pricing as part of the strategic mix, however, will be aware of such alternatives as market segmentation from country to country or market to market, competitive pricing in the marketplace, and other market-oriented pricing factors." Cateora then reviews the alternatives of variable cost pricing or full cost pricing, a familiar decision in U.S. domestic pricing, but then counsels "If the firm regards itself as a world marketer, it is more likely to think in terms of full cost pricing for all markets."

There is no single, correct policy. Pricing for export depends on the nature of a business and the objectives of the management plus a heavy dose of end market factors. Alternatives are presented here because they are just that, alternatives. You must decide which is best for your business.

If you as a burgeoning exporter have as your objectives the building of a distributor network for long-term growth and penetration, then it is important in this discussion of objectives to consider two key principles. The first is that you should endeavor to *protect* your distributor from outside interference and to allow him to compete effectively against competitors inside his market. This does not necessarily mean that you must reduce normal or desired profits. What it means is that your marketing and some other costs in export are often lower than in domestic and this normally permits a slightly lower price to the distributor which, in turn, provides protection for the distributor. Now let us move from objectives to the matter of costing and pricing and learn why and how they are different in exporting.

FAMILIAR, MISSING, AND NEW COSTS IN EXPORTING

FAMILIAR COSTS

The first, obvious, and familiar cost is that of manufacturing the goods to be sold. Accountants usually call this *cost of goods* or cost of sales. (As a marketer and not an accountant, I could never understand the logic of calling the cost of the goods I was selling cost of *sales* but each profession seems to adopt its own special glossary and we are stuck with it.) There are several ways of stating cost of goods, depending on if you use variable, standard, or historic costing methods. But that is not the issue here. Whichever system you use, the first and most familiar cost will be for the product or goods you are going to offer to your new foreign customers. If you find you must modify the product, as discussed in an earlier chapter, the cost of these modifications should, of course, be included at the outset of your calculations. For example, you may have to alter electrical components to satisfy local country codes, or change products to meet safety and noise standards. Incidentally, the costs for changes such as these can often be shifted to your distributor in that market who is also in a better position to obtain design testing and approvals from local regulatory bodies.

Other old familiar cost friends will be *research and development* and *general and administrative* costs. The former is self-explanatory and the latter usually include legal, accounting, executive, and other such administrative costs.

Taxes are another obvious cost and, at this stage, it is important to also list your desired profit expressed as a ratio or percentage of the selling price.

So, on our Profit & Loss pro forma so far we have these familiar categories:

Gross revenues	$000	100%
Less:		
Cost of goods	00	
General & administration	00	
Research & development	00	
Gross profit	00	
Less:		
Taxes	00	
Net profit after taxes	00	

Absent from this list are marketing costs. There will also probably be additional expenses for packing, shipping, insurance, and after-sales service. This is where the differences begin to creep into the equations. Packing for export is usually more elaborate and more expensive than for domestic sales. This makes sense because of greater distances, more handling, wider temperature extremes, and so on. The same applies to insurance and shipping.

Missing Costs

It is in the marketing category where significant savings can occur. This is because the distributor is taking over many of the marketing tasks you fund in the United States. For example, the distributor is fielding a salesforce, generating and filling orders, funding collection and credit, and contributing to advertising and promotion expenses. True, you will have some of those same expenses when selling to overseas distributors but usually not to the extent you have when servicing the entire U.S. market. This is an important principle that we will return to shortly.

New Costs

Additional expense for packing and shipping must be considered. There will also be additional costs for travel and probably for after-sales service and maybe for commissions, but all of these are part of your new marketing calculations. There will also be new costs for translations, freight forwarders, and international postage, cable and telephone.

In this "new" expense category, probably the most unfamiliar newcomer is *duty*, which is a tax on imports. A *tariff* is technically a list or system of duties but it is often used interchangeably with the word duty. Duties are levied in three forms: specific, ad valorem, or a combination. A specific duty is a flat charge, expressed in cents or dollars (or in the currency of the importing country) per item or piece imported. Ad valorem is a percent of the stated value on the shipping documents or invoice, such as 12 percent on watches. A combination duty does just that; it levies both a specific and ad valorem tax, such as 10 cents per unit plus 12 percent of the value of each unit.

Duty schedules are developed over long periods and occur for various reasons, the most common ones being to (1) protect local industries, or (2) discourage local consumers from purchasing luxury imports which then sends valuable currency reserves abroad. Another way to accomplish both of these is through *nontariff* barriers. This simply means that the government in the importing country has raised obstacles other than taxes. These other obstacles vary from quotas to licenses to prior deposits and an ingenious variety of similar disincentives.

The General Agreement on Tariffs and Trade (GATT) is an accord among 95 nations to nurture and encourage world trade. For the past several decades, negotiations through GATT have successfully reduced both tariff and nontariff barriers. In 1976 negotiations, for example, many categories of goods had tariffs reduced by as much as 60 percent over a period of 8 to 10 years. Eliminating or reducing nontariff barriers has not been as simple, but overall the GATT discussions have achieved good results.

Duties are paid by the importer, so while they are not an expense to you on your profit and loss statement (P&L), they are an additional and new expense in determining your end selling price in the market.

Two other factors affecting costing and pricing are *inflation* and *currency rate fluctuations.* Inflation is a cost familiar to all and can properly appear on P&L sheets. In some countries, inflation has run amok and is termed hyperinflation. In hyperinflationary countries like Brazil and Argentina, where inflation rates have commonly run 100 percent or more per year, costing and pricing become a complex chase. In those countries, governments resort to indexing, where all expenses—retail prices, wages, interest rates, exchange rates—are routinely and regularly raised to keep pace with inflation. Imagine a country with a projected inflation rate of 100 percent a year, where every month all wages, salaries, prices, rates, and so on, are raised 8.5 percent simply to keep even with inflation. That is what is meant by indexing.

Exchange-rate fluctuations will not affect your P&L but they will affect the end selling price in the market. As the U.S. dollar rate moves up or down against another currency, your distributor must either pay more or less of his currency to buy dollars to pay you. This, obviously, affects his cost and that cost will be reflected in the end selling price. In the event that you must make quotations or sell in another currency, it would be wise to obtain the assistance of a foreign exchange expert at your local bank. Dealing in other currencies, especially when dealing with future commitments, can be a risky business. A foreign exchange specialist can provide forecasts for currency exchange rates and advise you on such measures as *hedging* which means taking out contracts to avoid losses from currency rate fluctuations. But playing the currency exchange rate games is best left to professionals.

COSTS AND PRICING: DOMESTIC VERSUS EXPORT

Now that we have listed some of the different costs affecting pricing, let's examine how they compare in domestic versus export conditions.

A sample *domestic* pricing calculation, or P&L might look like this:

		Percent
Sales (or revenues)	$1000	100
Less:		
Cost of goods	400	40
(Includes packing & shipping)		
	——	
Gross margin:	600	60
Less:		
Marketing expenses:		
Market research		
Field sales		
Advertising		
Promotion		
	350	35
	——	

Net margin	250	25
Less:		
General & administrative	50	5
Profit before tax	200	20
Profit after tax (assume 50%)	100	10

Such P&L pro formas are always problematic because each business is different. For this exercise, it makes little difference— just insert your own.

The purpose here is to dramatize that, first, for export it is extremely important to construct a P&L based on *actual* costs; second, your price to your overseas distributor should be equal to or lower than the lowest price to a domestic dealer; and third, this exercise will eventually demonstrate *price escalation,* or how your price will naturally increase as it travels overseas accumulating duty expenses, distributor marketing expenses, local taxes, and other piggybacked expenses. Americans traveling in other countries are often surprised to find American products selling at much higher prices than at home. This is a result of the price escalation process.

Now let us take that same pro forma P&L for *export* sales. Remember, the objective is to provide your distributor with a price *equal to* or *lower* than your lowest domestic price. For this example, then, let's assume a price 5 percent lower:

		Percent
Sales (or revenues)	$1000	100
Less: 5 percent for distributor	50	5
Net sales	950	95
Less: Cost of goods	427	45*
(increased by 5 percent because of increased packing and product modification costs)		
Gross margin	523	55
Less:		
Marketing expenses:	266	28

* This is 45% of the net sales amount.
Note: These should be *less* than in a domestic situation for the reasons stated—that the overseas distributor is

bearing normal costs for field sales and part, or all, of advertising and promotion.

Net margin	257	27
Less:		
General & administrative	50	5.2
Profit before tax	207	21.8
Profit after tax (assume 50%)	103.5	10.9

AFFECT ON END SELLING PRICE

Now let us examine this matter of price escalation. We will take the domestic and export sales price in the examples above, and show what happens as each is used in their respective marketplace.

	Domestic	Export
Factory price	$1000	950
Export documentation, freight, insurance (assume 20 percent)		190
		1140
Import duty (assume 10 percent on landed cost)		114
		1254
Domestic wholesaler markup (15 percent)	150	
	1150	
Export distributor markup (30 percent)		376
		1630
Retail markup (50 percent)	575	815
End selling price	1725	2445

This illustration demonstrates several points in this chapter. First, price escalation almost invariably causes your end selling price to be higher in export markets versus domestic markets. Second, in order to compete effectively, your end selling price in foreign markets should therefore be driven as low as possible. Third, this means a carefully constructed, separate P&L for export sales that covers all *actual* expenses. And fourth, it means you should endeavor to protect and help your distributor by offering him prices at least equal to, and if possible lower than, your lowest domestic prices.

The duty rate plays an important role in determining what elements might go into your pricing. Let's say that you include a cost factor of 10 percent for advertising, meaning that you include in your price to the distributor an amount equal to 10 percent of the selling price with the intention of spending that 10 percent within the market on advertising. Duty is charged on your selling price to the distributor, and often on selling price plus insurance and freight. That means the importer is also paying duty on the 10 percent amount you have allocated for advertising. This is not too significant in a market with very low duties. But once the duty reaches double-digit levels, then your distributor pays duty on an advertising allowance. Therefore, as a general rule, for markets with high duty rates, it may be wise to eliminate all commissions, rebates, allowances, and so on, from your selling price in order to achieve a net-net-net price; in other words, the lowest possible base price on which duty will be levied. This is a matter best discussed and negotiated with your distributor.

What happens if your export prices are *higher* than prevailing prices to customers in the U.S. market?

The answer is two things can happen, both bad. The first consequence is, as a result of natural price escalation when selling overseas, your end selling price becomes even more uncompetitive. The second result is that pirating or trans-shipping can result. This occurs when demand for your product becomes strong enough that individual customers in foreign markets decide to avoid your distributor and try to buy your product on the open market, usually in the domestic market. As we have seen in the earlier illustration, if a U.S. wholesaler can sell your product for 1150 compared to your overseas distributor at 1630, it is possible that those individual customers of your distributor overseas will find ways to buy directly from the U.S. wholesaler, bypassing the distributor.

Such trans-shipping, as it is sometimes called, can easily occur when, for example, a domestic marketing organization offers a special price promotion. If demand overseas is strong for that product, and if there are opportunistic domestic wholesalers who have developed their own foreign market channels, the result is that those price-promoted products in the U.S. market could easily end up overseas. This has the effect of undercutting your distributor, creating disruption among the trade, and lowering the morale and loyalty of your distributor.

Another term in this irregular commerce is "the grey market." A manufacturer of construction equipment describes the grey market this way. A Japanese company manufactures a line of excavators for a single customer in the United States who sells those excavators through distributors. Then, the Japanese supplier turns around and sells the same basic machine to others in the Far East who ship it into the United States at a lower price by eliminating service responsibility and shaving profits. While this is probably not ethical, it is also probably not illegal, which is why it is termed grey.

The same might happen to your products unless you carefully honor your foreign distributor agreements and support them in all possible ways. Bear in mind that once you sell a product to a customer in the United States, according to U.S. laws, that customer can resell it wherever he or she wishes; furthermore, if you refuse to sell to a U.S. customer on the basis that you do not agree with the final destination of that product, he can charge you with restraint of trade and, if successful in the courts, receive compensation for damages.

Another policy in export pricing is "uniform" pricing versus "variable" pricing. This issue may arise if and when you contract with more than one distributor and where some markets charge higher duties than others on the importation of your product. In this case, a distributor in a high-duty market will argue that you should lower your price to him to allow him to compete more effectively. Under this policy, you vary your export prices, charging less for high-duty markets and more for low-duty markets. This has been called variable export pricing. The danger here is that an unscrupulous distributor in the market receiving special, lower prices might be tempted to divert or re-export your product to another market. Also, it becomes difficult to administer variable pricing because, as the old adage goes, "the squeaky wheel gets the oil," meaning that the distributor who argues the most forcefully may get the lower prices. Under uniform pricing, you establish one, and only one, export price and every distributor no matter where the location must pay that price.

EXPORT PRICING INGREDIENTS

Following is a list of factors that might be considered when constructing your export price list. Keep in mind that many items may not apply to your business. It is also important to remember that your goal is to keep the costs, and resulting export price, as *low* as possible, for the reasons presented. This sometimes makes the pricing game difficult and complex.

Sales or Revenues This may be listed as: before or after returns, special discounts, and other special reductions to sales. As a result, some companies show *Gross* Sales and then *Net* Sales.

Cost of Goods This will reflect your system of costing: standard, actual, historic, etc. As pointed out in this chapter, any additional costs for modifying your product for export should be included here. Some firms also include costs for packing and shipping in this category. But, as we will see, many exporting firms pass the shipping expenses on to the customer.

Export Documentation This is often expressed as "Export Administration" because some experienced clerical help, either within your firm or provided by an outside freight forwarder service, will be required to provide the documents required for export shipping. This process will be explained in more detail in a subsequent chapter on how to ship goods overseas.

Insurance This covers risks during shipment and is often passed on to the end customer, but some firms absorb it on their P&L and therefore it should be considered.

Credit and Collection This might be an allocated cost for this service from your domestic credit and collection department, or actual costs incurred for collections, when providing discounts, or bad debts for foreign customers.

Inflation Allowances This is a factor only when delivery dates are far in advance and some allowance must be made for the costs associated with rising inflation in the interim.

Freight Forwarding This is part of your shipping expense. The role of the freight forwarder will be explained in Chapter 9.

Commissions You may encounter middleman commissions if, for example, Export Management Companies (EMCs) are involved. Another practice is that exporting companies include a separate commission for their overseas distributors, including it in the price, and then remitting it to the distributor later. This practice allows some measure of control over a distributor, but in markets where duties are high it also has the effect of uplifting the landed price.

Rebates and Allowances You may wish to include some costs for rebates to distributors if certain sales targets are reached or for allowances to cover defective merchandise.

Market Research This is a marketing expense if and when you find it necessary, or it might be considered part of Research and Development.

Marketing Administration This covers the cost of export marketing managers and sales personnel, travel, phone, postage, telex, cable, and other such expenses attendant with sales.

Advertising and Promotion Again, this is a familiar expense in most any business but in exporting it could be slightly higher to cover special translations, special packing and shipping of materials, and so on. On the other hand, your overseas distributor might also contribute advertising and promotion funds.

Commercial and Political Risk Insurance If you extend credit to foreign customers, you may obtain payment protection from the Foreign Credit Insurance Association (FCIA). This association sells several types of policies on behalf of the Export-Import Bank (Eximbank). The policies cover both short-term and medium-term credit sales. Offices of the FCIA are located at 40 Rector St., 11th Floor, New York, NY 10006, (212) 306-5000. As for investors overseas, one branch of the U.S. State Department called Overseas Private Investment Corporation exists to offer investors insurance against currency inconvertibility, expropriation, and damage or insurrection, and civil strife. In addition, OPIC makes direct loans and may participate in the financing of pre-investment surveys where investments are being made or contemplated by small U.S. firms.

Warranties and After-Sales Service This expense may be comparable to your domestic experience, but will possibly be more costly to administer if only because of extra distances involved.

Training and Education Entering new markets may require special training for sales specialists, retail clerks or repair and maintenance crews. At minimum, translation of instruction or service manuals may be a new, additional expense.

General and Administrative Usually, this is an allocated cost to the export operation which covers and legal, accounting, tax, personnel, and other executive services.

Value Added Tax (VAT) This tax is encountered more and more in foreign markets. It is not used—yet—in the United States, therefore it is not a cost to be considered here. However, it is a common taxing device overseas and therefore could be a factor between your net selling price and the end selling price. This is a tax applied to the value that has been added at various stages on the road to the final customer. For example, if you sell your product to a distributor and he adds some ingredient plus his mark-up, a tax is levied on the value of the ingredient plus his mark-up, and that tax is passed along and reflected in the final selling price.

EXPORT PRICING TERMINOLOGY

There are a few key terms and abbreviations that are essential to know; in fact, you probably know them already from domestic selling experience. Nonetheless, it is important to spell them out here. These are also known as terms of sale and should be clearly specified in any sales proposal or transaction.

FOB This stands for "free on board" and signifies the selling price of an item loaded on board at a specific point. The most common point is the originating factory, thus FOB Factory is a very common term in export selling. In everyday terminology that means "This is my selling price to you from the factory shipping dock, but costs for transportation and insurance must be added to this price." There are several variations of FOB such as:

—FOB (and the name of the inland point of origin)
—FOB (and the name of the port of exportation)
—FOB vessel (and the name of the port of export)

EX This is another variation of FOB and is expressed as Ex Factory or Ex Warehouse or Ex City of Origin.

CIF This is another very common designation and stands for "Cost, Insurance, Freight" and is accompanied by a designated overseas port of import, such as Hong Kong or London. When you quote a CIF price, you are saying "This is cost for the product plus the cost of insurance and all transportation and miscellaneous costs to the point named." Importers appreciate knowing the CIF price because it tells them exactly how much it will cost them to have the item delivered to their nearest port of entry. To quote CIF prices, you must obtain the services of an international freight forwarder who is experienced and qualified to calculate transportation and insurance expenses. When you provide a freight forwarder with a description of your product with its weight and cubic measurement when packed, the CIF price can be calculated. There is usually no charge for this service.

C and F This is a variation on CIF and means "cost and freight" and *not* insurance which the buyer must purchase.

FAS This signifies "free alongside ship at a named U.S. port of export." This sales term means the price includes the cost of the goods and the cost of delivering the goods alongside a vessel at a specified port. The buyer must pay for the cost of unloading and wharfage, as well as loading, ocean transportation, and insurance.

Prices Subject to Change Without Notice Unless a specific price is guaranteed over a specific period, it is a good business practice to include this condition on all price lists.

Quote in U.S. Dollars Another recommended business practice is to always quote your export prices in U.S. dollars. The logic of this policy is that you normally want to be paid in U.S. dollars to avoid any risks of currency fluctuations. The overseas buyer, if he is an experienced importer, is accustomed to converting dollars into the local currency so it should provide no problem to him.

PRICE QUOTATIONS AND PRO FORMA INVOICES

A typical first-time export sale begins with an inquiry for the purchase of your product, or a proposal from you to an end customer or distributor. The next step is usually for you to prepare a quotation or a pro forma invoice. This document is exactly what the name implies and provides the following information:

▶ Names and addresses of both the buyer and seller
▶ Date and reference number
▶ Description, listing, and quantity of the products requested

▶ Price of each item, in U.S. dollars, specified as FOB or CIF or whatever

▶ Gross and net shipping weight (in metric where appropriate)

▶ Total cubic volume and dimensions (in metric where appropriate)

▶ Trade discount, if applicable

▶ Delivery point

▶ Terms of payment

▶ Insurance and shipping costs

▶ Period for which the price quotation is valid

▶ Total charges to be paid by the customer

▶ Estimated shipping date from factory or to U.S. port

▶ Estimated date of arrival

Pro formas also customarily certify that the pro forma invoice is true and correct along with a statement of the country of origin, or origins, of the goods. The Department of Commerce also strongly recommends that such an invoice be conspicuously marked "pro forma invoice" and special emphasis should be given to the period for which the price quotation is valid. Also, emphasize the shipping date from the U.S. port of export since the overseas buyer has no way of estimating inland transit time within the United States.

SUMMARY

At this point, export pricing may resemble a cumbersome collection of new terminology and additional costs. But remember Mr. Kurban and "the game." Proper pricing of your product will determine if you win or lose and, like most games, the process can be both challenging and stimulating.

It is absolutely essential to bear in mind that because of distances, duties, and special middlemen your costs will necessarily increase before they reach the marketplace. This places you at a disadvantage against indigenous competition. Therefore, for your price to be competitive, you must carefully craft your cost calculations with accuracy and completeness. Obviously, you want the best, most effective end selling price. Also, to build a strong pipeline, you want to support and protect your distributor. All of these elements enter into the game.

If, as is often the case, you find that your price is still higher than local competition, there is always the traditional triad of strengths that American goods have relied on for decades: quality, service, and innovation. These three attributes often mitigate a higher price. "Made in U.S.A." is still a hallmark respected around the world. Pricing is not the only determinant in winning or losing the game.

Back in 1968, on my visit to Beirut, Mr. Kurban, his Phoenician eyes twinkling, added this story to my lesson in pricing which helps encapsulate much of the message in this chapter.

> An international committee, he claimed, once began a search for the first person to travel to the planet Mars. The committee first approached a former American astronaut, reasoning that he was especially qualified and experienced for such a unique assignment. "How much would you charge to go to Mars?" they asked. "For such a journey, I would want to be paid $1 million," he replied. So the committee turned next to a Russian cosmonaut, asking his price. "I would need $2 million," he explained. "Why so much?" they countered. "Well, I would want $1 million for myself and $1 million for the State, because that is the way we do it here in the Soviet Union."
>
> The committee pondered this and finally decided to talk to a Lebanese because, after all, everyone knew they were descendants of the first and perhaps greatest explorers. "How much would you charge?" they asked. "Oh, for such a dangerous journey I would require at least $3 million," he replied.
>
> The committee protested, "Why $3 million? That's three times as much as the American."
>
> "It's very simple," said the Lebanese. "One million for me, one million for you, and one million for the American to make the trip."

Moral: Pricing is, indeed, something of a game. And, as history has proven innumerable times, while price is extremely important, it is not the only element of a successful game plan.

8

Export Financing
and Payments

**There is no sale until the check is
cashed in the bank.**

An Accountant's Creed

Everything discussed so far in this text about export sales is almost
useless until payment has been safely received for your efforts.
This chapter deals with both how to obtain additional financing for
your export campaign and what types of credit instruments are
used for payment in international business.

Harold E. Tower, former treasurer of the Beloit Corporation,
the largest exporter of paper-making machinery in the United
States, claims that most foreign creditors are more experienced
and more ingenious about paying bills than we are in this country.
"The reason," he says, "is that, first, they have a longer history in
international trade than we do here in the United States, and the
second reason is that in high-inflation countries, where cash flow
is critical, any delay in making payments is literally like money in
the bank."

Another veteran international manager echoes Tower's remarks, but in a slightly different way: "I manage 143 distributors
around the world and I visualize each of them waking up every
morning with the first thought on their mind being 'How can I
avoid paying my bill today and still not risk being cut off.' Many
of my distributors are absolute masters at finding ways to delay

payments. So, my job is to be just a touch more clever and a tad faster than they are."

There is a bit of hyperbole in that view, of course, because not *all* foreign accounts act this way. On the contrary. Most are fully aware of the importance of strong credit ratings and prompt payment. Yet, as more new markets are added to your collection of export territories, you will undoubtedly encounter more new payment experiences and more new payment excuses. One market will claim your payment is being delayed by his government's central bank. Another will request an additional 30 days credit because the ship carrying his order was delayed by a longshoremen's strike. And a third will claim there was some defective merchandise in his latest shipment and payment will be delayed until this has been resolved.

To help you steer away from these storms and shoals of costly delays, get expert advice and help in financing and credit instruments. One of those instruments will be a letter of credit and, as international banker Ingeborg Hegenbart says, "with the right letter of credit you will not have to worry about prompt payment." Next, you will find a listing of places and programs where you can obtain credit assistance. Then, you will learn about the basic financing instruments which become essential everyday tools in export sales. We also will review the offering of credit terms and datings to overseas distributors.

Because getting paid in international trade can be a complex specialized field, the purpose of this chapter will be to acquaint you with the fundamentals only. Your best resources will be your international banker with additional advice from your domestic credit and collection manager plus the trade specialist at the U.S. Department of Commerce. This chapter on financing and payments in export and the next chapter on shipping goods overseas dwell on two essentials in the export process, but they are essentials best managed by specialists. You, as the manager, must know what is involved in each and make the basic policy decisions in both categories, but the details are best left to the specialists.

WHAT KIND OF FINANCING HELP DO YOU NEED?

Your first task will be an assessment of what type of financial help you may require to either launch an export program or to finance your sales until revenues arrive. You will want to ask yourself certain questions. For example, will there be any problem in covering the costs for the first stages of exporting—the planning and exploration that usually involves only your time and perhaps some travel expense? Will you have to buy expensive raw materials to create the products for export? Will you need any new machinery or new processes to produce your products for export? Next, in your sales kit you will want to carry details of the payment terms you plan to offer customers and this usually depends on competition or customary terms for payment in your industry. Can you offer these terms to international customers without special financing?

When considering this, keep one new factor in mind: the extra time it takes to get your product to the overseas market. You may have to allow an extra 30, 60, or even 90 days for your shipment to reach your new customers. Can you comfortably finance this extra time?

New customers involve new risks, whether domestic or international. The creditworthiness of a customer is always a worry and, while there are many ways to determine this in overseas markets, it remains a risk nonetheless.

Another start-up expense is the cost of a marketing manager, support staff, and eventually perhaps an export administration department to handle incoming orders and outgoing shipments. Finally, if your product must be modified, you will want to determine what up-front costs will be encountered and include those in your overall financing considerations.

Having done this self-examination, you are ready for the next stage.

WHERE TO GO FOR HELP

Two predominant questions are: Where can I get help financing this new exporting venture and, after I begin receiving orders, what payment and credit practices should I use to assure I am paid in full and in a timely fashion?

You should start with the trade specialist at the U.S. Department of Commerce. He or she will undoubtedly be acquainted with all of the federal government and probably your state government export finance programs. For example, the Department of Commerce has printed a pocket-sized pamphlet titled *A Guide to*

Financing Exports that relates why credit is important and lists which government agencies assist both investors and exporters in international trade. The pamphlet also lists the methods used to finance your exports once orders have been received and reviews other related areas, such as foreign exchange risks, export licensing, tax exemptions through a Foreign Sales Corporation (FISC), U.S. Foreign Trade Zones, and some of the Commerce Department programs to assist exporters.

Your second destination should be the international department of a commercial bank. Of the thousands of commercial banks in the United States, however, only several hundred have international departments. Again, your trade specialist at DoC probably knows which banks in your city or region are most active in dealing with international finance. The technicians at your bank are usually fully knowledgeable about both credit assistance and methods of payments. Furthermore, they will not only be pleased but anxious to see you because you are a possible new customer. Here are some questions you should ask: What branch correspondent or affiliate banks do they have overseas and in what specific markets? Can the bank provide buyer credit reports? If so, at what cost? Does it have experience with government programs for financing trade and exports? What are the charges for letters of credit, processing drafts and collecting payments, if necessary? The larger international departments will have a host of other services involving trade, financing, and money management, but at the outset it is best to concentrate on just those services you require. More sophisticated services, such as lease financing or private placements or Eurobond trading, can wait for another day.

A third source of information is your state government agency dealing with commerce and international trade. More and more states are providing credit assistance, and a select few also even offer low cost loans for start-up expenses dealing with export. In these cases, low interest loans are offered to help pay for translations and printing of promotional material and for sales trip overseas.

Here are some examples of state-financed export programs for selected states:

California In 1985, California established a $3 million fund for counseling and both pre- and post-export loan guarantees.

Connecticut A $1 million fund has been established in Connecticut for both counseling and loans. Here, loans are made direct to exporters after sales have been made, but loan guarantees are also available for pre- and post-export expenses.

Illinois Illinois is the big spender in terms of export finance assistance. There, $100 million has been authorized for a variety of services: counseling, credit insurance administration, and loans to lenders for both pre- and post- export cases. The Illinois finance authority relies on bonds with guarantees from the Export-Import Bank and was the first of its kind in the country. Other states are examining its organization and considering how to emulate it.

Ohio In 1983, Ohio created an allotment program with $100 million for what they call a "linked deposit" program. Using state funds, the state deposits money that the bank then lends to a qualified small business at below market rates. This is a variation on the loans-to-lenders approach.

Other states with diverse export lending programs are as follows: Colorado, Indiana, Louisiana, Maryland, Michigan, Minnesota, Missouri, South Carolina, Tennessee, and Washington.

Another source of information and help will be the Export Management Companies (EMCs) who, as we have explained before, are professionals in helping small companies generate exports. Some of the larger EMCs will even participate in the financing, but most serve as commission agents and therefore leave credit matters to you.

There are two private sources of financing assistance. They are called factoring houses or confirming houses. The former are well-known in domestic financing circles for purchasing receivables at discounted rates. Factoring houses will also "buy" export receivables. "Confirming" is a financial service in which an independent company confirms an export order in the vendor's own country and makes payment for the goods in the currency of that country. These are common in Europe, but new and somewhat rare in the United States.

FEDERAL GOVERNMENT PROGRAMS

Most of the federal programs described here are designed to be implemented through local commercial banks with international departments. They are presented here to save you time and allow a nodding acquaintance with them in advance before sitting down with your local banker. The type of information you will receive on these federal government finance programs from your Department of Commerce trade specialist includes:

Export-Import Bank (Eximbank) This is the principal U.S. government banking institution for international trade. It offers direct loans to foreign customers for large projects and equipment sales that usually require long-term financing. It also guarantees loans made by cooperating U.S. and foreign commercial banks to U.S. exporters and to foreign buyers of U.S. products and services. One key for using Eximbank is to prove that you have competition from foreign sellers; the more competition you can demonstrate, the better your chances for financing help. Eximbank also provides credit insurance, through a private insurance association, the Foreign Credit Insurance Associations (FCIA), that enables exporters to extend credit to overseas buyers.

The programs offered by Eximbank that seem especially applicable to small businesses and companies expanding into exporting are as follows:

1. *Working Capital Guarantee Program* This program can guarantee loans for working capital needed before actual sales. The loan is made by a commercial lender to a U.S. exporter; however, Eximbank guarantees repayment of 90 percent of the principal. Thus, the lender retains only 10 percent risk on the loan. The purpose of the loan must be for a specific export-related activity, such as inventory purchases or the development of export marketing programs that may include foreign marketing trips, trade fair participation, and other promotional activities. The term of the loan generally ranges from one month to one year, but may be of longer duration if required. Security for the loan must have a value of at least 110 percent of the outstanding balance (in contrast to 150 percent to 200 percent that would be required *without* Eximbank's guarantee). The total cost for the loan is similar to the cost of regular commercial loans.

2. *Export Credit Insurance* Credit insurance is available through FCIA to cover 100 percent of losses for political

reasons (war, expropriation, currency inconvertibility, etc.) and up to 95 percent of commercial losses (nonpayment by the buyer due to insolvency or default). Having such insurance can encourage the exporter to extend credit or more favorable terms to foreign buyers and thus to be more competitive. Credit insurance also encourages commercial banks to extend credit on the basis of covered accounts receivables. Policies can also be purchased by a single exporter. A special new-to-export policy is offered with greater coverage than for policies available to more experienced exporters. While FCIA policies offer considerable protection, they do not make exporting completely risk-free. The exporter is expected to exercise good credit judgment and to assume a portion of the commercial risks. Also, FCIA will normally want you to buy coverage for low-credit risk countries as well as high-credit risk countries. Like all insurance, the exporter must also consider the administrative time to file claims and resulting delays of payment if a buyer defaults.

3. *Commercial Bank Guarantees* Eximbank offers guarantees against nonpayment of foreign purchases on medium-term (181 days to 5 years) export loans by U.S. commercial banks. Loans may be used to finance capital and quasi-capital goods and services. A minimum 15 percent cash payment must be made by the foreign buyer. Eximbank's guarantee covers 100 percent of political risk and up to 90 percent of commercial risk. Coverage is currently available for approximately 140 countries.

4. *Small Business Credit Program* Because interest rates vary, commercial banks generally prefer to extend floating rate loans. Foreign purchasers, however, are usually unwilling to accept fluctuating interest rate risk in addition to foreign exchange risks. This small business credit program enables US. banks to offer medium-term fixed rate export loans. This program also covers loans made to finance capital and quasi-capital goods and services under these conditions: the purchaser makes a minimum 15 percent cash payment; the bank loan covers up to 85 percent of the export contract; and the terms range from over 1 year to 5 years. Interest rates are fixed according to the classification of the country to which the export is shipped.

Eximbank and FCIA also provide other credit programs for medium- and long-term financing. Long-term financing, meaning 5 years or longer, is generally for export of capital equipment and large-scale installations. These loans are either in the form of a direct credit to an overseas buyer or a financial guarantee assuring repayment of a private bank credit.

Whether you use the services of Eximbank and FCIA will depend a great deal on the nature of your business, your financial resources, and your willingness to work with government agencies. At the Parker Pen Company, for instance, in over 80 years of exporting we never once turned to Eximbank for help, yet 10 miles away, the largest exporter of huge paper-making machinery worked closely and successfully with them.

Small Business Administration (SBA) The SBA also offers financial assistance programs to U.S. exporters, some of which are similar to Eximbank's proposals. SBA generally defines a small business as one that is independently owned and operated and is not dominant in its field. One program offered by SBA is its Export Revolving Line of Credit Loan program. Operating as the name implies, this allows withdrawals and repayments up to a prescribed limit within a stated maturity period, which is not over 18 months. These funds can be used for the following activities: to finance labor and materials needed for manufacturing, to purchase inventory to meet an export order, and to penetrate or develop foreign markets.

Private Export Funding Corporation (PEFCO) This is a private corporation comprised mainly of commercial banks that provides additional funding to supplement major Eximbank bank loans. PEFCO makes medium- and long-term loans to borrowers in foreign countries for the purchase of U.S. goods and services. All of its loans must be covered by an unconditional guarantee of Eximbank for principal and interest. PEFCO generally does not make loans of less than $1 million.

Department of Agriculture The Foreign Agricultural Service (FAS) of the U.S. Department of Agriculture provides financial support for U.S. agricultural exports through the Food for Peace program and the Commodity Credit Corporation. Under the Food for Peace program, Title 1 of the Agricultural Trade Development and Assistance Act of 1954 authorizes

U.S. government financing of sales of U.S. agricultural commodities to friendly countries on concession credit terms. Sales are made by private business firms usually by bids. FAS administers agreements under this program. Among those commodities that have recently been included under this program are: wheat, corn, grain sorghum, rice vegetable oil, wheat flour, dry edible beans, blended/fortified foods, and cotton.

This synopsis of government-related financing for exporting is what you can expect to learn, in greater detail, from your U.S. Department of Commerce trade specialist. It is a large subject in itself. In 1984, a 200-page handbook was published by the Machinery and Allied Products Institute that elaborated on each of these agencies, programs, regulations, and restrictions.

How to Receive Payment

Now that you have determined how to finance your export activities, it is time to learn how you will be paid for them. Once again, two experts—your trade specialist and your international banker—will be invaluable allies. In addition, there are seminars and courses on this subject offered frequently by local colleges, universities, vocational education institutes, trade clubs, and banks. These courses, usually well-attended, are vital for the person in your organization charged with the responsibility for credit and collections of export sales.

"Getting paid in international sales is similar to getting paid in the United States except the distances and different cultures make getting information about your customer more difficult," according to Harold Tower. "In the United States we have many efficient ways to determine the creditworthiness of a customer. The same with making collections. But overseas, while there are some credit rating and collection services, they are not as common or often as effective as here in the United States."

Tower emphasizes that, as in all credit matters, someone has to make a judgment about creditworthiness. In international business, the banks are usually the best intermediaries to do this, aided by special documents or credit instruments used to facilitate payment. But because of the great distances involved and lack of knowledge and confidence about certain customers in remote countries, collections in international business become a bit more complex. Two commercial services to investigate for help are Dun & Bradstreet, who provide information on many countries similar to their service in the United States, and Business International, a global business information and advisory service (One Dag Hammarskjold Plaza, New York, NY 10017, (212) 750-6300.)

There are several basic methods of receiving payment. You will recognize that some of these methods are quite similar to domestic payment terms and instruments, but it is important to learn those commonly used in international trade. There are five basic methods of getting paid, and three of those are common in domestic sales. The methods, in order of risk, are as follows:

1. Cash in advance
2. Letter of credit (Figure 1)
3. Documentary drafts for collection
4. Open account
5. Consignment sales

Two of these are uncommon in domestic sales—letter of credit and documentary drafts—and these, plus open accounts, are the most common in export sales.

Obviously, *cash in advance* is the most desirable from the seller's standpoint. In export sales, it is rare. That is because of the extra time it takes for the product to reach the market, plus the fact that most overseas traders are experienced in commercial affairs and know the importance of establishing credit and obtaining extended payment terms. On occasion, you may be surprised, however. Some overseas buyers may offer cash in advance in order to impress you with their worthiness. Other buyers may have quite different motives. One sales manager in Latin America tells of a large customer in the Caribbean who always placed orders and asked for "double drawer" invoicing. This meant the order should be divided into separate invoices, one to go into his drawer marked "payment by cash" and the other for a drawer marked "payment under open account." The sales manager suspected that the "payment by cash" invoice was never recorded in the buyer's account books, thereby possibly avoiding taxes in that country. So, there are occasional unusual requests and surprises when it comes to payment methods.

Letters of credit are very common in export, especially when the overseas buyer has not established any credit record. These have several features in common with documentary drafts. See the example shown in Figure 1, p. 164.

In both cases, documents such as shipping and insurance forms must be presented to the bank to insure that the conditions of the sale (which are repeated on the letter of credit) are met.

Letters of credit (L/Cs) are actually agreements between two banks. The buyer, your customer, goes to his bank and arranges to buy or take out a letter of credit. The bank in his country makes out the letter of credit to you, the seller, and sends it to your bank. It is best if the buyer's bank confirms this letter of credit through a U.S. bank, probably one specified by you. As soon as you present to the confirming bank the shipping documents that prove that you have shipped the merchandise as specified, you can receive payment immediately, if that was the term of the sale and it was so specified in the L/C.

There are two types of L/Cs, revocable and irrevocable. You as an export seller should always insist on irrevocable L/Cs because that means once the letter of credit is issued to you the payment cannot be canceled or the terms changed without your approval. Therefore the key phrase to remember is that you will want "an irrevocable, confirmed letter of credit." Confirmed means that a bank acceptable to you, either overseas or in the United States, has confirmed that the money has been obtained and is ready for payment to you once satisfactory proof of shipment (i.e., shipping documents) has been made. You will also probably want to be paid in U.S. dollars and this would be specified in the letter of credit.

L/Cs can be worded so that payment is made on the very date that the shipping documents are received by the confirming bank, or, if you wish to give the buyer extra time, an L/C can also be worded so that payment is made 30, 60, or up to 180 days, which is the customary maximum. It is vitally important, though, that the wording in the L/C be clear and specific and equally important that the words in the shipping documents conform precisely with the wording of the L/C. Even slight variations can cause delays in payment until the questions are clarified and answered.

Letters of credit can be extremely flexible. An unlimited number of provisions can be specified. For example, the buyer can even indicate what types of marking should appear on the shipping containers. The key elements to remember about confirmed,

Swift: **MARBUS 44**
Telex Number: **191115**
Answer Back: **BANK ONE MIL**

BANK ONE, MILWAUKEE, NA

ADVICE OF IRREVOCABLE DOCUMENTARY CREDIT
FURTHER TO OUR ADVICE OF June 24, 1988

DATE: July 7, 1988   ISSUING BANK NO.: SND-2194/Z34

BANK ONE, MILWAUKEE, NA ADVICE NO.: 34219   CABLE

BENEFICIARY: ISSUING BANK:

John's Bolt Company   Development Bank of Singapore
2578 North Sun Highway   DBS Bldg., Shenton Way
Sommer, WI 54817   Singapore

APPLICANT:

Sembawang Machine Fty.
5 Orchard Road
Singapore

AMOUNT: USD 3,200.00   EXPIRATION: September 9, 1988,
        (Three Thousand Two Hundred and   our office
        00/100 U.S. Dollars)

Gentlemen:

At the request of the Issuing Bank indicated above, we are enclosing their Letter of
Credit established in your favor.

All Banking charges outside of Singapore are for the account of the Beneficiary, and
will be deducted from the proceeds remitted to you.

We confirm this credit and therefore undertake that all drafts drawn and presented in
accordance with the terms of the credit will be duly honored by us.

Please check the terms and conditions of this documentary credit closely on receipt to
ensure that you will be able to comply with its exact requirements. If there are any
conditions which you consider in variance with your contract with the buyer, or which
you will have difficulty in fulfilling, please arrange to have the credit amended by
contacting the buyer direct.

Except so far as otherwise expressly stated, this credit is subject to the Uniform
Customs and Practice for Documentary Credits (1983 Revision) International Chamber
of Commerce Publication No. 400.

Very truly yours,

SPECIMEN

Authorized Signature
/swb

Figure 1 Letter of Credit. This document is advising the exporter (John's Bolt
Company) that his bank (Bank One Milwaukee, NA) has received irrevocable
documentary credit for US$3,200.00 from a Singapore bank on behalf of Bolt's
customer. The letter explains that the money will be paid assuming all the
conditions of the contract with the buyer are fulfilled. (Provided through the
courtesy of Bank One, Milwaukee, NA.)

irrevocable letters of credit are: they offer you security when it comes to payment, they are flexible, and it is vitally important to observe and heed every word of the document lest the bank refuse to pay until every condition, no matter how trivial, is met.

The cost of obtaining a L/C is normally charged to the buyer. It is customarily based on a straight fee plus a percentage of the value, usually a fraction of a percent. The confirming bank is also paid a fee but, like many dealings with a bank, this is negotiable.

In summary, a L/C is a method where your buyer must obtain the payment funds in advance from his bank and pay for a document that assures you that payment. It is a very flexible document and can be written to accommodate just about any conceivable situation. L/Cs are extremely common in international trade and international departments of local banks will undoubtedly have extensive experience in dealing with them.

After doing business with one overseas customer for a long period of time using L/Cs, be prepared for a request to shift to an open account. The reasons are obvious. This will save the buyer not only the fees for each L/C, but the necessity to arrange for financing for his purchase with his bank. From your standpoint, however, an L/C is a very secure method of payment.

Here is a short glossary of the most important terms dealing with letters of credit:

Account Party The party, usually the buyer or importer, who instructs the bank to open a letter of credit.

Amendment A change in the terms or conditions of a letter of credit after it has been issued; changes must be in favor of the beneficiary and, if not in their favor, you need the beneficiary's prior approval.

Assignment Using a letter of credit to obtain additional credit.

Back-to-Back Credit Issuing another letter of credit on the strength of an original L/C.

Beneficiary Usually, the seller or exporter; this is the person who receives payment as directed in the letter of credit.

Bill of Lading This is a document issued by the transport company which verifies movement of goods from one location to another. It is a receipt and a contract for delivery and sometimes represents title to the goods. It is a vital document in conjunction with a letter of credit.

Confirmed Credit When a letter of credit is backed by a second bank.

Discrepancy Whenever there is a variation or failure to comply from the original stipulations in the letter of credit.

Irrevocable The important term which signifies that a letter of credit cannot be changed or cancelled without the consent of all parties involved. Almost all letters of credit are irrevocable, but this must be stated on the face of the document.

Opening Bank The bank that issues the letter of credit; the bank that is obligated to make payment.

Revolving Credit When a letter of credit provides a credit limit that can be used repeatedly to cover repetitive shipments.

Sight Credit A L/C that is paid when the beneficiary first presents the draft and accompanying documentation, usually when the goods are in transit and when the documents are in proper order.

For anyone interested in learning the complete set of rules and guidelines involved in letter of credit transactions, they are contained in a publication issued by the International Chamber of Commerce titled *Uniform Customs and Practices for Documentary Credits*.

Documentary drafts have some similarities to L/Cs but are less secure and can even be likened to payment by ordinary check. However, these drafts in their several forms are used almost exclusively in international trade, therefore it is important to understand exactly how they work.

First, some terminology. The document itself is called a *draft* or *bill of exchange*. When you sell your product to a customer overseas, you ask your bank to prepare such a draft and present it to your customer through its branch or affiliate bank in the country of your customer. When the customer is presented with this draft, if he signs it, it is *accepted,* which means he agrees to pay it on the predesignated date. Drafts can either be *sight drafts* (Figure 2) or *time drafts* which means exactly what the terms imply: a sight draft must be paid "on sight" whereas a time draft must be paid according to the time period specified. The buyer is called the *drawee* or *signer* of a draft and once it has been accepted, the draft is termed a *trade acceptance.*

BANK≡ONE.
BANK ONE, MILWAUKEE, N A
111 East Wisconsin Avenue • P. O. Box 975 • Milwaukee, Wisconsin 53201 U.S.A.
International Banking Department • Telex 191115

DATE   July 8, 198–

DIRECT COLLECTION LETTER

PLEASE REFER TO
COLLECTION NUMBER
▼
DCL - 79930

DRAWER

MAIL TO	
Banque Nationale de Paris International Department Rue La Fayette Paris, France	ABC Company 123 Water Street Milwaukee, WI 53202

INVOICE NO.   DRAFT NO.

We enclose for collection and remittance the items(s) described hereon. Please accept for account of Bank One, Milwaukee, N.A., International Banking Department, P. O. Box 975, Milwaukee, Wisconsin 53201 USA to whom you should acknowledge receipt and advise promptly of acceptance, maturity, or payment by airmail. Do not protest unless indicated below.

SHIPMENT	DATE OF B/L	TENOR
machine parts	6-30-8–	*****Sight*****

DRAWEE:
XYZ Company
P.O. Box 1648
Paris, France

AMOUNT

$10,000.00

**PLEASE NOTE INSTRUCTIONS
ON REVERSE SIDE**

Subject to Uniform Rules for the Collection of Commercial Paper adopted by the International Chamber of Commerce as in effect on this date.

DOCUMENTS	DRAFT	INVOICES			CERTIFICATES		WEIGHT LIST	PACKING LIST	AIRWAY BILL	BILL OF LADING	P.P. RECEIPT	OTHER
		COMM.	VISAED	CONSUL	ORIGIN	INS.						
	1	4			1			3		2/2		

PLEASE FOLLOW INSTRUCTIONS INDICATED (X):

☒ DELIVER DOCUMENTS AGAINST   ☒ PAYMENT   ☐ ACCEPTANCE

☐ PROTEST

☐ ALLOW DISCOUNT OF $ IF PAID

☐ COLLECT INTEREST @   % P.A.
   FROM

☐ OTHER INSTRUCTIONS

☐ HOLD ACCEPTED DRAFT AND PRESENT FOR PAYMENT AT MATURITY

☒ ADVISE NON-PAYMENT/NON-ACCEPTANCE GIVING REASON(S) BY AIRMAIL

☒ COLLECT ALL CHARGES FROM DRAWEE
   INCLUDING BANK ONE, MILWAUKEE, N A
   CHARGES OF 1/8 of 1% - MINIMUM U.S. $20.00

☐ WAIVE CHARGES ONLY IF ABSOLUTELY REFUSED

☒ REMIT PROCEEDS BY   ☐ MAIL TRANSFER   ☐ CABLE TRANSFER   ☒ SWIFT
IN CASE OF NEED REFER TO:

WHO MAY ASSIST IN COLLECTION ONLY

1) ORIGINAL—Shipping Documents attached hereto
0236 (00-035) 4-88

DETACH HERE FOR DRAFT

$ 10,000.00   July 8, 198–   Draft or Invoice No.   1976

***** Sight *****   OF THIS SOLE OF EXCHANGE

PAY TO THE ORDER OF   BANK ONE, MILWAUKEE, N.A • MILWAUKEE, WISCONSIN, U.S.A.

Exactly Ten Thousand and 00/100 US Dollars ---

DRAWEE'S NAME & ADDRESS

XYZ Company
P.O. Box 1648
Paris, France

(AUTHORIZED SIGNATURE)
John Smith, Controller, ABC Company

Milwaukee   Wisconsin
CITY   STATE

DCL - 79930

Figure 2 Sight Draft. The lower portion of this collection document is a typical *sight draft*. The top part provides instructions for payment. In this case, the exporter, The ABC Company, through its home bank in Milwaukee, is notifying a bank in Paris that it can deliver the shipping documents to the end customer, the XYZ Company, on payment of the amount owed, $10,000. (Provided through the courtesy of Bank One, Milwaukee, NA.)

For you as an exporter, sight drafts are obviously better than time drafts because payment is made "on sight" of the shipping documents. A time draft delays payment (Figure 3).

Drafts are simple payment vehicles that are not guaranteed by any bank. There are risks for both parties on a sight draft, and for the exporter alone on time drafts. Costs are much less for drafts and usually shared by exporter and importer.

Open accounts are common in international trade, especially in Europe, but limited, as they are in domestic commerce, to credit-worthy customers who have established good ratings and good re-payment records. Payments are based on trust and faith. Under open account credit terms, you agree to receive orders and make shipments on the understanding that the customer will pay you according to prearranged conditions. Those conditions are often called *datings,* meaning they will pay, say, 30 days after the date of the shipping invoice, or 30 days after the merchandise is received in the end market, or 60 days or 120 days, or whatever time period you agree upon. Other variations on datings are to offer special small discounts if payment is made by a certain time. For example, you might specify "2 percent, 30 days" meaning you will allow a 2 percent discount, meaning a reduction in the amount owed if the buyer pays you within 30 days. In international trade, be prepared for strong arguments to grant long and liberal datings. This is be-cause the buyer will claim it takes 30 or 60 or 90 days for him to receive your merchandise, place it in inventory, sell it, and then receive payment himself. There is validity to this when, for example, your merchandise must be shipped by ocean transport where weeks

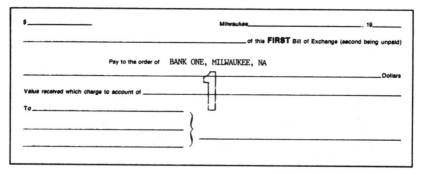

Figure 3 Bill of Exchange. This is a *draft* or *bill of exchange.* It is a legal demand for payment. When it is signed by the customer, it has become "accepted" and is called a *trade acceptance.* Drafts can either be *sight drafts* or *time drafts.* (Provided through the courtesy of Bank One, Milwaukee, NA.)

and months can elapse before the buyer has access to what he has purchased.

It is also possible to consider offering extraordinarily long payment terms to a newly appointed distributor. This is a means to help finance a new distributor's start-up with your product line. In cases like this, firms may offer as much as 180-day payment terms, which gives the new distributor a full six months to receive his first shipment from you, generate sales, and begin to receive payment from his own sales. This should only be done, naturally, if you have either strong credit references or some other form of security. Another extraordinary situation occurs when a distributor has a damaging fire or some other serious business interruption. In this case, offering extra-long payment terms is a welcomed form of assistance and goodwill. Also, bear in mind, as pointed out earlier, that letters of credit can be issued for payment at almost any advance date agreed upon by the two parties. This is another form, a much more secure form, of offering datings to the distributor. His objection will be, first, that he must still arrange for financing locally with the issuing bank and, second, he must pay the bank a fee for the letter of credit.

In general, many exporting companies who have long and trusted relationships with their distributors, customarily offer terms and datings mutually arrived at over a period of years. Just as in the domestic market, this is often influenced by competitors. If competitors offer longer datings, your customer will pressure for you to do the same. An overseas distributor will undoubtedly tell you when his other accounts in the United States provide more liberal payment terms and argue that you should do likewise.

Consignment is considered the least desirable form of selling and receiving payment because the buyer bears little or no risk and your payment is delayed until the so-called buyer turns around and sells it to someone else. True, you retain title to the goods, but they are usually located far away and out of your control. To most international trade sellers, consignment is a dirty word.

Here is a short glossary dealing with international collections:

Bill of Exchange Another term for a draft.

Clean Collection When a draft or other demand for payment is presented without additional attached documentation.

Collecting Bank Usually a bank near the buyer that acts as an agent for the seller's bank (called the "Remitting Bank").

Documentary Collection When a demand for payment is presented along with shipping or other documents.

Documents Against Acceptance A payment term when documentation accompanying a time draft is released to the buyer when the buyer "accepts" the draft; by "accepting" it means the buyer agrees to pay the amount owed.

Documents Against Payment A payment term meaning that documents will be released when the buyer pays the amount of the draft, usually a sight draft.

Draft A banking instrument that looks like an ordinary check which is used for payment in a business transaction. (See Figures 2 and 3.)

Presentation When the collection instrument is presented to the payer.

Remitting Bank The bank that represents the seller in a transaction and deals with the "Collecting Bank" in the vicinity of the customer.

Sight Draft A draft signifying payment at first presentation, or literally on sight of the draft.

Time Draft A draft signifying payment on the date indicated in the draft. This is also sometimes called a *usance draft*.

Trade Acceptance When the buyer acknowledges and agrees to pay a time draft on the date specified.

HANDLING DIFFICULT COLLECTIONS

One reason letters of credit are so important in international trade is because collections of money owed can be sticky, difficult, and time-consuming with accounts overseas. In many cases, persistence and patience will bring rewards because often a delayed payment is a result of misunderstandings or unhappiness over some small aspect of your shipment.

When more serious disagreements occur, you can use the services of your bank or legal counsel, or specific groups such as The National Association of Credit Management or the collection services of Dun & Bradstreet, assuming the latter have facilities in the market in question. If some form of arbitration is required, The International Chamber of Commerce handles the majority of these.

The American Arbitration Association also handles international disputes.

For general disputes over all aspects of a trade deal, go through your local district office of the DoC. However, before you appeal to them, you must show that you have made every effort to settle the complaint without U.S. government assistance and that the claim is more than $1000. Simple collection claims are not accepted.

SUMMARY

The natural inclination when embarking on new sales overseas is to concentrate on marketing. A common attitude among even the best marketers is "If I can get the sales volume up, the profits will take care of themselves." This is short-sighted and without proper attention to financing and payments it can lead to ruin.

Getting paid for exports can be especially problematic because of the distances, the barriers to communication, and the legal differences between countries. One well-known consumer goods company hastily decided to terminate a distributor because they found the firm guilty of flagrant trans-shipping. The problem was that, at the time, the distributor owned them $346,000 on open account. It took years of negotiation and large concessions before the debt was ever settled. Never terminate a distributor until all debts are settled, or some secure method is arranged for payment.

As recommended at the outset of this chapter, financing and payments in international trade are specialty fields. However, any executive, no matter what his or her position in a firm, who plans to travel abroad to find new outlets for sales must be acquainted with financing methods and payment terms. The reason is that foreign buyers want decisions on the spot. They do not want you to say "Well, I must check back with the home office on that question." The traveling executive must have both the knowledge of company policies and authority to make decisions about financing and payment on the scene. Lacking this, the overseas buyer will lose patience and insist on dealing with someone who has such authority.

In this chapter, nothing was mentioned about certain other collection documents such as commercial or consular invoices. That is because they more properly fit in the department of shipping and shipping documentation. That is our next stopping point on the road to exports. Meanwhile, while the phrase "No sale is complete until the money is in the bank" is worn, tattered, and prosaic, it is nonetheless solid gold truth in international business. If customers overseas awaken each morning wondering how to delay payments, it stands to reason that you should go to bed each night muttering that time-honored phrase about a true sale is one where the money is safely in the bank.

9

Shipping

We are the "supply" in supply-side economics . . .

Shipping company manager

The transportation industry in the United States is, at once, a marvel and a maze of complexity. Shut down the highways and the nation would stiffen with paralysis. Block the airways, the railroads, and the sea lanes, and the country would quickly suffocate as well. Considering this, one can rationalize the pride of the shipping company executive quoted above who maintains that if demand and then supply are the keys to the whole economic system, it is the shipping industry that carries the lifeblood of supplies to energize the market.

Shipping overseas is really just an extension of the U.S. transportation and shipping business. "It just means shipping farther," one freight forwarder explains. But shipping is so important to exporting and international trade that any high school or college graduate wishing to break into international trade would be well-advised to take courses in export shipping early is his or her career. For aspiring international careerists the most popular single seminar, night course, workshop, or college course offered is the one on export shipping and documentation. These specialists perform the role of the navigators of the shipping business. Good ones can turn the captains of international trade into heroes, while bad ones can threaten the very existence of the business.

This chapter will *not* prepare an international manager to be a qualified shipping specialist. That takes months and even years.

However, this chapter will introduce the terminology and the language of shipping, packing, documentation, labeling, and insurance.

Because this area is such a specialty, it will be no surprise to learn that a whole cadre of service specialists exists to help you. They are called "international freight forwarders" and names, addresses, and phone numbers for these specialists can be found in the Yellow Pages of almost any large city.

ROLE OF THE FREIGHT FORWARDER

Freight forwarders act, first, as your agent in moving your product overseas. Second, they are knowledgeable about import duties, documentation, credit transactions, crating services, insurance, and bonding in addition to their fundamental role of moving your goods from one point to another.

"We do for cargo what travel agents do for passengers," explains Del Brahm, professional international freight forwarder and instructor. "There is no law that says you must use a freight forwarder. Just like the airlines or advertising, you can book your own ticket or buy media space directly. Freight forwarders operate like travel agents and advertising agents who, in those cases, receive commissions from airlines and the media. Freight forwarders receive their commissions from steamship lines. To qualify for these commissions, freight forwarders must be licensed by the Federal Maritime Commission and post a bond of $30,000 with that commission as a warranty for proper service."

Many forwarders also perform these same shipping services on imports as well. But this is possible only if they have obtained a license from the U.S. Customs Agency to be a customs house broker. Therefore, a properly licensed forwarder can help you with both outgoing and incoming shipping and documentation and, in the case of imports, with clearance of your goods through U.S. Customs.

Here is a synopsis of duties performed by a typical U.S.-based international freight forwarder:

- ▶ Pre-shipment counseling
- ▶ Issuance of quotes for transportation costs
- ▶ Booking of space

- Advice and booking of containerization
- Production of all shipping documents
- Consular documentation
- Handling of credit transactions between banks
- Tracking and follow-up from loading of goods to payment of letter of credit
- Handling at gateway port
- Insurance and bonds

For the *importation* of products, a freight forwarder who is licensed as a customs house broker will also do the following: handling "in bond" storage at ports and at duty free zones; arrange for customs bond; work with the international carrier conveying the goods; track your cargo shipment; clear your shipment at U.S. Customs; arrange for consolidation services for either air or ocean freight; and provide general counseling for clients.

International freight forwarders are independent businesses that vie for clients, so you will find competition in both rates and scope of services. While some rates are regulated by federal law, it is recommended that you periodically obtain several different bids on rates and also compare from time to time the services being offered.

The role of the freight forwarder can begin with your very first overseas order, since even for a price quotation to a potential new customer you will want to indicate the cost of packaging, shipping, insurance and possibly duties. Only in this way will your customer know the full and true cost to buy your product and bring it to his doorstep. As indicated in Chapter 7 on Pricing, the cost of packing and shipping overseas can be crucial part of developing your P&L so a close and confident working relationship with a freight forwarder is essential. Remember also that many exporters sell on an FOB basis, which means the *buyer* has the responsibility for shipping costs. That means the buyer has the responsibility to not only pay for that service but to direct how the goods should be shipped. You will either work with the freight forwarder designated by the buyer, or the buyer will agree to work through a forwarder you recommend. Keep in mind, however, that the buyer's forwarder will have the buyer's interest as a priority.

A sequence of events in a typical export transaction follows that demonstrates the general routine of a freight forwarder:

1. An inquiry is received and you must determine freight and insurance costs in addition to your selling price.

2. A freight forwarder is contacted who makes cost calculations based on the following: FOB factory value, weight, size, method of shipment, destination, and so on. In addition, the forwarder may obtain an option on shipping space.

3. A quotation is sent to the buyer.

4. If accepted, you prepare a confirming contract and obtain formal acceptance. You agree on method of payment, such as a letter of credit.

5. The forwarder will help prepare a *Shippers Export Declaration,* as required by the U.S. Department of Commerce for presentation to U.S. authorities.

6. The forwarder will book space and obtain confirmation.

7. The forwarder will prepare a bill of lading and have it accepted by the shipping line.

8. The forwarder will prepare a dock receipt and have it properly signed by the shipping company.

9. The forwarder will assure your commercial invoice is proper for the full transaction.

10. When required, the forwarder will prepare a consular invoice and have it properly authorized or legalized.

11. The forwarder will obtain an on-board certification from the ship line.

12. The forwarder can provide insurance if you, as the shipper, do not have your own insurance coverage.

13. The forwarder can assist in providing documentation for the bank to obtain payment.

Like all service companies, the international freight forwarder provides an extremely valuable service if they are efficient, reliable, cost-effective, and trustworthy. It is important to develop a solid working relationship with one or more forwarders and to assure that you are receiving full value for your dollar. Del Brahm urges shippers to visit several freight forwarders to compare the range of services. Find out what services are provided free of charge, what generic documents can be reproduced by word processors and what the fees are for preparing specific documents like invoices and packing lists.

PACKING

There are four obvious problems when packing for export: breakage, weight, moisture, and pilferage. A carton destined for export can run the gamut of torture and abuse. Consider its mini-odyssey: dollied from your shipping department to a waiting truck, hauled over roads and highways to a warehouse, unloaded and loaded again, subjected to heat and humidity, stored for days or weeks at a time, lifted by forklift trucks or slings, bumped or dropped repeatedly, shaken and stressed by different vehicles and temperatures. If that isn't enough trauma, your carton may be stealthily invaded by some of the most professional thieves.

In the quantity of products streaming through this massive transportation system, it is easy to assume one would not give much attention to such things as pens—ballpoint and fountain pens. But in my three decades with the Parker Pen Company, pilferage was a constant threat. The reasons, once considered, are fairly clear. Quality pens often contain gold parts. Pens are also small in size and, consequently, many of them can be packed into relatively small cartons. And, finally, if the brand name is well-known and respected, the products are easily marketed to a wholesale or retail distribution system. Parker took great pains to disguise its shipping cartons because placing the brand name conspicuously on the cartons became an open invitation to thievery. As a result, the name of "E.C. Frederick," a loyal and knowledgeable export manager at Parker, was stamped on the side of each carton instead of any corporate identification. Over the years, his name became well-known to the 153 importing distributors around the world.

Even so, crooks in New York, Lima, Toronto, London, Caracas, and dozens of other international sites found ingenious ways to burglarize pen shipments. In fact, regular pilferage in one of those ports became so serious that metal boxes were used inside corrugated cartons bound with metal straps. Still, the robbers found ways to cut through the cardboard and metal, remove the pens, replace them with junk of comparable weight, and re-seal the carton so that no one could detect a disturbance of any kind.

This example helps emphasize that packing for export deserves special care and attention.

Another factor to consider is that the handling of cargo overseas may not be as mechanized and as sophisticated as it is in the United States. Heavy crates should be packed on skids with provisions for forklift trucks. They should also have notches to facilitate the use of slings. Additional tips include: cement-coated nails hold better; packages should be strapped for added strength; plywood sheathing is economical and strong; use waterproof inner liners plus moisture-absorbing agents and rust-inhibiting coatings on finished metal parts; avoid overpacking since some customs offices overseas levy duties on gross weight rather than on the value of the package.

For either ocean or air shipments, the respective carrier can advise on the best packing method. Marine insurance companies also are available for consultation. "Containerization" is an increasingly popular method of shipment. Some containers are no more than truck bodies lifted off their wheels at the port of import for movement to an inland destination. Whether you use a container like this for shipment will depend, of course, on the size of your shipment and its destination. Your forwarder or shipping company agent can advise you on the pros and cons for your circumstances.

As a general rule, shipments by air do not require as heavy packing as ocean shipments. Protection is the critical word in both modes of shipment. For air shipments, standard domestic packing is usually acceptable.

Finally, packing is important in export if only because distances are greater and repeated handling and re-handling is so common. The buyer will often specify packing requirements, and insurance firms may also have suggestions for proper packing. In either case, the freight forwarder can be a helpful ally in advising on and solving your packing problems.

LABELING

The buyer usually specifies what type of labeling or marking should appear on your cartons, crates, or containers. These marks serve various purposes:

▶ They identify the shipper.
▶ They identify the consignee and reference number, contract number or purchase order number.

- ▶ They indicate the country of origin.
- ▶ They provide information on weight, in both pounds and kilograms.
- ▶ They tell the number of the package, especially if there is more than one in that shipment.
- ▶ They indicate handling instructions such as "fragile," depicted in international pictorial symbols.
- ▶ They provide cautionary remarks such as "store this side up" or "store in heated space," which should appear in both English and the language of the country of destination.
- ▶ They tell the port of entry and final destination, for example, Rome via Naples or Stuttgart via Antwerp.
- ▶ If hazardous materials are used, this should be indicated using the universal symbol identification system.

Markings should appear using letters at least two inches high, stenciled in black, waterproof ink and should appear on at least two adjacent sides, and preferably on top. Sacks should be marked on both sides prior to filling. Drums should be marked on both the side and top. Old marks should be completely removed. Legibility is important.

These labeling and marking rules are especially enforced in certain countries so it is important to abide by them carefully.

DOCUMENTATION

Documentation in international trade is more important than in domestic shipping. Export documentation must be precise and accurate, otherwise payment may be jeopardized. Most documentation is routine for customs brokers and freight forwarders, but the ultimate responsibility for accuracy is with the exporter. The amount and type of documentation required depends on the importing country. Each country has different import regulations. Another obvious difference is language.

Here is a list of the most important and more common documents used in exporting:

Commercial Invoice This is the same document used in domestic commerce but in exporting the buyer needs this invoice to prove ownership and to arrange payment. Also, in exporting, the customs agent overseas uses this invoice to determine the amount of duty to be charged.

Bill of Lading (Figure 4). This extremely important document is actually a contract between the owner of the goods and the carrier. The customer usually needs this as proof of ownership to take possession of the goods. They are two types of bills of lading: the straight bills are nonnegotiable, while shipper's order bills of lading can be bought, sold, or traded while the goods are in transit or when a letter of credit is involved.

Consular Invoice. Only certain countries require this and it is used to identify or control the goods. Some must be purchased from the consulate of the country to which the goods are being shipped. Some even must be purchased from the consulate office at the U.S. port of exit. And some must appear in the language of the country involved.

Certificate of Origin (Figure 5). This can be obtained through forms supply houses or from your forwarder. These certificates can be certified by your local chamber of commerce or, for Middle East destinations, by the Arab Chamber of Commerce in your area, and verifies the country of origin of the item being exported. This certificate is required by some importing countries such as Israel. Your forwarder will know both the process and which forms are required.

Dock Receipt (Figure 6). Also called a warehouse receipt, this document is used when the inland carrier leaves the shipment with the international carrier. It acts as a transfer of accountability.

Inspection Certification. If the buyers or the country of destination requires some documentation attesting to the specifications of the goods being shipped, this certificate can be obtained from an independent third party inspection organization.

Insurance Certificate. When the seller provides insurance, this document provides information on the type and amount of coverage.

Shipper's Export Declaration (SED) (Figure 7). Known in the trade as an "export dec," this is the one *required* document by the U.S. Department of Commerce. It is required for shipments valued in excess of $1500 and is used for three vital purposes: (1) to control exports, (2) to help compile trade statistics, and (3) for harbor tax.

BILL OF LADING

SHIPPER/EXPORTER	DOCUMENT NO.
	EXPORT REFERENCES

CONSIGNEE	FORWARDING AGENT · REFERENCES
	POINT AND COUNTRY OF ORIGIN

NOTIFY PARTY	DOMESTIC ROUTING/EXPORT INSTRUCTIONS

PIER OR AIRPORT	

EXPORTING CARRIER (Vessel/Airline)	PORT OF LOADING	ONWARD INLAND ROUTING
AIR/SEA PORT OF DISCHARGE	FOR TRANSSHIPMENT TO	

PARTICULARS FURNISHED BY SHIPPER

MARKS AND NUMBERS	NO. OF PKGS.	DESCRIPTION OF PACKAGES AND GOODS	GROSS WEIGHT	MEASUREMENT

FREIGHT CHARGES PAYABLE AT BY

	PREPAID	COLLECT
Land Origin Charges		
Port Charges		
SUB TOTAL		
Ocean Freight		
SUB TOTAL		
Port Charges		
Land Destination Charge		
SUB TOTAL		
GRAND TOTAL		

SHORT FORM BILL OF LADING

Received the goods, or packages said to contain goods herein mentioned, in apparent good order and condition unless otherwise indicated, to be transported and delivered, or trans-shipped as herein provided

This carriage is subject to the provisions of the U.S. Carriage of Goods by Sea Act of 1936. This Short Form Bill of Lading is issued pursuant to 46 U.S.C. 844, as amended. All the terms and conditions of the Carrier's regular form Bill of Lading, as filed with the Federal Maritime Commission and posted on board the vessel and available to any shipper or consignee upon request, are incorporated with like force and effect as if they were written at length herein, and all such terms and conditions so incorporated by reference are agreed by Shipper to be binding and to govern the relations, whatever they may be between those included in the words "Shipper" and "Carrier" as defined in Carrier's regular form Bill of Lading

IN WITNESS WHEREOF, the Carrier Master or Agent of said vessel has signed and the Shipper has received this one original bill of lading

Dated At_____ NAME OF CARRIER

By_____

MO   DAY   YEAR

B/L No.

Figure 4 Example of a Bill of Lading. This is a standard bill of lading which serves as a contract between you the shipper and the carrier of your goods. Also, your customer needs this document to take possession of the goods.

CERTIFICATE OF ORIGIN

SHIPPER/EXPORTER			DOCUMENT NO.		
			EXPORT REFERENCES		
CONSIGNEE			FORWARDING AGENT - REFERENCES		
			POINT AND COUNTRY OF ORIGIN		
NOTIFY PARTY			DOMESTIC ROUTING/EXPORT INSTRUCTIONS		
PIER OR AIRPORT					
EXPORTING CARRIER (Vessel/Airline)	PORT OF LOADING		ONWARD INLAND ROUTING		
AIR/SEA PORT OF DISCHARGE	FOR TRANSSHIPMENT TO				

		PARTICULARS FURNISHED BY SHIPPER			
MARKS AND NUMBERS	NO. OF PKGS.	DESCRIPTION OF PACKAGES AND GOODS		GROSS WEIGHT	MEASUREMENT

The undersigned .... (Owner or Agent), does hereby declare for the above named shipper, the goods as described above were shipped on the above date and consigned as indicated and are products of the United States of America

Dated at .... on the .... day of .... 19 ....

Sworn to before me this .... day of .... 19....... .

....

....
SIGNATURE OF OWNER OR AGENT

The ...., a recognized Chamber of Commerce

under the laws of the State of ...., has examined the manufacturer's invoice or shipper's affidavit concerning the origin of the merchandise, and, according to the best of its knowledge and belief, finds that the products named originated in the United States of North America.

Secretary ....

Figure 5 Certificate of Origin. This is a standard certificate of origin form. It verifies the country of origin of the goods being exported.

DOCK RECEIPT

SHIPPER/ EXPORTER	DOCUMENT NO.
	EXPORT REFERENCES
CONSIGNEE	FORWARDING AGENT - REFERENCES
	POINT AND COUNTRY OF ORIGIN
NOTIFY PARTY	DOMESTIC ROUTING/ EXPORT INSTRUCTIONS
PIER OR AIRPORT	

EXPORTING CARRIER (Vessel/Airline)	PORT OF LOADING	ONWARD INLAND ROUTING
AIR/SEA PORT OF DISCHARGE	FOR TRANSSHIPMENT TO	

PARTICULARS FURNISHED BY SHIPPER

MARKS AND NUMBERS	NO. OF PKGS.	DESCRIPTION OF PACKAGES AND GOODS	GROSS WEIGHT	MEASUREMENT

DELIVERED BY:

RECEIVED THE ABOVE DESCRIBED GOODS OR PACKAGES SUBJECT TO ALL THE TERMS OF THE UNDERSIGNED'S REGULAR FORM OF DOCK RECEIPT AND BILL OF LADING WHICH SHALL CONSTITUTE THE CONTRACT UNDER WHICH THE GOODS ARE RECEIVED, COPIES OF WHICH ARE AVAILABLE FROM THE CARRIER ON REQUEST AND MAY BE INSPECTED AT ANY OF ITS OFFICES.

LIGHTER
TRUCK ....

ARRIVED– DATE ....TIME ....

UNLOADED–DATE ....TIME ....

CHECKED BY...

PLACED IN SHIP LOCATION ....
         ON DOCK

502
WHSE NO. 0846
JOB NO. H 4771

FOR THE MASTER

BY...
                 RECEIVING CLERK

DATE ....

ONLY CLEAN DOCK RECEIPT ACCEPTED.

Figure 6 Example of a Dock Receipt. This is a dock receipt form and is used when an inland carrier leaves the shipment with the international carrier.

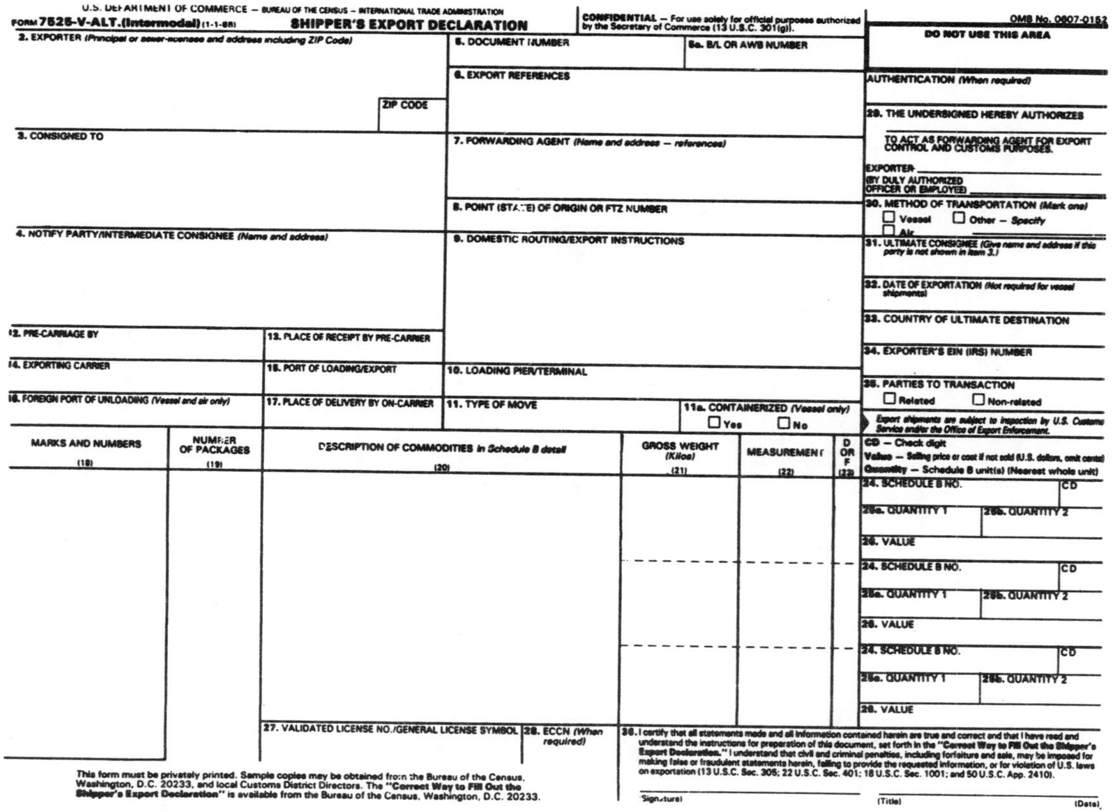

U.S. DEPARTMENT OF COMMERCE — BUREAU OF THE CENSUS — INTERNATIONAL TRADE ADMINISTRATION

FORM 7525-V-ALT.(Intermodal) (1-1-88)

SHIPPER'S EXPORT DECLARATION

CONFIDENTIAL — For use solely for official purposes authorized by the Secretary of Commerce (13 U.S.C. 301(g)).

OMB No. 0607-0152

DO NOT USE THIS AREA

2. EXPORTER (Principal or seller-licensee and address including ZIP Code)

ZIP CODE

5. DOCUMENT NUMBER

5a. B/L OR AWB NUMBER

6. EXPORT REFERENCES

AUTHENTICATION (When required)

3. CONSIGNED TO

7. FORWARDING AGENT (Name and address — references)

29. THE UNDERSIGNED HEREBY AUTHORIZES

TO ACT AS FORWARDING AGENT FOR EXPORT CONTROL AND CUSTOMS PURPOSES.

EXPORTER

(BY DULY AUTHORIZED OFFICER OR EMPLOYEE)

8. POINT (STATE) OF ORIGIN OR FTZ NUMBER

30. METHOD OF TRANSPORTATION (Mark one)

☐ Vessel ☐ Other — Specify

☐ Air

4. NOTIFY PARTY/INTERMEDIATE CONSIGNEE (Name and address)

9. DOMESTIC ROUTING/EXPORT INSTRUCTIONS

31. ULTIMATE CONSIGNEE (Give name and address if this party is not shown in item 3.)

32. DATE OF EXPORTATION (Not required for vessel shipments)

33. COUNTRY OF ULTIMATE DESTINATION

12. PRE-CARRIAGE BY

13. PLACE OF RECEIPT BY PRE-CARRIER

34. EXPORTER'S EIN (IRS) NUMBER

14. EXPORTING CARRIER

15. PORT OF LOADING/EXPORT

10. LOADING PIER/TERMINAL

35. PARTIES TO TRANSACTION

☐ Related ☐ Non-related

16. FOREIGN PORT OF UNLOADING (Vessel and air only)

17. PLACE OF DELIVERY BY ON-CARRIER

11. TYPE OF MOVE

11a. CONTAINERIZED (Vessel only)

☐ Yes ☐ No

Export shipments are subject to inspection by U.S. Customs Service and/or the Office of Export Enforcement.

MARKS AND NUMBERS (18)	NUMBER OF PACKAGES (19)	DESCRIPTION OF COMMODITIES in Schedule B detail (20)	GROSS WEIGHT (Kilos) (21)	MEASUREMENT (22)	D OR F (23)	CD — Check digit Value — Selling price or cost if not sold (U.S. dollars, omit cents) Quantity — Schedule B unit(s) (Nearest whole unit)
						24. SCHEDULE B NO. / CD 25a. QUANTITY 1 / 25b. QUANTITY 2 26. VALUE
						24. SCHEDULE B NO. / CD 25a. QUANTITY 1 / 25b. QUANTITY 2 26. VALUE
						24. SCHEDULE B NO. / CD 25a. QUANTITY 1 / 25b. QUANTITY 2 26. VALUE

27. VALIDATED LICENSE NO./GENERAL LICENSE SYMBOL

28. ECCN (When required)

36. I certify that all statements made and all information contained herein are true and correct and that I have read and understand the instructions for preparation of this document, set forth in the "Correct Way to Fill Out the Shipper's Export Declaration." I understand that civil and criminal penalties, including forfeiture and sale, may be imposed for making false or fraudulent statements herein, failing to provide the requested information, or for violation of U.S. laws on exportation (13 U.S.C. Sec. 305; 22 U.S.C. Sec. 401; 18 U.S.C. Sec. 1001; and 50 U.S.C. App. 2410).

(Signature) (Title) (Date)

This form must be privately printed. Sample copies may be obtained from the Bureau of the Census, Washington, D.C. 20233, and local Customs District Directors. The "Correct Way to Fill Out the Shipper's Export Declaration" is available from the Bureau of the Census, Washington, D.C. 20233.

Figure 7 Example of a Shipper's Export Declaration. This Shipper's Export Declaration is the one document required by the U.S. government. A new, "harmonized" system of product identification went into effect on January 1, 1989. After that date, weights must be listed in metric measurements, and a new eleven-digit number is used to identify your product according to government codes. This document has traditionally been printed on yellow paper for easy identification.

Your trade specialist at the Commerce district office can provide you with the booklet titled *Correct Way to Fill Out the Shipper's Export Declarations.* This is a form you can learn to complete yourself, or ask your freight forwarder if they will provide it free of charge.

Export License If your product must have one of the validated licenses issued by the U.S. government for export, as discussed in Chapter 2, this becomes one of the essential documents for shipping.

Export Packing List Just as with any domestic shipment, a packing list is essential. However, in export more detail is required because it must itemize the material in each individual package. It shows the various weights (net, legal, tare, and gross) and measurements for each package. This list should be in a waterproof envelope and is used by the shipper or forwarding agent to determine the shipment weight and volume. It also helps determine if the correct cargo is being shipped. Also, customs officials in both the United States and the foreign country may use the list to check the actual cargo.

INSURANCE

Just as with any inland, domestic shipment of goods, insurance is a separate and important part of doing business. Depending on your agreement with the buyer, either you must obtain insurance coverage, the buyer will arrange for it, or you will obtain it for him, at his cost and subject to his approval. Most large U.S. commercial insurance companies are fully experienced in providing all types of insurance for the exportation of all types of goods. A good insurance agent can be helpful in advising you on packing and labeling and even on modes of shipment. They also know which ports have the worst records in terms of pilferage and damage and therefore which ports to avoid. If your volume of exports is not sufficient for your own policy, most forwarders can arrange for coverage under their policy.

Since exported goods are handled more often over longer distances, the risk of damage is increased which makes insurance coverage all the more important. It is wise to shop around among insurance companies as well as asking your freight forwarder for information and advice. Some forwarders and customs brokers offer "blanket marine insurance," meaning they secure insurance that remains in continuous effect and automatically insures all cargo movements for the seller. Be certain you have "warehouse to warehouse" coverage. Forwarders can also arrange for "consolidation" of shipments which means your shipment is combined with others, which may then be put in a container which, in turn, provides additional security.

SUMMARY

At the outset of this chapter, we emphasized that the process of shipping, documentation, packing, and labeling was a specialty best delegated to experts. You will have no problem whatsoever finding these experts. Your trade specialist at the Department of Commerce can provide a list, or the phone book will have numbers and addresses. In addition, you can meet them personally by attending meetings of the world trade associations or clubs in your region. As your exporting experience and volume increase, it is possible you will want to hire your own in-house specialist to be in charge of all export administration. Later, you may want to add others to help with documentation and records. Even so, you will still probably work closely with freight forwarders.

Any international marketer will tell you that as he or she traveled the world calling on distributors, probably the first few hours of any visit were taken up resolving shipping problems. That is because for your buyer it is vitally important to receive purchases swiftly, efficiently, and at the lowest possible cost. Furthermore, precise attention to detail in "cutting" documents, as it is called, is exceedingly important. Errors in documentation lead to costly delays in transit time, to delay of payment of letters of credit, and to punishing penalties by the importing government as well.

In some countries, an inadvertence in quoting values or quantities on documents can result in harsh fines and, if the error was yours, the warning applies: "You drop it, you pay for it."

A 20-year international marketer confided that one of the wisest decisions he ever made was to take his shipping manager along with him on an extensive tour of overseas customers. "It was not until that trip that my manager could see for himself how important his job actually was. He saw for himself what the process was like at the other end. He saw first hand the importance of accuracy and precision in documentation. Furthermore, my customers established a good personal relationship with my shipping manager and from that point onward they worked more comfortably with each other."

In the past two chapters, we have become acquainted with three crucial areas in exporting: (1) financing—arranging the financing for either pre-shipment or project financing, (2) payment—how to assure proper payment from your customers, and (3) shipping—packing, labeling, documentation and the role of the freight forwarder. It is important to remember that two of these areas—payments and shipping—are specializations. Both require the services of experienced and competent experts. Fortunately, help is readily available from the international department of commercial banks and from freight forwarders. Like many aspects of management today, learning the language of any specialization is half the battle, and that is what we have tried to do in these chapters.

You are now ready to move into another form of management, the management of your distributor. You undoubtedly have already accumulated considerable experience in managing others, but that has probably been within the business culture of the United States. Managing overseas distributors is a new challenge because there are new elements: different languages, different business methods, and different attitudes. But, as one international manager explains it, "Shipping and finance, those are the necessary nuts and bolts of trade, but managing the people . . . ah, *there* is the real fun and the challenge. That is where the wonderful element of people makes management truly come alive."

10

Managing and Motivating the Distributor

**Call it style-flex, call it chameleon
management . . . whatever you call it,
you *need* it in international business.**

Just what is this "style-flex" or "chameleon" management that is so
important in being successful in international trade? Listen to one
experienced and successful executive:

> The great excitement for me in international business, aside from
> bringing home the business, is the challenge of change. For exam-
> ple, I work for three days with my distributor in Amsterdam where
> we have a prescribed set of rules according to Dutch business
> methods—that includes pricing, merchandising, discounts, termi-
> nology, attitudes of the distributor, and so on. Then, I board one
> of those fast, modern European trains and in less than two hours I
> am with my distributor in Brussels who is totally different from the
> Dutch distributor. In a flash, the whole game changes; not only a
> different personality with different methods and attitudes, but
> a different currency, a different culture, and not one, but in Belgium
> *two* different languages within one country. Now that's what I call
> a management challenge.

While those are the words of just one international manager,
they reflect the conviction and enthusiasm of most international

managers. They express the contrast and the extra challenge between managing in the United States and managing overseas.

If, as described here, the world of international commerce is a mosaic, each piece having its own separate identity, then your linkage with each is the distributor. Your appointed distributor (for convenience, we will refer to the distributor here as "he" although this individual may be either male or female) is your individual bridge into each market. Successfully managing that distributor becomes a key priority.

Your distributor represents an extension of your company in his assigned market. If he succeeds, you succeed. If you provide quality products and competitive prices, he can prosper. For that reason, he is motivated to work with you, to represent your product successfully, and to generate sales for both parties. He wants you to flourish; he wants you to bring out new products; he wants you both to have a long, secure future.

In this chapter, we will explain the vital reciprocal expectations of any distributor relationship: first, what services and duties you have a right to expect from a distributor, and second, the services and duties the distributor has a right to expect from you. We will also discuss the management of advertising and promotion, ways to evaluate a distributor's performance and, finally, how to conduct a typical visit with a distributor—the agenda to cover, the information to collect, and the type of reports to file.

Woven throughout this chapter is the theme that a distributor relationship is a two-way relationship. A good distributor can generate for you millions and millions of dollars in business each year with little or no investment risk on your part. Close collaboration can therefore be rewarding for both sides.

A CASE HISTORY

The following is a true story with names of the principals changed.

In 1958, Mr. J. was an employee at a distributorship in a small Far Eastern market. For various reasons, that distributor decided to close and abandon that market. Finding himself without a job, Mr. J. petitioned one of the distributor's suppliers, a U.S. manufacturer of quality razors, to allow him to take over as their sales representative in that market. Not having any start-up funding, he asked the razor company to also grant him a $10,000 revolving line of credit. Since the American managers knew Mr. J. and trusted him, they agreed because the alternative was to lose the market. For the next several years, Mr. J. would take his stock of razors and drive up the length of his small country, selling razors from the tailgate of his station wagon. Two or three weeks later, he would drive back down the same route collecting payments from his dealers. With these funds, he would replenish his supply of razors and start over. After several years of this, he was buying $500,000 a year from his U.S. source. This evolved into a license for local assembly of some of the razors and then a small plant to produce shaving creams and other accessories. After a few more years, Mr. J. expanded his operations into exporting, serving as a buyer for American department stores. As his capital accumulated, he negotiated a deal to buy another distributorship in the largest market in the Far East to sell—you guessed it—the razors for his original benefactor. With these separate and growing ventures, Mr. J. grew so large that at one point he was offered, and was capable of buying, a major competitor of the razor company. He declined. Remembering how he got his start, selling razors from the tailgate of his station wagon, his loyalty to the original razor company was too strong. Today, Mr. J. is an extremely successful and wealthy man with properties all around the Pacific rim. During the intervening years, he has aided the razor company in countless ways, and it all began with one very modest distributorship in an equally modest market.

WHAT TO EXPECT FROM A DISTRIBUTOR

Distributor arrangements will vary from market to market and from product category to product category, but here is a general checklist of services that a typical distributor might customarily provide for a U.S. exporter.

> *Knowledge of the market.* This must be the predominant requirement. No matter how long you work in international trade, you will never come to know the Venezuelan market like someone who has lived and worked there for decades; the same is true of Thailand or Belgium or whatever market you name. The first responsibility of a good distributor, then, is to know the nature and the system and the methods of his market.

Knowledge of importing and selling your type of product. A distributor must know all the mechanics of ordering, shipping, insuring, paying duties, obtaining import licenses, and the other routine tasks of importing. While it may not be necessary that he have specific experience with your type of product, it is indeed important that he have experience with allied products. For example, an agricultural importer might have great difficulty being successful importing and selling consumer goods. An importer of auto parts would probably be a poor distributor of expensive perfumes. On the other hand, in very small markets you will find importers who are, indeed, "general traders," meaning they import and trade in a wide variety of goods such as foodstuffs, auto parts, and perfumes. The ideal profile is a distributor who has some general knowledge about your particular product, who may have complementary but not competitive lines, and who does not have so many diverse lines that yours becomes lost in the crowd. Occasionally you will find single-line distributors who exist to handle only one product, but these are uncommon and usually joint ventures between a sourcing company and the importer. Speaking of joint ventures, when appointing a new distributor one way to protect yourself and plan for the future is to either negotiate a "first option to buy" for that time when the distributor may decide to retire or sell. Another twist is to buy a minority share of a new distributorship; this allows you access to financial statements and more control of management. Incidentally, when a distributor does decide to sell out, it is generally accepted that the right to sell your product is not necessarily or automatically part of the sale. In this instance, depending on the terms of your original agreement, you have the option to leave or remain with the new ownership.

He should not be selling directly competitive products. The logic of this policy is obvious, and it is generally understood by most distributors that such a built-in conflict of interest helps no one. Larry M. Greb, with 27 years in international marketing for the S.C. Johnson (Wax) Co., says "This, of course is the ideal situation. But with many large companies diversifying, there often becomes a conflict and if you have a very good distributor, you may not want to terminate the relationship because of one or two minor product conflicts. As an example, before Johnson got into the shampoo category, we had some distributors that also distributed Lever Bros. products. No conflict existed until we introduced shampoos and conditioners. It wasn't practical to change distributors because of this one conflict. We were able to get Lever to agree to allow the distributor to handle our shampoo as well as theirs. This, of course, must be negotiated on an individual basis and a lot depends on the relationship you have with the distributor."

How many other noncompetitive lines should a distributor have? There is no firm rule. Some distributors have dozens and dozens of lines; others have only a few. Good business prudence suggests that a distributor should not have all his eggs in one basket. One distributor in Kenya states his policy is to have no single line become larger than 10 percent of his total volume. "That way," he reasons, "if I lose one of them, I will only be losing 10 percent of my sales, and I should be able to accommodate that kind of loss."

Ability to thoroughly cover the assigned territory. The distributor should have the organizational capability of serving the entire territory assigned to him. Some distributors are strong in metropolitan markets but weak in outlying districts. Or they are proficient with one channel of distribution and inexperienced in others. You as a sourcing company have the right to expect your distributor to sell and service the entire geographic territory agreed upon and to sell to all potential customers through all appropriate channels of distribution. If this means adding sales personnel in order to carry your line, so be it. On occasion, a distributor in, say, Colombia will argue that he wants the territory surrounding Bogota but not the coastal region to the north. It is possible to create two distributorships within one market but this often leads to jurisdictional disputes and conflicts involving overlapping customers, pricing, or service policies. It is usually best to find one distributor who will be responsible for an entire market, which usually means an entire country.

Prompt payment. Without question you have the expectation and the right to be paid promptly. Payment terms should be agreed upon before any appointment letter is signed, and the distributor should honor those terms. Any departure should have your prior approval. You should expect periodic requests for more lenient payment terms, either on a temporary or even permanent basis. This is a normal business procedure, especially during an economic slump in a market. A drastic business reversal, such as a fire or water damage, is another occasion when your payment schedule might be suspended. When the Arno River burst its banks and flooded Florence, Italy in 1967, buyers and sellers around the world rushed to assist thousands of Florentine artisans and suppliers in the best possible way—financing, special discounts, longer datings, and the like. It is a time-honored, effective way to build good will and loyalty.

A sales organization. Before signing any distributor agreement, make certain you are thoroughly acquainted with how the distributor intends to generate sales of your product. Will the salesforce be part-time or full-time? Will there be a sales manager? A marketing manager? A service manager? How will territories be assigned? Will special channels—mail-order, door-to-door, franchise—be opened? In other words, while it is important to be flexible and allow for local customs and methods, you should ask questions like these until you are satisfied that the distributor has a selling organization suited for your product. What about sales' samples? Who pays for them? This can be negotiated, incidentally, but if samples are expensive, many firms provide one free set and then require the distributor to purchase, perhaps at special discounts, subsequent samples.

Administrative support. A distributor should provide warehousing of your product, inventory management, order-filling, delivery, credit, and collection and all the other customary administrative back-up required for your product. Once again, the distributor's administrative staff may not replicate the one you have in the United States, but be satisfied it can do the job. Also, bear in mind that a distributor usually spreads administration costs over several or all his imported lines. Therefore, your product will be one of many that is stored, inventoried, delivered, and so on. But you have the right to receive your fair share of administrative support and service.

Adequate stocks. This is usually a matter of repeated negotiation because a distributor rarely wishes to carry every product model and in the quantity desired by the supplier. While you must respect the distributor's knowledge of what sells and what does not sell in his market, he in turn must respect your desire to fulfill the needs and demand of the marketplace. Your mutual goal is to avoid missing one sale and your argument is that to achieve this the distributor must carry sufficient stocks of all available models.

Sales records. You have the right to periodically receive and examine sales data for your product. This does not apply to other lines of goods carried by the distributor. But, receiving regular data on sales of your product should be a requirement. Your argument is that the distributor must keep some record of outgoing sales and you merely wish to see copies or extracts of those records. As you study this data and observe the flow of sales, you can suggest that he should increase his minimum inventory of a given item or add new models. This is all part of the patient, friendly negotiation process when dealing with a distributor. One helpful tip about semantics that reflects the whole relationship between distributor and supplier is:

While it is natural for you to discuss your "sales" to a distributor, for him they are "purchases." He purchases the goods from you and makes "sales" to his customers. Try to use his framework: call what he buys from you "purchases" and use the term "sales" to refer to what he sells. This is just good psychology because, in the final analysis, you are *both* interested in *his* sales; if his sales are strong and steady, your sales to (purchases from) the distributor will follow suit. This may seem trivial, but consider the psychology and symbolism behind it. A distributor who becomes convinced you are truly interested in his "sales" is one that will become more cooperative and trusting in your relationship.

Forecasts of purchases. Very few customers like to be pinned down to forecasting what they intend to buy in future months, but as your relationship with a distributor matures, you should emphasize that this is the only way to assure uninterrupted supply. One unpleasant way for a distributor to learn the role of forecasting is when he is suddenly confronted with strong demand for your product and you cannot rush shipments because your factory was producing according to old, conservative forecasts. You should explain this possible set of circumstances to him, assuring him that forecasts are not necessarily commitments to buy but are used, instead, for production planning. One company's policy on forecasting was as follows: The distributor was required to provide a twelve month rolling forward forecast that was used for production planning only; it was not a firm commitment to buy. Then, the distributor was required to submit firm orders at least three months before shipment with modifications permitted in those orders up until 30 days prior to shipment. When the 30-day limit was reached, the order became a firm commitment and was shipped accordingly. This is just one way to manage sales and production forecasting with a distributor.

A marketing plan. It is perfectly reasonable to ask your distributor to prepare, with your help, an annual marketing plan. This, incidentally, is where a forecast of purchases becomes integral. Many foreign distributors may not be accustomed to sophisticated planning, so be patient. However, the need for basic planning for advertising, promotions, seasonal campaigns, establishing new channels of sales, and introduction of new products is understood almost everywhere. Once that is established, the next step is to assure six-month reviews and revisions, and even quarterly reviews, if possible. As more and more distributors are added, you will find that these separate marketing plans become essential for your own forecasting and marketing planning within your own company. It is important to reach an understanding *early* in the relationship about producing periodic marketing plans.

Competitive information. A basic ingredient of any marketing plan is intelligence about competitors—prices, models, methods of distribution, strengths, and weaknesses. It is reasonable to ask for and receive periodic reports from your distributor on the activities of your competitors in his market. A good example would be copies of advertising by your competitors in that market. These help you understand the marketing positioning of your competition and may also signal new products or new strategies being introduced by your competitor.

Reports on economic conditions. Your distributor may not supply these regularly without gentle prodding from you, but they are not only important to the conduct of your business but, again, they demonstrate that you are just as interested in the sales climate in his market as he is. Incidentally, it is prudent to verify the distributor's economic forecasts with other sources, perhaps with banks or U.S. State Department reports.

Price calculations. You have the right to receive basic price calculations showing how your distributor marks up your product for resale in his market. These calculations should show shipping, insurance, duty and other landing charges, inland freight to his warehouse, the gross margin he adds to cover his costs, local VAT taxes, and retail mark-up, if any. All of this will be converted into his currency, of course, and the exchange rate should be clearly indicated. A point of debate may arise over the breakdown of his gross margin. He may not wish to reveal his percentage of net profit, but you may certainly ask what portion of his margin he is contributing to advertising and promotion. Some distributors may offer gross margin information freely; others contend that their costs for administration, sales, service and other expenses, plus net profit, is privileged information. Gross margins, or mark-ups by the distributor, will vary from product line to product line. You will have to use your own good judgment on whether or not the distributor is applying unreasonably high—or low—margins. As an example, in the quality consumer durable field, it was reasonable for a distributor to have a margin of about 30 percent of his selling price to his customer. Within that margin, the distributor charges costs for administration, sales, service, and his profit. He may also contribute money to advertising and sales promotion from that margin. One of the leading determinants of pricing in each market will be competitive prices, and that is why it is essential that you receive periodic updates on what your competition is doing: prices, payment terms to customers, new products, and new marketing strategies.

Market research. Your distributor may provide empirical information about competitors and marketshare, but normally the cost of any formal market research is borne by you, the supplier. An alternative is to have the cost for market research shared between you and the distributor. "No matter who pays," says Larry Greb, "make sure some research is done. It needn't always be expensive—just enough to get a feel for the market and what the end user thinks about the product. You want to avoid big mistakes or surprises." An example proves this point:

Briggs & Stratton Corporation makes engines for lawnmowers and wanted to introduce its product in Germany, England, and France.

They first learned that changes were occurring in the German and English markets as the result of increasing numbers of mass merchandisers plus the aggressive entrance of Japanese engine and lawnmower makers, like Honda, into Europe. In the United States, 80 percent of lawnmowers are bought on the basis of price from mass merchandisers. In England, 80 percent of gasoline engine-powered mowers are purchased from lawn and garden dealers with virtually no consideration given to price. Just getting this valuable piece of research was tricky. Briggs found that it couldn't simply replicate its research methods from the United States to Europe. In Germany, for example, the law forbids researchers from maintaining a record of who was interviewed. This prevents follow-up research, as is done in the United States. Also, in Germany and England, people won't respond to a written questionnaire because it is regarded as an invasion of privacy. Interviewing must be done over the phone or face-to-face. This example demonstrates how research may involve different methods in different cultures. Also, it shows how the distributor's knowledge of the market is critical because of local laws or customs.

Advertising and sales promotion funds. You, the supplier, should not automatically assume that the distributor will contribute funds for advertising or sales promotion. That will depend on what margins the distributor has at his end; this is a matter for discussion and negotiation. In many cases, you the supplier provide all advertising and promotion funding. In other cases, the landed cost of your merchandise plus prices among competitors allows the distributor to generate funds for these expenses. One determinant, as mentioned in the Chapter 7 on Pricing, is that in high-duty markets, if you include an allowance for advertising on the invoice, your distributor will be paying a duty on that allowance. In that circumstance, it is perhaps better to negotiate with the distributor to omit any unnecessary costs at your end so that duties are levied on the lowest possible invoiced price, and for him to provide the necessary advertising and promotion funds from his margin.

Clear understanding regarding termination. As stated repeatedly, it is essential that you and the distributor have a clear understanding over how and when termination of your agreement can occur. See Chapter 6 for more information on terminating distributor agreements.

Visits to your home factory and offices. You have the right to expect your distributor to pay occasional visits to your home headquarters. These visits are extremely useful in developing the feeling of partnership. Who pays for these trips is, again, a matter of negotiation. One reasonable compromise is that the distributor pays travel expenses to the major airport nearest you and the supplier may then pick up all expenses for meals, accommodations and overland travel. You will find that distributors often make trips to the United States and visit all of their suppliers in one sweep.

Translations. Distributors should assure that your printed materials—from advertising to instruction manuals—are properly translated into the vernacular. This does not mean your distributor must provide formal translations for lengthy technical texts, but he should review all materials to assure they are acceptable for his market. Keep in mind, too, that usage within one language is often different from country to country. What is common in Mexico may not be proper in, say, Argentina (both Spanish-speaking countries). The best rule is to have the distributor in *each* country review your proposed translation. As for spoken translation services during your visit, if your distributor is an experienced importer he will probably speak English. If not, he will assure a translator is present for your visit and discussions. If he does not, you can arrange to hire a local interpreter to assist you. Johnson Wax sent some Argentine-developed advertising material for its bug killer product, Raid®, to Mexico and Puerto Rico. The Argentine advertising said "Raid kills bugs dead" which, in Argentine-Spanish was *Raid mata bichos.* But, as it happened, in Mexico and Puerto Rico the word *bicho* is a slang term, and there the message meant "Raid kills the male organ."

For more on this subject of translations in advertising, and for more examples of embarrassing goofs and gaffes, read the Chapter 11 on Communications. Now, let us turn the tables.

WHAT THE DISTRIBUTOR EXPECTS FROM YOU

Everything is negotiable in a supplier-distributor arrangement, of course, but here are common expectations of an overseas distributor from the company he represents:

Exclusivity. This ranks first, understandably. The distributor wants control over the agreed upon geographic territory. He wants no interference from the outside, although this is impossible to guarantee and you should discuss this problem in advance. For example, you may agree to ship directly to others in his market but only with his prior approval. Indeed, he may even generate orders for you to ship directly to that customer. That process is called "indent" orders, a British term. It means your appointed distributor may develop an order and send it to you for direct shipment to a third party within his assigned territory. In these cases, it is important that your distributor understands he has "del credere" responsibility, meaning he bears the final responsibility for payment.

One problem that frequently arises regarding exclusivity is that you cannot guarantee absolute protection. Products sold into the U.S. system, for example, can be legally resold to third or even fourth parties and exported into markets overseas. There is nothing you can do to prevent this. In fact, if you cut off a U.S. customer simply because they resold your product to a foreign market, that U.S. customer can bring charges of restraint of trade against you. As explained in Chapter 7 on Pricing, one way to discourage this is to give your foreign distributor lower, preferential prices so that he can negate this type of incursion. In summary, your distributor will want assurances that you will exercise every legal method to provide him with exclusivity in this territory. When you grant exclusivity to a distributor, you are therefore really saying "I will do my utmost to not knowingly sell to any other party in your territory without your permission but I cannot absolutely guarantee that my goods will not find there way into your market. If and when that happens, I agree to work with you to resolve and remove that problem within the limits of the law."

Patent and trademark protection. Your distributor may want assurances that your product and your brand names will not be legally imitated and that you will take appropriate legal action if such counterfeits are brought into his territory. This means you must register your trademarks and patents in advance in that market. Your distributor might be able to assist you with evidence and other information, but generally he assumes the final responsibility rests with you.

Quality. Is there anyone who doesn't want quality in the products and services they buy? Your distributor will want trouble-free merchandise and will also want the protection of a liberal warrantee agreement. Bear in mind that replacement of defective parts and products is especially costly in international trade because of the distances and tariffs involved. A distributor imports a product, paying shipping and duty costs, and if that product is found to be defective, he is inconvenienced for more than just his time. Even if you replace the product at no cost, the distributor must once again pay shipping and duty expenses. More about this in a later section on repairs, service, and maintenance.

Commissions. Depending on your arrangement, the distributor may expect to receive a commission on each purchase, or each sale, of your product. The same would apply to rebates or bonuses or awards if they are negotiated as part of a sales quota system. There are pros and cons regarding commissions. The pro argument says that a commission is one way to help control a distributor. If he fails to do what you expect or ask, you can withhold his commission and thereby exercise some measure of control. The con argument is that a commission becomes part of the invoice price on which duty is paid, and therefore he is paying duty on his own commission. Another common arrangement is to pay a distributor a commission of, say, 10 percent, on any merchandise that entered into the exclusive territory from a sale other than through the distributor.

Shipping services. A distributor automatically expects you to provide efficient export shipping services. This means proper export packing, labeling, and documentation. He may ask you to help arrange for insurance and actual shipment, subject to his approval, and reimburse you for those costs.

Favorable prices. The distributor expects you will provide him with the lowest possible prices because of the three compelling reasons discussed in Chapter 7: (1) because he is absorbing some of your normal selling costs, (2) because you both want your end price to be as low as possible versus competition in that market, and (3) because the process of price escalation occurs, meaning your end selling price escalates as it moves across oceans, over duty hurdles, and through several distribution levels. Your distributor will also want to receive advance notification of any price increases. As in the U.S. market, this is always problematic. A supplier is wise to regularly print on his price lists the words "prices subject to change without notice." However, because a distributor is a quasi-partner, a supplier might give some short prior notice and accompany it with a degree of leniency such as honoring all orders already "in the house" at old prices, or allowing one average-size order before applying the new prices.

Payment terms. This was discussed in Chapter 9. Suffice it to say your distributor expects leniency as his credit rating is established and proven to be reliable.

Advertising, sales promotion, and packaging. Whether or not you actually provide dollars for the purchase of advertising is a negotiable point, as was discussed earlier. However, your distributor has a proper expectation that you will provide your product in packages suitable to his market. That means packaging in the proper language and with colors, symbols, and designs that are suitable and inoffensive in that market. There may also be certain packaging or labeling laws that must be heeded, such as the bilingual requirement in Canada. Other sales promotion materials, such as display cases, banners, streamers, window cards, illuminated signs, customer leaflets, sales catalogs, are also customary in international trade and a reasonable expectation of any distributor.

New and modified products. Your distributor will assume you want to fill the needs in his market. That means modifying your product or introducing new products to suit that market. Your action may be as simple as a new color, or it may be a total innovation when compared to competitive offerings. The point here is that your distributor expects you to at least stay head-to-head with the rest of the competitors in that market-place and, if possible, well ahead of them.

Training materials. These are especially important, especially at the beginning of a distributor-supplier relationship. You may supply leaflets, manuals, slide presentations, videotapes, or even on-site trainers. Whatever the case, the distributor has every right to assume you will provide instruction in the operation and sales features of your product. The same applies to service and repair methods. In addition, you may offer full counseling on how to operate an after-sales service operation.

Updates. While this is often neglected, it is reasonable for a distributor to hope that you will provide periodic new information perhaps in for the form of a newsletter about your company, your products, your people, and your industry.

Periodic visits. Every distributor wants and expects you to visit his market. As a general rule, the higher the visitor is on the executive ladder, the better. There is no better way to truly understand a specific market than to visit it, not just over night, but for several days. Spend time with the distributor, visit the administrators and the salesforce, and, most importantly, visit the end customers. Your managerial prowess will be directly related to the time spent with your distributor learning about problems and opportunities in that market. If necessary, your distributor also has the right to expect your technicians—quality control experts, shipping managers, market researchers—to visit his market as well. Veteran export managers live by the slogan "nothing replaces travel." Also, time your visits carefully. Avoid national holidays or special events, like local elections. "The natural inclination is to visit Caribbean distributors in January, February, or March," says Larry Greb. "If you show up in July, they know you really care."

Frequent communication. More detail on this area is in Chapter 11. Your distributor expects efficient, clear communication with you and your subordinates. This can be in the form of personal visits, phone, telex, facsimile machine (fax), or mail. For most of your distributors, English will be an acquired second language, not their native tongue, and this makes it doubly important to communicate effectively. The most important single action is quick follow-up on everything you have discussed and promised. In international management, the worst affronts are inaction and silence.

Sales conferences. You know from experience that your U.S. sales organization needs and wants periodic recognition and rejuvenation and this is usually accomplished at sales meetings. The same applies to a foreign distributor. He is anxious to learn the latest information about your product and your sales programs, and he expects you to inform and teach him. He also enjoys meeting with other foreign distributors of your product in order to exchange ideas.

Rewards and incentives. While they may take different forms, it is human nature to respond positively to rewards, recognition, and incentives. The trick in exporting is to learn which rewards appeal to which cultures. In some countries, personal recognition is just as effective as cash awards. The Japanese respond well to travel awards involving golf or, say, gambling and wives are rarely included. Middle Easterners may prefer gifts of substance and value. Latins may prefer entertainment, and there it would be appropriate to include wives. Rewards should be tailored to the customs and tastes of each market and be characterized by personal attention, sensitivity, and sincere friendship.

THE DISTRIBUTOR DOSSIER

The conscientious exporter will build a comprehensive dossier on each distributor which, over succeeding years, will become invaluable for the management and motivation of that distributor.

There are several reasons why this dossier will be useful. First, each time you visit that market, a quick scan of the dossier will refresh your memory and help you remember fundamental facts. As you add more distributors, it is easy to confuse certain details between one and another. Second, American companies are known for rotating or replacing sales representatives. Most overseas distributors dislike this practice, incidentally, and prefer to deal with one person, or the same people. The reason for this is that personal relationships are extremely important in doing business overseas. Therefore, with a detailed file on each distributor, whenever a new person from your firm visits that market, much of the human relations spadework has already been done, and transitions are easier. Lastly, information about your customer and his market is fundamental to good selling, so keep it updated, keep it accurate, and don't leave home without it.

This distributor dossier, or file, should contain the following information, and it should be updated after each visit to that market:

▶ Full name, address, phone number, telex number, fax number, and so on of the distributor

▶ Complete names and correct full titles of each person in the distributorship dealing with your account; home addresses and phone number for each

▶ Normal payment terms

▶ Names, addresses, and phone numbers of popular hotels in the city, or cities, where you might visit

▶ A list of national holidays in that market, with dates and explanations of each, so that you do not innocently visit that market at an inappropriate time

▶ Customary office hours and time difference between your home office and the distributor office, with footnotes about daylight savings time

▶ List of electrical voltages or special requirements, and system of weights and measures

▶ Currency used (with correct designation for coins and paper bills) along with the current exchange rate

▶ Information on climate and recommended clothing for certain times of the year

▶ List of competitors in that market, with names of their respective importing distributors

▶ List of other firms that the distributor represents in that market

▶ Duty and other tax schedules applicable to your product

▶ Notes on insurance carrier, preferred method of shipment, and any special shipping, labeling, packing, or documentation requirements for that market. This might even be a separate "country shipping instruction" sheet.

▶ Notes on preferred entertainment: favored restaurants or nightclubs, popular sports

▶ A record of gifts presented on past occasions to avoid duplication in the future, plus a list of suggested gifts

▶ Family information about each of the principals: spouse's name, children's name and ages

▶ Notes on proper protocol: use of first names and titles, proper greetings, use of business titles, attitude toward punctuality, conversational taboos, useful toasts, proper business attire

▸ Names, addresses, and phone numbers for the following: U.S. embassy or consulate, branch or correspondent bank, your legal advisor (if you have one), and local hospitals

Additional useful information, if possible to obtain, might be: nature of the ownership of the distributorship, basic market share information among competition or product categories, trade discount schedules, pricing calculations, ages of key people, plus a listing of prior visits both to the distributor and your headquarters.

Paying attention to this type of detail can pay handsome rewards. For example, remembering the birthday of a child, or recalling a favorite gift or toast, or recalling precisely when the distributor last visited you in the United States—all of these demonstrate personal interest and sensitivity which help build a lasting relationship of trust and friendship.

ADVERTISING MANAGEMENT

Within international trade circles, there are two prevailing, but contradictory, theories about advertising management. They are *centralized* versus *de-centralized* advertising. Centralized advertising customarily means one basic advertising image and message in all markets so that consistency and repetition prevail. Furthermore, it may also involve having one U.S. advertising agency for all markets. In practice, what this means is using one major U.S. agency and their foreign-owned or affiliated offices overseas.

Under this *centralized* management approach, a U.S. agency will argue that they can, through one headquarters office, spread your message at minimum expense by creating and booking mutually agreed upon advertising in a host of different markets. Savings on artwork and production costs can result, they say, and "everyone is singing from the same hymnal." This does not mean that the advertisements themselves cannot be localized in various ways. For example, translations will be required in many instances, and illustrations and copy may be altered to fit local tastes and idiosyncrasies.

Large U.S. companies such as Coca-Cola, Kodak, IBM, and Pan American Airways usually prefer this centralized approach. It gives them tight control over both message and image as well as absolute discipline over their valued logotypes. The *decentralized* approach is just what the word implies. This school says "Each market is different and so we will let the best local advertising experts translate our messages, literally and figuratively. Furthermore, just because a large U.S. ad agency is strong in market A and market B, that does not guarantee that it is the best and strongest in other markets." A new-to-export firm might have no other choice than to begin with this decentralized approach because it will be starting in one market, then two, and then several and will, by necessity, appoint an ad agency for each. On the other hand, your U.S. ad agency may possibly have affiliations with other agencies overseas. However, your question should be: Is this the best agency in that market? This is where you and your distributor should confer. Your distributor, if he is experienced and knowledgeable about his market, will probably have opinions about which agencies are best.

As for management of the agency and the advertising, the proponents of this decentralized philosophy would say "We try to pick the best local agency, regardless of size or affiliation. Then we explain our fundamental philosophy about our product and what we are. Then we tell the local agency to translate that philosophy into the vernacular. They must use our logotype precisely as we instruct, of course, because we want constancy with our company name in all markets. But we want the local agency to decide how to convey our message most effectively to the audience in their market." The following story illustrates the importance of the local ad agency:

> The manufacturer of a line of prestige wrist watches created a basic advertising campaign that pictured a handsome, sophisticated couple standing in front of a Rolls Royce automobile while admiring each other's watches. This, the watch company believed, conveyed their marketing message of elegance, prestige, luxury, and quality. It was a safe, simple, and immediately understandable message. They sent this campaign to their distributors saying "This is the type of image we want to create."
>
> During a routine trip to one Latin American market, the watch company's international marketing manager asked the distributor "What about the advertising? Is it doing the job?" The distributor had no strong opinion about the tactics or message so they decided to pay a visit to the advertising agency. There, after the customary tour and review of other clients' successful campaigns, they sat down in front of the smiling-couple-in-front-of-the-Rolls-Royce campaign. At first the ad agency executives were positive and supportive of the campaign because, after all, the campaign had come from corporate headquarters. The watch company manager, sensing something was

wrong, finally put it to the ad executives in blunt terms: "Our sales are stagnant. It may be the advertising message. If there is something wrong with it, please tell me." After much shuffling of feet and shrugging of shoulders, one brave ad manager suggested, "Senor, if you wish to suggest prestige and luxury and quality, maybe there is a better way. You see we have no Rolls Royce automobiles in this country, and so no one knows what they look like or what they represent."

Realizing that the distributor and local ad agency were simply doing what they thought the watch company wanted, the visiting executive reacted instantly. "O.K.," he instructed, "you suggest the best way to convey elegance, quality, luxury, and prestige in this market."

Within a few weeks, the ad agency produced a campaign featuring an endorsement by a popular romantic baritone and within a few months the positive effects were seen at sales counters around the country.

Decentralized advertising means inconvenience in working with a variety of separate ad agencies. It also often means separate artwork and additional production costs. However, these inconveniences are often offset if the distributor has a voice in the selection of the agency and thereby works closely with the account executives. In that way, the distributor becomes part of the resulting campaigns, watching results more carefully, especially if some of his own money is involved.

You, as the exporter and supplier, should always hold final veto power over all advertising matters. You may defer to local judgments regarding which medium is the best buy per thousand, or which particular symbol is best in that country, but if the advertising does not support your basic tenets, you have the right to argue and even veto the campaigns. The best way to avoid such disagreements is to communicate over and over again to both the distributor and the advertising agency why your product is good, better, best, unique, or successful. Explain why your company has prospered and what qualities predominate in your product. Then ask them to convert those messages into the best possible advertising suited especially for that market.

AFTER-SALES SERVICE

Next to a dentist's office, or an IRS auditor's waiting room, probably the most disliked location in the United States is the place where you take something to be repaired. Fear and frustration accompany you as you enter the door. Galloping obsolescence, high charges, eternal delays, and lemon-sucking clerks seem to surround you. Shops that repair video cassette recorders now require advance payments of $25, or more, before even examining your wounded unit. Six to eight weeks of delay because "we must send it back to the factory" are common. The clerk who smiles and sympathizes is a slight balm, but that hardly provides appeasement.

Two decades ago, the Zippo lighter company based its entire marketing campaign on free, no-questions-asked repair service. Zippo turned that service program into a long-standing advertising campaign, illustrating lighters that had been battered by bullets and beaten by bull elephants. "We repair or replace any Zippo lighter," they trumpeted. "We do not believe in making a profit twice." Such a brave stand, and such a lonely one. In current marketing, the closest substitute for such an enlightened policy is the policy of a few manufacturers and retailers who offer "return it if you don't like it, no questions asked." Today, the Maytag Company is basing its whole marketing approach on the premise that their appliances rarely need service calls and repairs.

If you face frustration getting products fixed in the United States, imagine being in Singapore when your American luggage suddenly disassembles itself. Or you are in Venice and your watch needs a special battery. Or you are in the mountains of Colombia and a chain belt on your rough terrain forklift breaks and no replacement is at hand. The moral here is as obvious as it is important: after-sales service is important in the United States, but it is critical in exporting because frustration and rejection build in direct proportion to the distances involved.

There are four basic options for after-sales service:

1. Disregard service responsibilities.
2. Train and assist your distributor to provide service.
3. Train an independent agency to provide service.
4. Place your own service personnel in the market.

A repair or maintenance program in a foreign market, properly managed and run, can not only be a source of marginal profit to your distributor but it can literally turn a nonuser into a loyal repeat customer. Your distributor should understand and appreciate that fact and be willing to invest in training, inventories, and the time it takes to manage both. Furthermore, it is useful to have a liberal and speedy repair parts supply system. Depending on your product and your policies, replacement parts may be supplied at cost, or a cost-plus basis. Keep in mind that your distributor may have to obtain licenses to import his spare and replacement parts, and also pay freight and duty costs, and this additional expense will probably be passed along to the end customer. After-sales service and repair departments can be structured to be profitable or unprofitable or operate on a breakeven basis. That decision will depend on competitive factors in the market. The wise distributor will establish a smooth and efficient after-sales service facility; the wise exporter will support him at every step.

AGENDA FOR THE TYPICAL VISIT

A constant refrain has been that there is no substitute for visits with your distributor in his market. Planning for these visits is important and worth careful consideration. Here are some tips culled from a dozen well-traveled international trade managers:

> *Set the dates well in advance.* Weeks or months ahead, agree with your distributor on a mutually convenient time for your visit. Make certain there will be no disruptions such as national holidays, local political elections, or other supplier firms visiting the distributor at that time.
>
> *Arrive rested.* Few people, if any, can sleep soundly on airplanes. You may think you are rested, but jet lag is insidious—lassitude and thick-headedness creep in during your business discussions at unexpected times. If you will be passing through numerous time zones, depart on a Friday or Saturday to allow at least one day's rest. Some seasoned travelers allow for one full day's rest for every four hours of time difference. Former Secretary of State John Foster Dulles, in his memoirs, confessed that he probably lost the Aswan Dam project to the Russians in Egypt simply because of befuddled thinking resulting from jet lag. This, he said, set back U.S.-Egyptian relations for almost a decade. Even North-South travel can be fatiguing. Few people realize that Lima, Peru is actually

positioned east of New York City, so when you head to South America you will usually cross several time zones.

First class air travel. While first class compartments affords premier treatment, it comes at high expense. Many airlines now offer business class overseas travel which is almost as comfortable as first class and at considerably less cost. Some travelers save money by flying coach class and then taking an extra day at their destination and use the time to relax at their hotel.

Spend enough time. The length of your visit depends, of course, on the business agenda you carry with you, but bear in mind that in most parts of the world, business is conducted at a slower pace than in the United States. In addition to spending ample time with your distributor, allow time to visit end customers, service/repair departments or to visit banking and legal contacts. A luncheon meeting with an embassy official or someone from the American Chamber of Commerce might provide helpful views of trends and conditions in that country. Incidentally, make these appointments well in advance by phone or mail rather than trying to fix them on short notice after your arrival. In summary, a visit of two to three days, with the preference being three, is probably the norm among seasoned managers.

First on the agenda. Your first priority should be to deal with the distributor's immediate concerns and problems. It is highly likely that the distributor will have accumulated a list of problems, some major and some petty, that have been nagging since your last visit. Review all of these immediately. Clear the air. Refrain from presenting your agenda items until his mind is open and at ease. This process may take a morning, a full day, or even several days, depending on the volume and seriousness of the problems. But be prepared for glitches in shipping, customer complaints about delivery or quality, confusion over a piece of correspondence, and a host of other typical irritants that have accumulated.

Review sales results. You should have the distributor's purchase records in your trip folder; now is the time to review the distributor's sales figures and inventory status. Any surprises? Any questions? What preliminary conclusions can be drawn? Any new trends emerging?

Meet with sales representatives and customers. Take time to have face-to-face meetings with these key players. Even if these visits seem almost totally social or superficial, bear in mind that personal relationships are highly important in most business cultures. You may have to drink more colas and more coffee—some with enough caffeine to curl your toenails—but this is an important part of interpersonal relations. You will also be assembling bits and pieces of intelligence to help you with the next items for discussion.

Review marketing plans and forecasts. Once you have wiped away some of the aggravating problems, studied sales figures, and done some homework with the infantry, you are ready to open your briefcase and bring out your prepared list of new plans, new ideas, new samples, new support materials, or whatever you have concocted to brighten the future for the distributor. "Motivating a distributor is selling the future, and vice versa," says one exporter for a major manufacturer of household products. "If a distributor is convinced that the future will be good, most of the current problems drop away and disappear around his feet."

Other visits. Consider visiting the advertising agency for a status report and review. Remember the opportunity for entertainment—consider taking the distributor and his chief aides, possibly with their wives, for dinner or a show or to some sporting event. Other helpful places to visit: regulatory agencies, banks, law offices, importing firm, customs house, other government officials.

Summarize. Before quitting the market for your next destination, sit down with your distributor and summarize what was concluded during your visit and agree on the next steps. Write those notes in front of him, if necessary, to signal the importance of this part of your visit. This is also the time to use some of the techniques described next in Chapter 11 regarding communication and language to assure that, even though you may be using the same words, you also have the same definitions behind those words. This may seem peculiar, but for most of your customers English will be a second, or acquired language, and you may inadvertently be using unfamiliar terminology. This is also the time to pull out the distributor dossier and make any necessary changes.

Trip reports. Several executives who contributed advice for this section on distributor visits recommended that you write a draft of your report *before* arriving in the next market on your itinerary. "You'll be amazed how easy it is to confuse one market with another, to forget exactly what was agreed in Taiwan, when you are sitting in Hong Kong," one explained. These trip reports serve many purposes. They provide a permanent record for company files, they help the next visitor to the market and, while this is optional, they can also be sent to the distributor to reconfirm exactly what transpired and what was agreed upon. A concise but complete trip report also tells your superiors about the market, its problems, and what solutions are being undertaken.

After returning home. Your first act should probably be to write a simple thank you letter to the distributor. Also, in the same or a separate letter, it would be wise to once again summarize the major points discussed and agreed upon. Lastly, start *now* to consider when you or someone from your firm will make the next visit to that market.

WAYS TO EVALUATE DISTRIBUTOR PERFORMANCE

There are many obvious and common sense methods of evaluating distributor performance. These do not differ much from evaluating performance in the United States, with two important additions which will be explained at the end of this section.

Here is a checklist of ways to measure effectiveness of a foreign distributor:

▶ *Sales growth.* The emphasis here is on the distributor's sales, not necessarily his purchases from you. As explained earlier, if his sales are good, yours will be, too. Compare sales growth to other indices in that market, such as inflation, consumer buying, GNP, exports from the United States or any other data on sales you have pertaining to your product or industrial category.

▶ *Ratios and marketshare versus competition.* This is an obvious measurement of effectiveness, but in many foreign markets it is difficult and expensive to obtain this data.

▶ *Feedback from end customers.* This is always an excellent barometer of rising or falling satisfaction.

▶ *Check other sources for opinions.* The U.S. embassy in some markets has a rating system of distributors. Your banking contacts may also be able to offer information on the reputation and performance of a given distributor. Conversations with other American managers in that market might also be useful.

▶ *Rate one distributor against another.* Ask: How do they compare in payment promptness, marketing planning, inventory turnover rates, delivery to customers, and a host of other day-to-day activities? Attitude and receptiveness to new ideas is another less tangible but highly important quality. You may even establish a numerical rating system to help compare one distributor against another, as some exporting firms do.

There are two additional factors to consider when managing and evaluating an overseas distributor. The first deals with your personal relationship with the owner or manager of the distributorship and the second involves culture. Let's take the personal relationship first.

A senior vice president of a famous consumer goods firm in the United States always counseled young managers dealing with huge department stores to "get to know the clerks behind the counter. If they like and trust you, your job will become much easier. Then, if you're really good, establish a similar rapport with the department head. If you are a professional, you will also have a strong and positive relationship with the buyer. You will be considered a master if you can work closely with the merchandise manager above the buyer. But you will be an Olympic Gold Medal winner if you come to know the president of the store. The reason is that when he nods in your direction, or he becomes convinced that your product deserves support, all the rest becomes very, very easy."

The analogy here is that the head of a distributorship is like that department store president. He has the power to make major purchasing decisions. If he has faith in your product, the rest becomes easy . . . or easier, at least. Therefore, in managing, motivating, and evaluating foreign distributors, try to establish a strong, personal relationship with the top person. If you are un-happy with the performance of a given distributor, this personal relationship can usually come to the rescue. Like the president of a huge store, the owner or managing director of a distributorship can make decisions and implement them quickly. In summary, it is easier to cause constructive change from the top down than the other way around.

The next difference to bear in mind when evaluating a distrib-utor is the cultural differences. This means language, attitudes, and ways of doing business. As dissatisfaction rises in your dealings with a distributor, ask yourself if the roots of the problem could simply be cultural. For example, maybe the distributor does not act as swiftly as you desire. Or, perhaps it appears to you that more time than necessary is spent socializing than working. Or, perhaps you've noted that when you try to train or instruct your distributor, a glaze appears over his eyes. All of these could be attributed to cultural differences. They do not necessarily mean that a distribu-tor is ineffective.

The remedy to this problem is, first, patience. Second, seek advice from others in that market about the cause of your frustra-tion to learn if your problems are typical or not. Third, seek to have frank but friendly discussions with the distributor, explaining that each culture works differently and you want to learn as well as build strong, mutually prosperous relationships.

International executives frequently find their traveling man-agers returning from overseas trips frustrated and angry and ready to terminate a certain distributor. This is so typical that many cor-porations require that every market manager must prepare a com-prehensive analysis of what was wrong and specifically why the distributor should be dismissed. One such form poses no less than 34 separate questions to be answered. This process often results in the manager having second thoughts, and concluding that the problems stemmed more from the manner of doing business rather than actual malfeasance in business.

When evaluating distributors, one senior international execu-tive in Europe counsels his people to "Accumulate all the evidence showing why a distributor should be terminated and then, if it is justified, proceed. However, and this is highly important, make cer-tain you have a *better* one to replace him." This is profound advice. It is profound because, while other business cultures can be frustrat-ing to the point of divorce, there is no guarantee that a replacement distributor will be better. Therefore, the message is "try to work out differences . . . a divorce can be devastating . . . you may just be trading a large headache for an gigantic upset stomach."

It is essential to regularly review distributor performance using familiar and standard methods, but in international trade there is an extra dimension caused by distances and culture. It is therefore important to try to resolve misunderstandings and problems through patient discussion, ideally with the top person in the distributorship. Sacking a distributor, as was explained earlier, can be a costly and traumatic experience.

SUMMARY

The words "style-flex" and "chameleon management" were used to begin this chapter on managing and motivating foreign distributors. They should now both have more meaning and application in international trade because each market requires a tailoring of individual management style.

"Even in Europe where the Common Market is heralded for its achievement in harmonizing trade, the term 'Common Market' is, in truth, a misnomer." So says Peter C. Ward, a 30-year veteran of managing distributors in and around the European continent. "In truth it should be called the 'Uncommon Market' because no two markets there are alike. Each requires an individual set of management tools and attitudes. Carry different hats with you, one for each market, and put them on depending on where you are. I can go right through the list: Northern European countries are vastly different from their Southern neighbors; France will never in a million years become mirrored by any EEC partner; the Dutch are strong individualists, and the Belgians have cultural schizophrenia; and within the Nordic countries, the Finns are uncomfortable being lumped with the Swedes, Danes and Norwegians and, among the latter three even they have proud and separate identities. No, the Common Market is far from being common. In fact, there is very little common about them and a good manager should remember that."

In addition to pliability, it is important to be honest and sincere in all your dealings with the distributor. Visit him often. Follow-up quickly on agreed upon requests. Try to make the distributor feel like "family." Several successful U.S. companies honor distributors by inducting them into employee service clubs which helps build this familial attitude.

This chapter has provided ideas on how to effectively manage and motivate distributors. It has offered reasons why flexibility, patience, honesty, and perseverance are so important in this new business relationship and this new business challenge.

While business practices and attitudes vary, there is one common denominator among the mosaic of markets around the world, and that is the subject of Chapter 11. The one phenomenon linking all of us together is the need for good communication. In addition to our need for flexibility and chameleon management, we must communicate clearly and effectively to survive and thrive. Miscommunication becomes the enemy. It can create untold anger, frustration, misery, delay and financial loss. The next chapter will arm you with information and advice on how to avoid all of those maladies.

11

Communication

Words are like loaded pistols.

A French philosopher

English is the *lingua franca* of international business. That's the good news. The bad news is that we Americans have messed it up with idioms, jargon, colloquialisms, slang, euphemisms, sports and military terminology, and buzz words. When you consider that there are 2231 words and phrases in English just for the word drunk, pity the poor person who has learned English from a text-book, or more horrors, learned English/English.

We in the English-speaking countries are fortunate to have our language as the universal language of business. Americans are hardly known for their linguistic skills. Among the Japanese there apparently is a joke that says:

> *Question:* What do you call a person who speaks three languages?
> *Answer:* Tri-lingual.
> *Question:* What do you call a person who speaks two languages?
> *Answer:* Bi-lingual.
> *Question:* Well then, what do you call a person who only speaks one language?
> *Answer:* An American.

Ours is an opulent language with over 750,000 words, not counting highly technical terms. English is a dynamic language and that it makes it difficult for the foreigner who has tried to learn English only to discover it is a moving target.

American business is among the most guilty when it comes to proliferation of the language. Your overseas correspondent has learned from textbooks what the "insurance" department does only to one day receive correspondence from the person in your company in charge of "risk management." Likewise, the personnel department has become "human resource management." Perhaps the most glaring example of this propagation of words is in the field of public relations. That is an area where professionals in communications are supposed to reside, yet they cannot agree on a title for their own job. It is variously called public affairs, publicity, corporate communications, corporate affairs, or public relations. Overseas the term "public relations" is not commonly used. For example, in England the term public relations is known and understood but "publicity" means "advertising" and not free, editorial material. Public relations is identified with the United States, and, where the craft is practiced overseas, it is probably called "social responsibilities."

The purpose of this chapter is to make you more sensitive about communications in international trade. Words can be very damaging, especially in new relationships. "Words are like hand-grenades," as one observer said, "handled carelessly they can blow up in your face." We will begin with examples of how businesses have been embarrassed overseas by mistakes, like exploding cigars, that left them startled and shaken. Next, some tips are provided on improving day-to-day communication through the mail or telephone.

English-English was mentioned earlier, referring to the language spoken in the United Kingdom. George Bernard Shaw, commenting on the differences between American-English and English-English described "two great nations separated by a common language." There are thousands of differences between the two countries, some amusing and others serious, and some of these will be reviewed to help you avoid confusion. Finally, this chapter concludes with specific advice on how to avoid and overcome misunderstandings, whether they come from speaking, listening, corresponding, or even gesturing.

A Chinese proverb says "We get sick from what we put in our mouths, but we get injured by what comes out of our mouths." The purpose of this chapter is to build an awareness, a sensitivity to an area we often take for granted—language and communication. Experts and consultants in this field caution that we must communicate clearly because when we don't understand something we also don't like it. Further, in marketing the communication of information is the first step in the whole process. All of this is true, but especially true when dealing with people who not only have different national outlooks but different national languages as well.

This chapter will try to prepare you for effective communications with your new business contacts. It will present the mistakes of others and offer ideas and prescriptions for avoiding accidents from those loaded pistols called words and make certain no one is injured by what comes shooting out of our mouths.

THE TOWER OF BUSINESS BABEL

Through advertising, businesses create a constant cacophony of messages, each competing for our attention. It is like the Biblical Tower of Babel, a heaven-reaching tower whose construction was interrupted by the confusion of different tongues. Some of that confusion persists today when businesses communicate carelessly. Following are a dozen or more true examples showing how businesses mis-communicated, some with humorous results.*

▶ Two examples of marketing malaprops have become classics in international trade classrooms. The first involves General Motors who introduced its Chevrolet Nova model auto into Latin America without realizing that the words *no va* in Spanish mean "no go." Hardly a stimulating name for a car. The second involved the Parker Pen Company who, in the 1950s, promoted in the United States their "SuperQuink" bottled ink as "safe for your best social correspondence," and so, the message continued, "to avoid embarrassment use Parker SuperQuink." Parker decided to expand the campaign to Mexico and had 2000 metal signs printed with that message. The direct translation of "to avoid embarrassment" in Spanish is *para evitar el emborazo* . . . . It wasn't until later that the Parker people learned

---

* Thanks to F.A. Bowen, retired international advertising professional, for contributing many of these bloopers. Bowen has made a special hobby of collecting communication gaffes from around the world.

that this phrase happened to be an idiom in Mexican Spanish. What their signs were saying was "to avoid pregnancy use Parker SuperQuink."

▶ Another famous faux pas was recorded by Pepsi Cola in the country of Taiwan. There the familiar slogan "Pepsi Comes Alive" was translated into Chinese but came out saying "Pepsi Brings Your Ancestors Back From the Grave."

▶ Until 1927, the Jockey International Inc. of Kenosha, WI, makers of underwear, sportswear, and hosiery, went by another name. In that year, the symbol of a horse jockey was adopted because it had a masculine connotation in any language. Prior to that, however, the company had a different name: The Kenosha Crotch Co. Imagine marketing that name overseas.

▶ More recently a brewery in Queensland, Australia decided they might like to export their product to the United States. The well-known Australian brand name of this firm was "X X X X," known and pronounced as "Four Xs." Then the firm learned that in the U.S. there was a trade name already registered called "Fourex," a brand of condoms. Plans to enter the United States were halted.

▶ An American company marketing tomato paste tried to market it in the Middle East only to learn that in Arabic the term "tomato paste" translates into "tomato glue."

▶ In Japan, there is a bias for adopting English-sounding names for consumer products. Thus, there is a soup mix called "Kitchy," a candy name "Carap," and a Gatorade-type drink called "Pocari Sweat." "Crunky" is a chocolate bar, "Creap" is a nondairy creamer, and chocolate candy in a small metal box is called "Hand-Maid Queer Aids."

▶ The S.C. Johnson Co., makers of home products such as deodorizers and waxes for floors, researched the Japanese market and learned that many Japanese families kept pens of chickens adjacent to their small homes. This created an odor problem which Johnson decided to resolve with a special new spray deodorant designed to blot out the smell of chicken droppings. Larry C. Greb, former international marketer with Johnson, says they were tempted but resisted calling that product "Chicken Shot."

▶ Certain American trade names cannot, for various reasons, be exported. "Tang" is just that in all export markets except West Germany where that name was already registered and so there "Tang" is called "Cefrisch." A ballpen made by Parker Pen was known almost everywhere as the "Jotter," but that name could not be used in certain Latin markets because it connoted a jockstrap.

▶ Products with the prefix "diet" cannot be marketed in some non-English speaking countries because it would require that they be sold only in pharmacies.

▶ An American hosiery company tried to tell a Spanish audience that anyone who didn't wear its brand of hosiery just "wouldn't have a leg to stand on." When translated, the copy said the wearer would "only have one leg."

▶ In French-speaking Quebec in Canada, a manufacturer of laundry soap described its product on packaging material as "the best one to use on especially dirty parts of the wash." The phrase "the dirty parts" was translated into French as *les parts de sale* which, it turned out, was slang in that country for "private parts."

▶ One international magazine has learned from experience that corporate logotypes should never be translated but, instead, should appear in original form. They learned this lesson when Caterpiller tractors in Japanese turned out to be "bugs that crawl" tractors.

▶ A large U.S. cosmetics firm featured the image of the armless statue of Venus de Milo in its advertising and instructed an ad agency to promote the product in the Middle East. The agency alertly replied that in the Middle East an armless figure denotes a punished thief. Also, an ad for anything as personal as face cream would be offensive in printed type form. It should look like handwritten script, they advised.

▶ Want to use the word "ball" in your communications? One American company researched this question and learned that in Latin American markets, there are four distinct meanings for the Spanish word "bola," depending on the country. In one country it means "ball," as intended, in another it means "revolution," in another it means a lie or fabrication, and yet in another it is an obscenity.

▶ Spanish-speaking customers of Braniff airlines were once startled to read advertisements for new airfares which also invited them to try the leather seats in all Braniff aircraft. *Sentado en cuero,* or "to be seated in leather," looks like *sentado en cueros,* or "to be seated naked." Braniff seemed to be advertising low airfares for travelers without clothes on.

▶ Finally, the well-known vacuum machine company Electrolux was purchased by a Swedish firm who designed new ads and sent them back into English-speaking markets without first checking on American slang. The ads read: "Electrolux sucks better."

COLORS COMMUNICATE, TOO

Even colors communicate hidden meanings in different parts of the world. Here is a sampling:*

▶ Green has been the nationalist color of Egypt and should not be used in that country for packages. Yet the French, Dutch, and Swedes associate green with cosmetics and toiletries. In Malaysia, consumers complained about a green product because it was associated with the jungle and disease. In the Orient, green symbolizes exuberance and youth, but don't wear a green hat in China. Steve Renk, President of Renk International, learned this while watching competitors hand out green sport caps so popular among farmers in the United States. He noted that the Chinese quickly stuffed the hats in briefcases and didn't wear them. When he inquired about this, his interpreter confided that a green hat advertises that your wife or sister is a prostitute.

▶ Red is regarded as an "old" color in England, yet in Japan the combination of red and white is widely regarded as appropriate for happy and pleasant occasions. However, in Japan, don't wrap gifts in bright colors, such as red. In England

* Thanks to F.A. Bowen and also Visual Research International for this survey information.

and France, red is regarded as more masculine than blue. At the time of Chinese New Year in most Oriental countries, distinctive red envelopes are used for gift giving, usually gifts of money.

▶ White is right for brides in the United States but not in India, where red or yellow is used. White is the color of funerals in Japan.

▶ Yellow in England connotes youth and humor. In the Orient, it is considered the imperial color suggesting grandeur and mystery.

▶ Purple is the color of death in Brazil and Mexico.

▶ Gold, and its various hues, has meaning, too. Just about everywhere it signifies wealth. However, in the Middle East and parts of the Far East, gold products should be "dark"" or "orange," whereas in the United States a more "champagne" or "light" gold is preferred.

Communication in international business is both a skill and an art requiring special, new sensitivities. It is interesting to note that mathematicians and musicians from different countries who do not speak the same language can communicate effectively through their unique language of numbers and music. International business people, however, have English as a *lingua franca* and, as we have seen, it can be an imprecise and imperfect method of communication. When communicating in an international setting, the objective of everyone, from mathematicians to musicians to machinery salesmen, is to achieve what has been called the "Aha! I see!" factor. That is certainly the desired goal in our daily international dialogues.

EFFECTIVE EVERYDAY COMMUNICATION

In years hence, you will very likely communicate with your distributor overseas by punching numbers on a console and have his image beamed into your office via three-dimensional holographic imaging. Just like Captain Stark and Scotty aboard the Starship Enterprise, we will be able to see, hear, communicate with—but not touch—the image of our business partners. But that is long into the future. Sooner, perhaps, we will be communicating regularly through teleconferencing. With the advent of fiber optic cables capable of carrying 170,000 conversations over 12 hairlike strands of fiber, teleconferencing is expected to reduce travel time and costs substantially. Using compact, inexpensive video systems, we will see and hear the person at the other end of a telephone line on a TV monitor. Through this medium, we will be able to see charts, drawings, models, facial expressions, and other body language that should improve person-to-person communication immeasurably.

Until these scientific advancements arrive, however, we are stuck with more conventional methods: mail, telephone, telex, and the most recent medium, facsimile machines, known colloquially as fax machines. The more experienced companies in international trade are using fax machines to improve and speed communication around the world. These sending and reproduction machines have created the added dimension of permitting diagrams, charts, pictures, and other illustrations to be sent and reproduced using telephone lines and satellite signals. Some senders and receivers separated by time zones of 10 or 12 hours load their machine at the end of a work day, turn off the lights, and the fax sends a raft of correspondence and other data automatically. On the other side of the globe, the recipients are greeted with all this information to help them start a new day.

Still, the typed or printed letter is the world's most common form of business communication; here are a few tips that might make such business correspondence more accident-free.

Robert G. Parkhurst, former international executive with General Electric Medical Systems relates this true incident. While traveling in Europe one Spring, Parkhurst arrived at his French distributor's office to find him furious over a delivery confirmation letter the distributor had received for a recent order. The date confirmed was 5/12/85, indicating May 12, 1985. The distributor, however, said he simply could not wait until December for the delivery. "What do you mean, December?" Parkhurst asked. After some consternation and sorting out, the solution was revealed. In most countries outside the United States, when dates are written using numerals, the day of the month comes first, then the month, and finally the year. Thus, to most people outside the United States the numerals 5/12/85 signal the 5th of December 1985. This holds true when writing out dates, as well. In international circles, the date is always specified with the day first, such as 5 December 1985.

Other unpleasant consequences can occur from this simple but important custom of writing dates. I was once traveling with a colleague who was not permitted to enter a certain country because to the admitting health official my colleague's record of inoculations indicated the expiration date for his yellow fever shot had passed. My friend tried to explain that the American numerical system of stating dates was used by the medical facility in his home city and that the inoculation was still effective. But he was unsuccessful. He was denied entry and required to board a plane for our next destination and wait for me there.

When writing letters to overseas contacts, especially if you know their English is limited, it is important to remember these additional tips:

▸ Use short, simple sentences.

▸ Avoid idioms or slang.

▸ Shy away from sarcasm or innuendoes.

▸ Be polite.

▸ "The written word doesn't smile," one counselor warns. That means, of course, that you may write a paragraph in a light-hearted vein, but for a person with restricted knowledge of our language, such light-heartedness may be completely misinterpreted.

▸ Repeat important or complex statements in several ways.

▸ Double-check your finished letter for typographical errors and try to read the letter objectively to see if there could be any possible misinterpretations.

▸ Be particularly careful with numbers to assure they are correct.

▸ Don't be concerned if you receive letters from correspondents overseas with what we might consider flowery and formal language at the beginning or the end. That may be the custom in their land, and they are simply translating that protocol into English. It is not necessary to emulate them. However many Middle Easterners and Japanese often have a gracious style of writing, so it is diplomatic to include similar sentiments in your replies.

For telephonic communication, a good first rule is to simply know what time it is in the country you are calling. Desk clocks and wristwatches are now commonly available showing international time zones or indicating the current time in New Delhi or Amsterdam. Direct dial is now available for most large cities which is more economical if you are certain your party is present and ready for your call. In some cases, it is helpful to telex or telegraph in advance that you will be phoning at a specific time. An irritating feature often encountered in transoceanic phone conversations is the one or two second pause or echo between your voice and the respondent. The result is often we trip over the other person's last words, thinking they have concluded speaking. Those delays are often caused by the time taken for signals to be bounced off orbiting satellites, so consider it a miracle of our communications network rather than a minor nuisance.

Another useful trick is to conduct overseas conversations using a conference phone system so that others can participate in the conversation. It is also an efficient way to manage those moments when certain words need to be instantly translated or verified. Once again, speak in simple sentences. Speak slowly and clearly and pause from time to time to ask if the last point is clear. You may even wish to tape record the conference conversation, although courtesy suggests you notify the person on the other end that you are doing so. Finally, it is always wise to confirm telephone conversations in writing; that is just one more way to avoid misunderstandings and frustrations.

Telex machines have been standard means of communication in international business for several decades. They are less expensive than telephones and provide a written record of both your message and a response. It is also possible, if you are at the site of the telex sending machine, to carry on a dialogue of sorts by sending and receiving messages in sequence. At the risk of repetition, however, be extra cautious about certain words or phrases that might be misinterpreted. Here is one example:

> Jack L. Ottiker, the director of the American Chamber of Commerce in Lima, Peru tells of a telex sent to the factory manager of a U.S. subsidiary in Lima which said: "Please send a headcount of the people in your factory and in your office, broken down by sex. Information needed urgently." The local manager, a Peruvian, replied as follows: " Here is your headcount. We have 30 in the factory, 15 in

the office, 5 in hospital on sick leave, none broken down by sex." The Peruvian manager added "If you must know, our problem here is with alcohol."

AMERICAN/ENGLISH VERSUS ENGLISH/ENGLISH

For Americans, English is considered the "mother tongue." Even the word business comes from the Old English word *bisignis,* which in turn comes from *bisig,* meaning to be occupied or busy with something. Incidentally, the earliest meaning of the word, in the tenth century, was anxiety, solicitude, and uneasiness . . . which many people might argue is an apt definition even today. It wasn't until the eighteenth century that the modern spelling and meaning developed: dealing with trade and commerce.

Just as words change over time, they also change as they cross over oceans. Just where and how words get caught in crosscurrents of misunderstandings is unknown, but what is clear is that any world trader must beware of the many variances between American/English and English/English. Following are numerous examples that will keep you from being innocently and unexpectedly "tonked" (English for "clobbered") in your next British business dealing.

During World War II, Winston Churchill recorded that a misunderstanding over a single word at a high-level meeting resulted in "long and acrimonious argument." The word was the verb "to table" an item for discussion. For Americans, it means "to shelve" or to delay action, whereas to the British it means precisely the opposite, "to bring up for immediate consideration." No wonder we went to war 200 years ago; maybe it was all just a misunderstanding over the same words.

American tourists and businesspeople who visit England delight in relating stories about certain English phrases that result in double-takes. The head of a Wisconsin printing company owned by British interests once visited England and was entertained there by a leading businessman and his wife. He was more than startled when the wife casually said she would "knock him up in the morning." He learned later that it meant in the vernacular that she would call on the telephone in the morning. "Give me a tinkle" is another British way of saying "call me on the telephone." And, if you play tennis, don't be disconcerted if your opponent asks "Would you like to knock up first?" It merely means "Would you like to warm up first." Another red-flagged word is "pecker" which is a common English word for "chin." So don't be nonplussed to be told to "Keep your pecker up."

Conversely, a whole host of innocent American phrases are rude to English ears. Two notable ones are "fanny" and "sharp." In England, fanny refers to a woman's genitals and not her derriere, and a "sharp" person means a devious and unprincipled person. Also, Americans should not blanch when an English person describes someone as "pissed." It is not a blue word for "angry," as in the United States. It merely means the person was sloppy drunk. And be careful about adopting the common British adjective "bloody." While it is heard often there, it is strong language and should be used with care.

While winnowing out these differences can be an amusing search, in business the problem can become deadly serious. With the current spate of English buyouts of American companies, legal contracts become translation projects as well. In one recent sale, a two-inch thick purchase contract written by U.S. lawyers had to be completely "vetted" (a wonderful English word for "reviewed and checked over for accuracy") and rewritten to satisfy English word-smiths.

Here is a "dog's breakfast" (English for "mixture") of examples of different word usages that might be helpful to any American doing business in the United Kingdom.

▶ A barrister in England is a trial lawyer, and a solicitor is an attorney who does not appear in court.

▶ In the financial area, stocks are not called stocks but, instead, "shares." In Britain, stocks are considered as government bonds.

▶ The bathroom is, of course, the bathroom but you should know it is also referred to as the "WC" (for "water closet") and also "the loo." A quaint phrase for going to the bathroom is "spend a penny" which originates from the days when the large English penny coin was required to open the door to a bathroom stall.

▶ A gallon in England is actually 1.2 gallons by our standards and is known as the Imperial gallon. A barrel differs in weight depending on if it is soap, butter, beef, flour, or gunpowder. If you want to buy some grain, a ton is actually 2240 pounds and a "windle" is three bushels. "Going a ton" refers to speeding at 100 miles an hour on a highway.

▸ A million is a million, but a billion is officially called a "milliard" and customarily referred to in terms of "a thousand million."

▸ In America, you might innocently say "I made a presentation to the board today and bombed, and then when I got home I found a notice from my bank that I had a large overdraft." Most Americans would interpret that to mean you failed, miserably, at your presentation, and at the bank you had overdrawn your account. Both circumstances would deserve sympathy in the United States. But in the United Kingdom just the opposite reaction would result. "Oh, grand!" they would say. "You went like a bomb. Splendid. And then a large overdraft. Congratulations." The reason for these opposing reactions would be that to "bomb" in Britain means to succeed. And an overdraft (spelled "overdraught") at a bank means a line of credit, which every businessperson covets.

▸ When asking for whiskey in England, you will receive Scotch, not bourbon. A dinner jacket is often called a "smoking" and the first floor of a building is the ground floor to an Englishman. This latter peculiarity can lead to all kinds of confusion because then an American second floor becomes their first floor, and so on.

▸ The English customarily do not say "you are welcome." It is not because they are impolite, it is just a phrase that is not used. (But in Scotland, they do use it.) The normal response to a thank you in England is "thank you."

▸ If you are curious about Cockney, forget it. That rhyming bit of seemingly nonsensical dialect is truly a language unto its own. For example, the "stairs" are referred to as "apples and pears."

▸ If you weigh yourself in England, you may find yourself caught between two worlds, the "olde world" which used "stones" as a measurement for body weight and the new world meaning metric. In days past, and even today in some parts of England, a "stone" means 14 pounds and therefore a person weighing 180 pounds weighs "12 stone and 12 (pounds)." With England switching to metric it is now more likely you will be measured in kilograms, which convert at 2.2 pounds per 1 kilo and so 180 pounds converts to about 82 kilos.

▶ Spelling is another area of difference. Here are just a few examples: honour, colour, centre, criticise, jeweller, inflexion, defence, licence, cheque, gaol, kerb, pyjamas, tyre, aluminium, and manoeuvre.

▶ You should also know the difference between England, Great Britain, and the United Kingdom. The latter refers to the joint kingdom of England, Scotland, Wales, and Northern Ireland. Great Britain refers to that island containing England, Wales, and Scotland. So, when you refer to "England" you are technically referring to only that specific part of the island, and not Scotland and Wales.

Finally, there will not only be word and spelling differences but confusion about proper names and nouns as well. For example, a college group that fosters international exchange reports that American students have asked their English counterparts "how they go about celebrating the 4th of July and Thanksgiving in England." One wry British student reportedly replied, "We have neither, of course, but I suppose you could say we celebrate Thanksgiving every 4th of July."

England is not the only English-speaking country where confusion can reign. Australia is another. The "Aussies" are not only known for their gregariousness ("Chicagoans with an accent," one traveler calls them) but for creative slang as well. Here are some examples:

Australian	American
Avro	Afternoon
Bloke	Man
Cozzle	Bathing suit
Fair dinkum	The real thing, genuine
Footpath	Sidewalk
Jumbuck	Sheep

Jumper	Sweater
Lollies	Candy
Pommie	An Englishman
Station	A large ranch
Sandshoes	Sneakers
Ta	Thank you
Ta-Ta	Good-bye
Taxi Rank	Taxi stand
Tinny	Can of beer
Tube	Can of beer

Now that we have become amateur lexicographers, it is time to examine ways to avoid misunderstandings right from the beginning of a relationship. Adopting a few simple rules will minimize frustration, costly delays, anger, and losses in business.

HOW TO AVOID MISUNDERSTANDINGS

Giving advice on averting misunderstandings is difficult because the field of opportunity is so vast. A 12-year-old student once did research on Socrates for an essay and boiled it down to two sentences: "Socrates was a very wise man who went around giving advice to the people. They poisoned him."

Notwithstanding what they did to Socrates, here is some advice to help you avoid the poisons resulting from misunderstandings.

> *Watch the eyes.* If the eyes are the mirror of the soul, they also have a more practical use as barometers of comprehension. As you hold discussions with your foreign business associates, especially if they are not thoroughly fluent in English, watch the eyes. When they glaze over or stray, your words are probably not penetrating.
>
> *Summarize.* Stop and review from time to time. Make certain that everyone involved is riding along on the same train of thought.
>
> *Paraphrase.* This helps avoid the word traps discussed earlier. By rephrasing key points in several different ways, the whole message does not hinge on a few critical words.

Echo. Ask the person to repeat what has been reviewed or agreed upon. This can be done diplomatically by saying something like "Sometimes I speak too fast. Maybe it would be good to stop and have you review, in your words, what has been discussed thus far."

Speak slowly. While it is not necessary to be ponderous, adopting a slow meter is always wise. As stated earlier, it is claimed that experienced international managers can be distinguished by their steady, slow speaking pace.

Shortcut shortcuts. Try to avoid contractions (say "we will" instead of "we'll). Shun acronyms ("ASAP" for "as soon as possible.") Do not use "ditto." Try to stop saying "You know?" at the end of every statement.

Enunciate. Speech therapists call it "lazy lips," but whatever the term, try to avoid mumbling by speaking clearly and distinctly. If you have a regional accent, remember than your counterpart is probably not accustomed to it nor to regional phrases like "Y'all." "Y'all" is dangerous for other reasons. One Southern businessman reports that he innocently used that term in Saudi Arabia, saying "Y'all come visit us" and learned later that he offended his host who wondered why "all" the people in attendance had to come—was he, himself, not sufficient?

Avoid idioms. Raining cats and dogs, flatter than a pancake, when in doubt punt, safe as Fort Knox, coming up roses—the list is endless. Try to avoid them. I once heard an American radio news interview where a government official commented "We don't have deep pockets. This could be the straw that broke the camel's back, and then the whole project would go down the drain." For many people trying to learn and understand English, these statements could be completely unintelligible.

Body language. Communicate using the whole body. Facial expressions add visual meanings to your words. Gestures and body position send more than just superficial signals.

Assume nothing. Check, recheck, and double check. Write numerals and figures on a chart or blackboard so everyone can see. Put a summary of conversations in writing. Confirm phone messages by telex. At the least hint of a misunderstanding, stop your conversation and review.

Take the blame. Call it courtliness or diplomacy, if there is a misunderstanding, take the blame. Wherever the fault originated, this smooths over a rough spot and gets everyone back on track quickly.

Use visual aids. Communication experts suggest we use as many of the senses as possible to communicate effectively. Take along charts, diagrams, samples, photographs, slides, or videotapes if they will help you convey your message.

Listen. A University of Minnesota study indicates that 60 percent of all misunderstandings come from poor listening. As you converse, grace your partner with good eye contact, good posture, and avoid distracting mannerisms such as tapping fingers or scratching. Nod often to show visually that you are following along. Follow the dictum of my wife when she demands "Are you listening to me? Well, if you are, for goodness sakes at least make some listening noises."

Liquor won't help. Some people maintain they speak a foreign language better after a few drinks. This may help reduce inhibitions, but liquor is not a quick formula to better comprehension. On the other hand, a quiet conversation, after office hours, over a cocktail and away from the office might be a good way to confirm or summarize discussions held that day.

It's O.K. to "parlez," but within limits. By all means try to learn some of the language of the country you are visiting. "Please" and "thank you" are musts, and "hello" and "goodbye" are simple courtesies. Another helpful phrase, of course, is "Where is the bathroom?" Just as we appreciate it when foreign visitors make an effort to learn and speak even a few words of English, the reverse is true as well. On the other hand, don't assume that your three years of high school German qualify you for a certificate in fluency. Don't ever attempt to conduct serious business with limited knowledge of another language lest you give away the store with an errant tense or verb ending.

Finally, two specific pieces of advice from long-time U.S. State Department veteran Ralph H. Graner. "We forget how often we use our now nearly unique measuring system in our conversation." Graner points to phrases like "a miss is as good as a mile," or "grandfather's 100-acre farm," or "our daily 10-mile commute," or "30 inches of rainfall," or "a six-foot man," or "a 100-degree day."

These are meaningless to the majority where metric prevails. Graner also counsels that when in a public setting overseas never assume that a side conversation in English is in any way private and not understood by others. There is always the risk that someone overhears and understands, which could be embarrassing.

In conclusion, there is one single tool of communication that is invariably understood and useful in every country and for almost all circumstances. Even remote tribes who see outsiders for the first time know and recognize this signal in human communication. It is one of the few universally known symbols. It is the smile. As babies, we smile before we talk. The smile instantly communicates friendliness, openness, and happiness regardless of culture. The smile, by itself, will not avoid all misunderstandings in business communications, but it will surely help salve and heal some of the bumps and bruises that will invariably occur.

SUMMARY

In this chapter, we have emphasized that mis-communication can be the enemy. Conversely, good communication is an ally in successful international trade. Few companies succeed without it. Moreover, because of differences in language and culture, communication with our foreign business contacts becomes especially difficult. We require a new sensitivity to words. A new empathy must be developed. It is all part of that glorious challenge described in Chapter 10 where we described the marketing of your product in diverse cultures is unlike anything experienced in the U.S. market.

If, while reading this chapter, you have felt a desire to dust off and review the fundamentals of good communication—good writing, clear speaking, attentive listening—that is a bonus payoff. Most of us think we are good communicators, but like any skill it deserves refresher training. The businessperson who can write a clear, concise memo or report stands out among peers. "Good writing," it is said, "is nothing more than clear thinking made visible" and we all aspire to be clear thinkers. As for public speaking, on a list once compiled of "greatest fears," the fear of death ranked fourth; topping the list was having to stand up and make a speech. Therefore, the manager who has developed and practiced public speaking talents carries a talent that most others fear and ignore.

Finally, the skill of listening is barely taught in high school or colleges, so we can all afford to improve that most basic of all communication skills. Remember, "a closed mouth gathers no foot."

Now we turn to probably the most unique and enigmatic culture of all, Japan. If communication is a challenge in England and with other European markets where most of America has ethnic roots, then finding how to communicate effectively in Japan, the most unique and insular nation in the world, rivals finding the Holy Grail. Chapter 12 tells you why and how the Japanese are different and how you can not only cope but succeed with America's strongest rival for economic stature.

12

Dealing with the Japanese Mystique

No country is more important to our economic future than Japan.

Senator Bill Bradley (NJ)

Several years ago, the CEO of a major international company handed me the book *A Book of Five Rings* by Miyamoto Musashi saying, "If you want to understand the Japanese and how they plan strategies for business, then read this book." Reinforcing his claim, the subtitle of the book called it "The classic guide to strategy." On the flyleaf was another endorsement by the chairman of a New York firm which said "I have some advice for American business-men who are trying to figure out why the Japanese excel in business. Buy and study a copy of [this book]."

Who is this Musashi? He lived in the seventeenth century and was Japan's most renowned Samurai warrior. By age 30, he had fought and killed 60 opponents in duels. He eventually withdrew to a cave and wrote his biography which consisted mainly of his theories of battle strategy "for any situation where plans and tactics are used."

I read this book not once but several times. Frankly, I found it difficult to fully understand. Musashi speaks of "the way of strategy" and explains that "the way" is found in "five books" (represented by the five rings mentioned in the book's title). These five books are: ground, water, fire, tradition, and void. He writes at length about *kendo*, the Japanese art of fencing, and offers pages of abstract advice on how to defeat an enemy. "Hold down the shadow" when you can see the enemy's spirit, he counsels, and "release four hands" when you and the enemy are evenly matched. After deciding that the book was just too deep for me, I set it aside concluding I would never be able to learn the complex thinking of Japanese strategists.

More recently, the head of the East Asian Studies Department at the University of Wisconsin recommended a book to me titled *Japanese Etiquette & Ethics in Business* by Boye De Mente (Passport Books). De Mente writes that Musashi lived from 1584 to 1645 and was "a samurai warrior whose only claim to fame was that he became incredibly skilled with a sword and killed over sixty men in duels by the time he was thirty. In the later years of his life he wrote a small treatise called *A Book of Five Rings,* which gave his philosophy on how to defeat opponents in battle. The book was published in English in the 1970s for the martial arts trade. An offhand mention of the book by a New York newspaper columnist turned it into a bestseller among American businessmen, much to the amusement of the Japanese."

So here we have serious American businesspeople struggling to understand the mysteries of Musashi, and all the while the Japanese are smiling in amusement. I suppose the reverse of this anecdote would be if the Japanese, in their search to discover the formula for successful American business strategy, stumbled across a certain book, made it a bestseller in Japan, and it turned out to be a biography of Davy Crockett.

In our desire to unmask the Japanese, to resolve the mystique, Americans seem to have overlooked the obvious: The Japanese work harder. Asian scholars give us abundant evidence of this characteristic in the Japanese ethos. Historians say that island people try harder. Contemporary observers report that in Japan, work is almost a religion. According to the respected British publication, *The Economist,* Japanese workers put in 2100 hours per year which is 500 more than in West Germany and 200 more than in the United States. The work week in Japan is just now slowly being reduced to five days a week, and educators tell us that 95 percent of all Japanese high school students graduate and leave school with the equivalent of an American college degree.

Then, 40 percent of those go on to higher education. Competition for entry into a top Japanese college is so intense that when the lists are publicly posted each spring the suicide rate jumps among youngsters who have failed.

Former Colorado Governor Richard D. Lamm, at a Denver international trade conference, stressed one other difference between the Japanese and American outlook on business in this way. "Each year," he said, "for every 1000 engineers we graduate from college in this country, we also graduate 10,000 lawyers. In Japan, for every 1000 lawyers that enter the workforce, they graduate 10,000 engineers. Now, I have studied history and I have yet to find a nation that sued itself to greatness." (Some educators dispute these figures explaining that while lawyers, as we know them, are few in number, there is a separate group of "legal administrators" who provide many of the same roles and services.)

My own experience turned up this anecdote about the Japanese and their dedication to work and thoroughness. After I compiled and edited the book *Do's & Taboo's Around the World*, the largest publisher in Japan, Kodansha, came to us to discuss a Japanese language version. "We are pleased and honored," we replied, "but we are certain you will want to re-write the book because it is written in the American vernacular. We speak of Dr. Seuss and his cats and King Kong on the Empire State Building and O.J. Simpson running through airports. Your readers will simply not understand those peculiar references." The Japanese executives were quick to reply. "Oh, no," they said. "We want to publish it verbatim. In that way, our readers will not only learn how to act in Indonesia or India or Ireland, but they will also be reading the text through an American's eyes and consequently receiving a double message and a double benefit. You see, we here in Japan are an insular nation and therefore we must simply try harder to understand the ways of the world."

There is no special mystique about the Japanese. They may be enigmatic, true, but Americans must rid themselves of any perception that there is some inscrutable Oriental philosophy or formula that makes them more clever and more successful in business than the rest of the world. Their only special power or quality is that they are willing to work harder, especially when it comes to international commerce.

This chapter deals with how to do business with the Japanese, whether on our shores or theirs. It will provide insights and advice and help equip you with "management styleflex" techniques described in Chapter 10. With this type of homework, plus more study and experience, you will be able to work comfortably and effectively with the Japanese. The motivation to do business with the Japanese should be especially strong, as we will now learn.

HOW IMPORTANT IS JAPAN?

Facts and figures abound on how Japan has risen economically, like the fabled phoenix, to become a near equal with the United States. "[Japan's] economic drive is pushing it toward center stage," says Yale History Professor Paul Kennedy. "The American century is over," says Clyde Prestowitz, formerly of the U.S. Department of Commerce and author of *Trading Places: How We Allowed Japan to Take the Lead.* Here is evidence to support these claims:

▶ Japan's huge trade surplus and its high savings rate combine to make it the world's largest creditor nation. Their economic condition is a mirror image of the United States with our low savings rate and debtor position. This availability of capital allows the Japanese to make extensive investments overseas, with the United States the favorite target.

▶ Japan is the third largest foreign investor in the United States with over 10.5 percent of the total foreign direct investment. Japanese investments in the United States were $590 million in 1975 but rose to over $19 billion in 1985.

▶ Japan is our second largest trading partner (Canada is the first). In 1985, U.S. exports to Japan were $22.6 billion.

▶ For the past several years, Japan has been responsible for the largest number of foreign investment transactions in the United States. In 1985, 24 percent of all transactions originated in Japan, double the number in 1980.

▶ Among the individual states in the United States, competition is fierce for Japanese investment. Some 40 state governments and port authorities now have offices in Japan, with more in the planning stages.

▶ In 1987, the Japanese government launched an internal drive to buy imported products. Bowing to pressures from their trading partners, especially the United States, the Japanese government officially proclaimed a policy of encouraging consumers there to buy products made outside Japan.

While many trade barriers still protect Japan, they are slowly being battered downward by U.S. government negotiators armed with heavy imbalance of trade statistics between the two nations. The dollar-yen currency exchange relationship is another reason why export products are more attractive to Japanese buyers than ever before and, conversely, why Japanese investment in the United States hits new peaks each year.

In June, 1988, U.S. Department of Commerce Secretary C. William Verity signed a new pact with Japan designed to promote increased U.S. exports of sporting goods, leisure products, furniture, jewelry, processed foods, and pet food to Japan. Additional products are expected to be added in the near future. Furthermore, the Japanese government will give the United States information on Japanese buyers and help move our products directly to Japanese consumers.

The message is clear. Anyone interested in international trade, whether it be exporting, joint ventures, licensing, or reverse investment would be foolish to ignore Japan.

Rules for Dealing with the Japanese

Japan and the United States are appropriately called "the odd couple" by John C. Condon in his excellent book *With Respect to the Japanese* (Intercultural Press). "No nation is more different from America than Japan," he writes. Herman Kahn, the respected futurist and government-retained consultant to Japan, called the Japanese "the most nationalistic nation in the world, unique, xenophobic, and insular." Consequently, Americans wishing to do business with the Japanese face a formidable learning period. One could spend a lifetime learning just the language, and the rest of the culture is equally complex and foreign, especially to Americans. But there are some fundamental guidelines that can be learned fairly quickly that will help you bridge the gaps and impress your Japanese counterparts with your sincerity and desire to accommodate their ways.

Ten general rules follow for dealing with the Japanese regardless of whether you are selling, buying, or negotiating with them.

1. *Seek the highest possible introduction.* Victor Kiam, president of Remington (Razor) Products Inc., preaches this advice at dinners and seminars across the country. He tells of meeting with the buying officer of a large retail chain, telling his whole story, and being summarily rejected. Kiam retreated, found a middleman who helped communicate the Remington pitch to a much higher level in the same retail group. Kiam was then invited back but found himself confronted with the same buying officer who had rejected him at the outset. "I already told this person my whole story," Kiam objected. "Say it again," his advisors counseled, and Kiam did. At the conclusion, the buyer smiled, agreed, and signed a huge purchase order.

The Japanese live in what is called a vertical society which, by itself, is not unique since all societies have some form of "pecking order." However, in Japan, according to De Mente, "there is always one single, distinctive relationship between individuals and between groups—or no relationship at all. It is the character of this relationship, or lack of relationship, that underlies not only the etiquette and ethics of Japanese businessmen but also most of 'Japanese' behavior." De Mente adds that it is a common joke among Japanese businessmen themselves that when playing golf it is customary to see them tee off according to salary rank.

How do you know you are dealing with a top decision-maker? It is often very difficult. A South Carolina banker once attended a meeting in Japan and collected six business cards indicating that all six Japanese were the "Public Relations Manager" of the same firm! All you can do is patiently try to sort out the hierarchy. While doing this, it is important to remember that the Japanese like to deal with an outsider of equal rank. Therefore if you are a company president you will have a better chance of meeting with someone they consider of equal status. But don't try to completely by-pass middle management—these are the people who implement decisions. In the Japanese structure, decisions go round-and-round and then percolate upward for final approvals. A Japanese middleman employed by you is helpful in discerning the exact strata system in the industry or company you are interested in. Japanese management is shaped like a box and the top person normally does not act without first gaining a consensus from all members of the box. For Occidental minds, all this is terribly complex, but that is our problem, not theirs. Suffice it to say, use all subtle and available resources to determine the ranking of the person you are dealing with and use patience and diplomacy to reach the highest possible person.

2. *Take a good supply of business cards.* While this tenet applies throughout international business regardless of culture, it is exceedingly important in Japan. The exchange of business cards (*meishi* in Japanese), done so casually in the United States, is a true ritual in Japan with important nuances. First, make certain that your own title on the card is clear and conventional. Even in our society we have difficulty distinguishing between Assistant, Associate, and Deputy. If we have difficulty with these shades of difference, imagine the consternation of the Japanese. Second, on the reverse side of your card, have everything translated and printed in Japanese. Also, make certain the graphics and ink are of comparable quality lest you give the impression that you consider the Japanese version less important. Third, cards should be exchanged at the very first encounter—that means often even *before* handshaking or bowing. Visitors hand out cards first and the customary procedure is for a Japanese to take your card, read it carefully (he is trying to determine your level in the pecking order), and then bow and shake hands, or the reverse order. Americans tend to glance at a card and slip it quickly into a shirt or coat pocket. This could give your new Japanese acquaintance the impression that you really are not interested in knowing him. Another nuance—resist writing on the card in front of him because that suggests lack of respect for his card and therefore his identity. If you must write notes, do it later in private.

When shaking hands, don't expect the strong, firm handshake taught in America, and don't pull away too quickly. The Japanese consider that abrupt and unfriendly and prefer a prolonged handshake often employing both hands to enfold yours. Don't expect direct eye contact. The Japanese are taught that direct eye contact makes the other person uncomfortable. This is particularly true among Japanese women. Elevator girls in department stores, for example, are taught to *not* have direct eye contact, especially with men. However, Japan expert Professor Sol Levine says "They are getting better with eye contact. I suspect much of what appears to be shyness is connected with their hesitancy over language." Levine explains that smiling is virtually a national trait, so be prepared to see lots of smiles. Other experts caution, however, that the belly-shaking laugh is not as common because any display of the open mouth is considered rude throughout the Orient. This explains why many Orientals cover their mouths with their hands while laughing.

3. *Do your homework.* Research of all kinds is vital for doing business in Japan. Such things as product modifications, distribution channels, and which niche you might fill are basic business research considerations. Entry to the Japanese market is possible through all the channels outlined in this text: a distributor (usually a general trading company in Japan), joint ventures, licensing, or setting up your own sales office or manufacturing subsidiary.

But because the culture is so unique, your research should go far beyond how to gain a marketing foothold in Japan. Levine urges visitors to study Japanese history. "They think we don't take them seriously," he says. "Take the time to study something about the last 200 years in Japan, and then find the occasion to display that knowledge. This can earn enormous respect." At a different level, be absolutely certain to brief yourself on ordinary, everyday business protocol. The reasons are because that is where first discussions begin and, as emphasized so strongly here, style is all-important in Japan. Here are some tips involving routine business protocol:

▸ Punctuality is respected.

▸ Don't expect meetings one-on-one in private offices; they will more likely be with several Japanese in a reception area or conference room.

▸ Bring printed materials, preferably translated into Japanese, about your company as well as your product. The same with video presentations—have the narration in Japanese. Such thoughtfulness will be appreciated and remembered. The Japanese like to know everything possible about the people with whom they are dealing.

▸ Be prepared to answer searching questions about your company, prices, delivery dates, warranties, and so on.

▸ You will probably speak in English, but Japanese will be the operational language. Use the advice given earlier in this text on working effectively through interpreters.

▶ Conversations will begin informally and then slowly ease into business. Let your hosts lead the way. The senior person on the Japanese side may remain quiet. Side conversations in Japanese will occur often; this is not a discourtesy but a necessity since they are very likely checking back and forth on comprehension. The Japanese normally comprehend the written English word better than the spoken word.

▶ Periods of silence are common. Americans find this vexing. One Japanese explained it with a question: "Do Americans think and talk at the same time?" He was politely saying that silence is O.K. because that's when we should be thinking.

▶ Business attire is conservative and conventional; so is posture and general decorum. Humor is difficult to translate but there is much smiling, which is good.

▶ A meeting ends with polite thank-yous from your host. Don't expect quick decisions. On the contrary, be prepared for long waits.

▶ If you are invited out socially, by all means accept. This is an extremely important part of the business culture. Among themselves, many Japanese believe that they truly cannot come to know a co-worker until they have had drinks with him socially. Expenditures for business entertainment in Japan are probably the highest in the world. In 1986, it accounted for 1.2 percent of the GNP, where defense spending amounted to 0.9 percent. This may change in the near future, however, with new tax laws now being considered that would limit such entertainment as a tax deductible business expense.

▶ Don't expect to be invited to a Japanese home. It is just not the custom.

▶ Remove your shoes, as you will see others do, upon entering restaurants, temples, homes, and wherever you see this custom practiced.

4. *Style is just as important as substance.* With the Japanese, the way things are done is just as important as what is done. To implant this in your mind, visualize the Japanese tea ceremony. It appears to outsiders like a carefully choreographed ballet where,

just incidentally, tea happens to be served. Another example is at the dining table where the appearance of a platter of food is just as important as the taste. This is what is meant by "style over substance." It permeates the Japanese culture.

Here is how one American firm took this principle and successfully orchestrated a visit to company headquarters by 25 key Japanese customers:

> The visitors' plane was met personally by company representatives and the guests whisked to waiting limousines, no more than two guests per auto. Each limo was fitted with standards holding miniature American and Japanese flags. Inside, each visitor received a welcome packet, printed in Japanese, explaining the complete itinerary, including sights of interest along the journey. In a park at the entry to the headquarters' city, the visitors were greeted with a large welcome banner in Japanese, a delegation of Chamber of Commerce "ambassadors" in colorful matched blazers and ties, the local City Manager, photographers, local Japanese women in traditional dress recruited as hostesses, speeches, gifts, and flowers—all the touches some hard-bitten American executives might consider corny. Lunch was held at a nearby country club so the guests could observe an American golf course; a driving contest was arranged and golf hats distributed; the menu featured dishes coveted by the Japanese, such as fresh melons, good beef plus American novelties like corn-on-the-cob.
>
> The emphasis on business was light and informal: a tour of the factory and offices, a brief slide presentation on the product line and opportunities for questions and one-on-one conversations. On the return leg of the trip, the American hosts made certain the flight stopped at Las Vegas so that the visitors could sample a Japanese favorite, gambling.
>
> In summary, the visit was a success because of the obvious attention to detail, to image, to style, and to sincerity, all of which conveyed caring and friendship to the visitors.

5. *Harmony is a key word.* De Mente tells us that the Japanese word *wa* is one of the most important words in the Japanese vocabulary. It means peace and harmony. Levine prefers to translate it as "calmness, a reconciling of conflict." This concept pervades all relationships: family, business, government, and employee-employer. In business, it is best seen in the consensus form of decision making. Anything that breaks the harmony of a relationship is terribly wrong. The standard adage in Japan is "the nail that sticks

up will get hammered." Negativism is bad, which explains why the Japanese have such a difficult time saying no in almost any circumstance. Furthermore, lack of impoliteness is a form of discord and therefore shunned. Japanese language experts explain that there are very few swear words in Japanese. One of the worst would be *baka*, meaning horse-deer, an insult because there can be no such animal. Instead of using swear words, the Japanese use a different level of speech to convey an emotion, and there are about eight levels. It is not surprising that when American audiences are asked for single words describing the Japanese, they often say gentle, polite, or modest. This obsession with harmony helps explain those stereotypes. In Japanese society, it is said that calling in lawyers to settle disputes is like performing the last rites at a death scene. Etiquette is a virtue. Embarrassment is a sin. The worst affront possible is to publicly embarrass a Japanese. This concept of *wa* is one area that can create friction between the two cultures. Americans consider forthrightness and thrashing out opposing views as a virtue whereas the Japanese have been conditioned to speak in vague, general terms. In fact, the verb comes at the end of a Japanese sentence, which helps the speaker watch the reaction of the listener in order to end on a positive, or at least neutral note. So, be very conscious of peace and harmony. Become supersensitive to the mood of your surroundings and the conduct and tenor of your business meetings.

The marketing vice president of a large Iowa consumer goods firm tells of a three-day negotiating session in Tokyo which seemingly produced few results. Finally, tired and frustrated, the American lost his temper, pounded the table, and demanded action. By the stunned, pained look on the faces of the Japanese, he knew he had committed a terrible breach of conduct and etiquette. Just at that instant, a rumbling was heard, the building shook, and everyone realized they were experiencing a minor earthquake. After it settled and the group realized it had passed, they looked at one another and all broke out in relieved grins. The tension had been broken, the American apologized, and talks resumed—eventually with success. "I now realize that earthquake was a happy portent," said the American. "I had violated the first rule in the Japanese culture, and it took a true subterranean signal to restore 'face.' If it hadn't been for that earthquake at that particular moment, I am certain our talks would have disintegrated completely and considerable business lost."

6. *Have patience.* It is said that Americans think in terms of days, weeks, and months, and the Japanese think in terms of years and decades. Americans pride themselves in being decisive, action-oriented in business. "Take action," is the credo, "and if it isn't right, correct it and resume." The Japanese are much more deliberative and cautious.

Tatsuo Yoshida, managing director of the Industrial Bank of Japan explains (*Nation's Business*, May 1986, p. 48) that the Western business culture is like hunting, whereas in Japan it is conducted more like rice farming. Japanese business vision is long-term as in farming, where American businesses aim for immediate returns on investment as in hunting. This analogy pervades much of the thinking in Japan. On one trip I made to Tokyo in 1976 during the Watergate scandal, the U.S. Ambassador said the Japanese were dismayed that Americans would react so strongly to that affair: "The Japanese believe we are cutting off the roots of the tree when all that is needed is careful pruning of the branches," he explained.

The Japanese tend to resist pressure on deadlines or delivery dates and agreement on a date may have been only to achieve harmony, according to authors Philip R. Harris and Robert T. Moran in their text *Managing Cultural Differences* (Gulf Publishing Co.). The Japanese are punctual but they expect you to wait for group decisions that take excessive time by American standards. Once a decision is made, however, implementation usually follows quickly.

Among themselves, Americans can become close business associates within weeks, but among Japanese and outsiders it may take years. The president of a New York firm reported that he conducted business with a Japanese counterpart for over 11 years before his associate there finally revealed that the American was no longer considered a *gaijen*, or "infidel" foreigner. Even then, the American confessed, he knew he would always be a *gaijen* and the Japanese gentleman was saying, in effect, "you are still a foreigner but we are comfortable having you in our inner circle among our several circles of relationships."

Edward T. Hall, highly respected social-anthropologist and consultant writes, "In the United States, schedules are sacred; in Japan scheduling cannot be initiated until meetings are held at all levels within the organization to permit essential discussions. Input from everyone is solicited and eventually a consensus is reached. Once consensus is reached, Japanese expect immediate action."

7. Gift giving is a must. Along with politeness, harmony, and a high sense of etiquette, the Japanese are also extremely gracious. So it should be no surprise that gift giving is more common than in almost any other culture. If you are visiting Japan or receiving Japanese guests in the United States, be prepared to receive and to give gifts. In Japan, gift-giving is both a skill and an art. Once again, style is just as important as substance. For example, gifts in Japan are almost always wrapped with paper—and not just any type of paper. Bold colors should be avoided; rice paper is preferred; white is bad because it represents death; and don't use fancy bows. The gift itself need not be extravagant. Bold logotypes printed on the gifts should be avoided. In fact, company identifications should either be very subtle or avoided entirely and replaced by simply inserting your business card inside the gift box. Also, don't insist that the receiver open the gift in front of you. The reason is that he or she fears their reaction to the gift may be insufficient and, in some way, *you* will lose face. Almost any gift will be appreciated, but the following seem to be especially prized: beef steaks, fine cognac, pen sets, good leather, commemorative coins, American Indian art or jewelry, and golf equipment. The best gift is one that shows forethought. For example, if you noted or learned that your Japanese associate collected glass figures, the mere remembrance would be impressive and appreciated as much as the gift itself. But above all, remember that gift giving is important.

8. *Entertainment.* This will almost always occur in the evenings. Breakfast meetings are rarely held, and lunches are normally brief. In the evening, however, you may be confronted with lavish entertainment in the form of first class restaurants, hostess bars, night clubs, or a dinner at a traditional geisha house. While geishas are, indeed, paid entertainers and hostesses, they are not present to provide sexual favors. They will fuss and giggle over you, serve your food and drink, and possibly play what we in the Western world might call simple parlor games. In keeping with the harmony of the evening, it is best to follow the lead of your host and let him make selections from the menu for you. Business may be discussed, but usually only lightly. The main purpose of entertainment is to bond friendships. A Japanese euphemism for the entertainment trade is "the water business," which is descriptive indeed because drinking is the staple. "Because the Japanese must

be so circumspect in their behavior at all 'normal' times, they believe it is impossible to really get to know a person without drinking with him," De Mente advises. "Foreign businessmen should be
very cautious about trying to keep up with their Japanese hosts at
such drinking rituals. It is all too common to see visiting businessmen being returned to their hotels well after midnight, sodden
drunk. The key to this important ceremony is to drink moderately
and simulate drunkenness," he says.

9. *"Yes" does not necessarily mean "yes."* The Japanese word
for yes is *hai,* pronounced like the English word high. However, it
does not necessarily mean assent or agreement. It conveys "Yes,
I hear you. Yes, I comprehend. But it doesn't necessarily mean I
agree with you." The explanation for this idiosyncrasy goes back to
the concept of *wa,* or harmony. The Japanese have extreme difficulty saying an outright "no" to anything because it disrupts the
harmony of any situation. Verb forms can be made negative, so
the word "no" is not prominent. How do you know when a Japanese
is saying yes but meaning no? Here are 10 ways the Japanese say no
or avoid saying no.

▸ In conversation, a flat no will rarely be heard, But on written forms where no one can be offended, it might appear.

▸ When refusing more food or a drink, they will more likely
   reply in a positive form ("I'm fine") rather than "No,
   thanks."

▸ Rather than say no, the Japanese will deflect the question
   with silence, or a sucking of air through the teeth, or perhaps a noncommittal "Oh, that would be very difficult."

▸ Another device is the counter question: "Why do you ask?"

▸ Appearing to ignore the question by shifting to another
   topic is a clear signal not to press further.

▸ Some Japanese will equivocate simply to save face for the
   Westerner, assuming that he will understand the truth.

▸ The qualified no might come in the form of "I will do my
   best, but if I cannot, I hope you will understand."

▸ A favorite is the "Yes, but . . ." answer. One agrees, but
   then states his real state of mind and this is commonly
   recognized as no.

▶ Delaying an answer, or "killing with silence" is another accepted method of conveying no. On the other hand, be patient—what you perceive as delay may just be the normal time required to arrive at a decision.

▶ Among themselves, the Japanese may accept a task they know they cannot perform by saying "I accept" but add an apology which signals no. Apologetic words are usually negative verb forms. For example, the Japanese phrases for "I am sorry" are expressed literally as "I'm not able to assume that," or "It cannot be helped."

Sol Levine explains that the Japanese know perfectly well how to refuse a request, ". . . it's just that they can do it so indirectly and diplomatically." An executive from Tennessee, visiting Japan with a delegation from his firm called on a company and hinted that he and his colleagues would very much appreciate a tour of the Japanese factory. All responses were evasive. The American tried everything in his power to eke out a yes, but failed. Finally, realizing that his Japanese hosts were becoming increasingly embarrassed, he phrased his question this way: "I have advised my friends that it would not be appropriate for me to ask you to show us your factory. Is that correct?" With much relief, the Japanese replied "Yes."

10. *Women in business*. As a general rule, women have great difficulty achieving equal status in Japanese business. Advancements have been made within their own society in recent years and more and more women are now seen in managerial positions, but for American women visiting Japan on business, the situation is best described as "strained politeness." Ingeborg Hegenbart, a highly respected and well traveled banker from Charlotte, NC, has visited Japan numerous times over the past 10 years. "There is no hard and fast rule," she reports. "Some Japanese bankers have been abrupt and rude to me, and I assume it was because I was a woman, and yet others send chauffeur-driven cars and are extremely polite." The male predominates in Japanese society and it is especially difficult for the senior Japanese businessman to accept women in responsible business roles. Western women visiting Japan on business should try to establish their business qualifications and authority—especially authority. Social situations will be strained but women will not be excluded, as was the custom a few short years

ago. The best advice for women who wish to conduct business in Japan is the same as for other countries: be 100 percent business-like, dress conservatively, don't look for special favors, answer what might be considered personal questions in a frank and direct way, and don't ever do anything that might be considered flirtatious. And while you carry these extra burdens of responsibility, take silent pride in the fact that you may indirectly be advancing the status of women in Japan by demonstrating how American women are just as capable as men in the world of business.

These are 10 general rules for dealing with the Japanese, just 10 among many. Entire books could be written elaborating on each facet of how to do business with the Japanese. At the end of this chapter, you will find the titles of several recommended books on how to conduct business in Japan. Meanwhile, let us move to the area of *negotiation* and review a few techniques and tips for face-to-face business discussions.

NEGOTIATING WITH THE JAPANESE

Perhaps the single most important concept to understand when negotiating a business deal with the Japanese is what Edward T. Hall calls "high context versus low context." High context communication is one where the information is mainly internalized; "implied" might be a good single word. Low context communication, on the other hand, is where the majority of information is contained in the explicit code. Our American culture is low context whereas the Japanese culture is high context.

This difference can lead to many misunderstandings when an American individual or team sits down across from a Japanese team to discuss a business negotiation. The American is searching for meaning by what is said, while the Japanese are more influenced by what is not said. The American message emphasizes specificity and accuracy, whereas the Japanese message is more circumspect and what Westerners would consider vague. Nowhere is this demonstrated better than in legal contracts. Americans tend to insist that every possible contingency be spelled out, letter for letter. The Japanese attitude is "Well, I will agree if you insist because I believe our arrangement should be friendly and harmonious, but if something happens where I simply cannot fulfill some detail, or if changes are required, we should be able to sit down and work out a positive solution."

Another point of friction deals with time. Americans pride themselves in being action-oriented, in getting things done *now*, and in quickly getting to the core of a problem and making a decision. The Japanese are cautious and gradual, and take what seems like an agonizing amount of time gaining a consensus before acting.

Of course, when negotiating we also have many interests in common. Both sides desire and respect the importance of honesty, integrity, friendship, and sincerity. In buying-selling relationships, both sides want quality, service, and favorable prices. Both sides are able to mix business and social pleasures, but with the Japanese these relationships are deeper and perhaps more profound than in the West. Americans are viewed as exceedingly friendly, especially at the outset of a relationship, but "shallow" in those friendships because we appear anxious to move along, to not become *too* close or revealing of ourselves. One manifestation of that is the frequent rotation of personnel in U.S. business positions. The result is that the Japanese business contact may just become acquainted with one U.S. representative only to find a replacement appear on his doorstep. If possible, it is best for the American side to establish a relationship and keep it constant, with the same U.S. person continuing to represent that side for as long as dealings are harmonious.

Here are some specific tips for negotiation:

- Never put a Japanese in a position where he can be embarrassed or helpless.

- Lean toward modesty and humility about your product or your service; let your literature present your virtues.

- Understand the concept of "face" and don't be afraid to use it to *your* advantage in negotiations when it is true and warranted. For example, if an agreement on a point is reached and the Japanese wish to renege on or reverse it, explain how this will cause you much personal embarrassment and difficulty with your superiors.

- Respect seniority and the elderly.

- Don't be disturbed by periods of silence or by lack of direct eye contact.

- Proper behavior, from dress to dining to decision making, is the cardinal rule in all relationships.

⟫ Avoid fixed schedules. For example, Americans visit Japan and allow, say, one week for business discussions. We expect to be done by that time and explain to the Japanese across the bargaining table that we wish to arrive at a decision by that time. The Japanese may use this as a negotiating weapon against you. It is far better to be flexible.

What about negotiations from Japanese eyes? A U.S. contractor in Japan happened on an unpublished essay written by a Japanese negotiator that provides a unique insight on how the Japanese view the negotiating process with Americans.* The very first sentence reflects much of the Japanese attitude toward modesty and humility. "At the start I must apologize for stating my ideas on this subject so boldly when my superiors already know more than I about the subject. I have only had more than five years of experience in dealing with U.S. negotiators."

The author then listed numerous reasons why American were difficult to understand during period of negotiations. Unlike the homogeneous Japanese, he explained, Americans come from different cultures, different parts of the United States, different size cities, and with different educations. He emphasized that Americans value "adversary proceedings" as reflected in the U.S. court system. The combination of these qualities made negotiations difficult, he suggested.

Americans, he said, also try to negotiate perfect and final agreements which they think will never need reinterpretation or adjustment. (The writer attributed this to the Christian religion "which promises perfection at some future time or after death.") In addition, he wrote, American negotiators often argue among themselves in public, "so it is safe to assume they argue even more in private . . . and seem to feel no shame about such embarrassing behavior.

"U.S. negotiators often have fallback positions which they can use if they do not win agreement to the first proposals. These fallbacks are worked out in advance almost as if they knew their first offers were unreasonable. Therefore it is necessary for us to learn what the final fallback is as early as possible. Once that

---

*This information comes from an article in the March 1983 issue of *Contract Management* magazine and these excerpts are reproduced here with the permission of that publication.

information is obtained, it is often possible to get the U.S. side to offer its fallback proposal in return for a concession of no consequence."

The Japanese negotiator also noted that Americans always prepare contingency plans, enjoy confrontation and rebuttal, and are exceedingly energetic and persistent. "Americans also like to concentrate on one problem at a time. They seem not to understand that the whole picture is more important . . ." As for protocol, "They often say that rank means nothing to them, but it really does. On the other hand, when mistakes are made they adapt easily and are not offended if the matter is quietly corrected."

The essay concluded with this observation on the American psyche: "When the talks are concluded the U.S. side always feels some kind of euphoria. They like to think they have won, which is part of the adversary style common to them. They may engage in some public gloating to justify themselves to their countrymen. This is annoying when they do, but I suppose we should try to understand such behavior and recognize that they actually cannot help themselves and do not mean any harm."

Another insight comes from Michael Almond, an attorney in Charlotte, NC, experienced in contract negotiations in Japan who advises that some Japanese negotiators are becoming more adept at Western ways than we realize. "A clever Japanese negotiator," Almond says, "knows about American habits involving eye-contact and the dislike of silence. The smart Japanese negotiator will respond to a point, or listen to the American's story, and then continue staring directly into the American's eyes without responding. The combination of the stare plus the silence usually unnerves the American."

Bradley K. Duerson taught negotiation seminars for Yasuda Trust Bank in Tokyo, instructing both Americans and Japanese on what to look for when negotiating with each other. "The Japanese are usually shocked at the informal posture of most Americans," he advises. "Slouching or crossing the legs and dangling feet are things a Japanese businessman would never do. Instead, you'll find the Japanese sitting upright and maybe even on the edge of their chairs. The Japanese were amazed to see a photograph of the Chairman of the U.S. Federal Reserve Board with his feet up on his desk and smoking a cigar." Duerson also reports that the Japanese normally work in teams, all sitting together usually on one side of the table so that they can converse in Japanese easily and also see their opposite number without having to switch heads back and forth as in a tennis match.

A small but significant negotiating tip pertains to numbers, specifically when numbers are *spoken* in Japanese. When they are written out there is no problem with comprehension, but some spoken numbers are problematic because of language differences, according to Duerson. The terms "one thousand" and "ten or twenty thousand" up to "ninety thousand" are common to both languages. However, when the conversation reaches "one hundred thousand" a language barrier arises because the Japanese express that figure as "ten, ten-thousands." Therefore, "two hundred thousand" becomes "twenty, ten-thousands" and so on. At "one million" the Japanese term is literally "one-hundred, ten-thousands." This example of dealing with something as commonplace as spoken numbers demonstrates how business discussions and negotiations in Japan require special knowledge and new skills.

In conclusion, it should become obvious that business negotiations in Japan test the best qualities in the aspiring international business manager. But three words can encapsulate the whole process: patience, perseverance, and politeness. Armed with these, chances for success and rewards are vastly improved.

WHERE TO LOOK FOR HELP

Help in doing business with the Japanese is not far away and, in fact, the first recommended source may even seem startling. Japanese External Trade Organization (JETRO) is a Japanese government-sponsored agency which exists for the purpose of encouraging and aiding with exports to Japan as well as helping their countrymen find good investments in the United States. JETRO maintains offices in many major American cities. If and when you face the prospect of doing business in Japan, this probably should be an early port of call.

While the bibliography on doing business with the Japanese grows each month, here are several valuable and readable books to start your library:

The Economist Business Traveller's Guides—Japan by Prentice Hall Press, New York, 1987. This is one book in a series on major areas in the world: Middle East, United Kingdom,

United States, with more volumes to be issued in the future. The bulk of this book is a conventional guide, with maps of cities and lists of hotels and restaurants. However, the first 100 pages are jammed with valuable facts and information on economic, industrial, political, and business facts.

Japanese Language and Culture for Business and Travel by Kyoko Hijirida and Muneo Yoshikawa, University of Hawaii Press, Honolulu, 1987. This is an extremely helpful introduction to the language of modern Japan. It focuses on business and travel language with excellent cultural insights along the way. A companion book, issued by the same publisher, is *Japanese Culture and Behavior* by Takie Sugiyama Lebra and William P. Lebra (Eds.), 1986. A collection of selected readings, this book is helpful to beginners in the study of Japanese culture and society.

With Respect to the Japanese, A Guide for Americans by John C. Condon, Intercultural Press, Yarmouth, Maine, 1984, is a short (92 pages) and readable book covering the basic principles of understanding the Japanese.

Japanese Etiquette & Ethics in Business by Boye De Mente, Passport Books, Lincolnwood, Illinois, 1987, has had over 100,000 copies sold in previous editions. This would be an extremely useful book for any businessperson to pack in his briefcase and read before, during and again after a first visit to Japan. De Mente carries the reader right through the fundamental principles of the Japanese culture as they apply to business, and finishes with a valuable glossary of key Japanese business terms and their meanings.

Hidden Differences: Doing Business With the Japanese by Edward T. Hall and Mildred Reed Hall, Anchor Press/Doubleday, Garden City, NY, 1987. This renowned social anthropologist has collaborated with his wife in producing an excellent, rounded guide dealing with everything from space and time concepts in Japan to how to start a small business there. It is short (172 pages) but each page is a golden nugget of helpful information worth examining over and over again.

How To Do Business With The Japanese, A Strategy for Success by Mark Zimmerman, Random House, New York, 1985, covers much of the same ground as the previous books, but adds sections on how to compete with the Japanese in the United States, in foreign markets or in Japan itself. Zimmerman, who died in 1983, served at one time as president of the American Chamber of Commerce in Japan.

From Bonsai To Levis by George Fields, Macmillan, 1983, has as its subtitle "When West meets East: An Insider's Surprising Account of How the Japanese Live." Fields, an Australian, served as Chairman of ASI Market Research in Japan and therefore writes from the eyes of a market researcher. He offers views of marketing, brand names, consumer habits, the role of women, and other insightful information about doing business in Japan.

All of these books are both informative and readable and make wonderful companions for travel to and business in the land of chrysanthemums.

The U.S. Department of Commerce and the trade specialists with the International Trade Administrations in your area are additional sources for help. They may be able to offer further readings on Japan, suggest private consultants in your area, and generally aid you with your research. Another resource is the Japanese "desk" within the Department of Commerce in Washington, DC. The specialists at this desk are fully knowledgeable about current laws and regulations, trade agreements, tariffs, and licenses, all as they pertain to Japan. A complete listing of these desk officers for all countries is included in the Appendix.

Local trade associations, world trade centers, and universities are staging more frequent seminars on Japan. Entire cities are also recognizing the need for closer business and cultural relationships with Japan by staging "Japan Weeks." During these celebrations, authorities are brought in to speak at seminars and workshops, and exhibits and demonstrations are arranged for everything from art to music to theater or foods from Japan. Watch for these in your communities. Your local Chamber of Commerce or world trade club or association will undoubtedly know if one is planned.

Finally, inquire with your state agency charged with economic development to learn if your state maintains a trade office in Japan. If so, write that office to ask what services it can provide you in doing business with Japan.

SUMMARY

This chapter, while dealing with perhaps the most complex culture in the world, is more a digest than a dissertation. It is a synopsis because in writing about the Japanese, it is far better to concentrate on a few vital characteristics and encourage the reader to read them over and over again.

The alternative would be to write and probe deeper and deeper into the Japanese ethos until a haze appeared to envelope them like modern-day Merlins. That has been our mistake. "It has been easy to attribute our problems in understanding the Japanese to the mystery we think exists there," Levine says. "That's the lazy way. The answer is to beware of stereotypes and mystiques. The answer is to simply work as hard as they do."

Doing business in Japan is not that complex. The Japanese are different in some important respects, that's all. They work harder than most. They view time differently. Harmony is essential. Details are important. Politeness is mandatory. Patience is a virtue. Consensus and compromise rule. Embarrassment and controversy are twin devils. Style is as important as substance. Communication is cloaked in inference, not specifics. But they also revere honesty and integrity, they prize quality and conscientious service, they admire innovation, they respect industriousness, they honor loyalty and friendship, and they value long-standing personal relationships. Sound like anybody you know?

After all this, If you still have difficulty with the so-called "mystique," then examine the roster of American brand names that not only are appearing in Japanese cities and retail stores but are familiar, everyday terms to all Japanese consumers: McDonalds, Kentucky Fried Chicken, Levis, Dunkin' Doughnuts, Parker Pens, Nescafé, Coca-Cola, Band-Aid, Johnson Wax, Avon, Max Factor, Tupperware, Schick, and hundreds of other American names. Yours could—and probably should—be among them.

From Japan, the most important country in our economic future, as Senator Bradley proclaims, we now move to what could be the most important *trend* in the world economy: countertrade and barter. This seems like an anachronism since bartering was undoubtedly man's first form of commercial trading. However, it looms on the horizon like a gigantic, rolling bank of fog because so few Americans have any knowledge or experience with modern-day barter. For this reason, it is important to be prepared by understanding the various forms and rules of countertrade as they are practiced today.

13

Countertrade

By the year 2000, fully half of all international trade will involve countertrade.

U.S. Department of Commerce Official

In 1985, National Semiconductor Corp. had two needs: to dispose of $3 million worth of computer games that were slow to sell, and to raise extra revenue for general advertising of other products. How to meet these needs? Answer: countertrade. They called in Richard Manney of Mediators Inc. who negotiated a deal with a South American country to take the computer games in return for bananas. Then Manney sold the bananas to a U.S. grocery store chain for dollars, which were turned over to National Semiconductor to use for buying advertising.

This is just one example of a burgeoning world business called *countertrade.* It is a complex business, risky but often loaded with deep profit margins for the negotiators. Most U.S. firms are totally inexperienced in it. Yet according to the *Los Angeles Times,* it is spreading at a rate that "alarms many in government, raises new challenges to the business community, threatens to write new rules for international commerce while undermining the international monetary system developed after World War II."

The earliest form of countertrade was barter, which is as old as the cave dwellers. In the United States, native American Indians were the first great commercial bartering experts, still in evidence today whenever someone refers to a one dollar bill as a "buck." That word originated from the use of buckskins as a medium of exchange between Indians and early settlers. Today in the United

States, when the word barter is mentioned, one probably thinks of young baseball fans studiously trading cards picturing past and present baseball stars. But, as we will soon learn, bartering is alive and thriving in certain select segments of American commerce and could well enjoy a renaissance as more and more international traders turn to this age-old means of exchanging goods.

Modern countertrade emerged in Europe after World War I when Germany tried to rebuild with an unstable currency. Another surge occurred after World War II. By 1981, it was estimated that about $1.2 trillion in international trade came in the form of countertrade. Presently, experts estimate that about one-third of all international trade is done through countertrade. Governments are not entirely happy with this trend because it is viewed as a regressive form of trade that could choke the flow of open, multilateral trade. Countertrade fosters an attitude of "I'll buy from you, but only if you'll take this stuff off my hands." Also, it is difficult for governments to tax profits when the profits take the form of, say, potatoes that are then traded for sewing machines that in turn are traded for vodka.

The purpose of this chapter is to acquaint you with the forms of countertrade, provide examples, and tell you how to prepare for it. Some sources for further information are also provided. This introduction to countertrade will hardly prepare you as a professional, but it will place you in an elite class of international business savants who can converse knowledgeably about this new-yet-old phenomenon.

CASE STUDIES

At present, international countertrade occurs most commonly among the following: (1) developing countries, (2) the state-controlled economies in Eastern Europe, and (3) large multinational corporations. It normally occurs in markets where hard currencies are scarce or carefully preserved. In those markets, governments hoard hard currencies to pay for vital necessities, forcing importers to resort to other means which usually leads to some form of countertrade.

Barter in the United States is also common and available, but perhaps not as visible. Here are some examples of how barter works within U.S. boundaries.

The oldest and largest bartering specialist firm in the United States is Atwood Richards Inc., New York, headed by Moreton Binn, dubbed by some as "The Baron of Barter." This firm does about $500 million a year in trading and has become especially adept in the bartering of "time disposable" services. That means such things as radio and TV advertising, airline reservations, and hotel and convention facilities.

If an airline seat is empty on any given flight or if a hotel room is vacant for one night, neither the airline nor the hotel can ever recoup that lost income. Therefore, faced with the prospect of an unused seat or room, they are pleased to receive almost anything in value in return for filling them. The same applies to a minute of radio or TV advertising. When program time goes unused or unsold, it is lost forever. Therefore, broadcast stations are fertile territory for barter.

But, it is far more complicated than trading one night in a hotel room for, say, a case of peaches. What Atwood Richards does is assemble a host of companies who want to barter something for something. In this way, the hotel owner who trades overnight lodging receives "trade credits" which qualify him to pick and choose from a catalog filled with other products and services. In 1984, Parker Pen turned over $1 million in pens to Atwood Richards thereby establishing a credit account on which it could draw airline tickets, TV time, hotel rooms, and a host of other products ranging from fur coats to outboard motors. However, this was not a simple case of being able to dip freely into a bag of goodies for an unlimited supply of free gifts. With the TV advertising, for example, to obtain good time slots Parker either had to "cash in" extra credits or provide additional cash.

Here is how the circle of bartering in the United States might work.

▶ A TV station needs $500,000 for studio expansion but would rather not borrow from the banks. So the barter company provides them with that amount in cash and, in return, gets $1 million in advertising time. At this point, the barter firm has something to sell that cost them 50-cents on the dollar.

▶ The barter firm scouts the market and finds a local manufacturer of mattresses interested in TV advertising time. A deal is negotiated and the barter firm gets $1.25 million in mattresses (at wholesale prices) in return for the $1 million in TV advertising. Now the barter firm has $1.25 million in mattresses for an initial investment of $500,000.

▶ The barter company then finds a hotel chain that needs mattresses and sells the lot to them in return for $2.5 million in room accommodations. At this stage, the barter firm has a service (i.e., room space) worth $2.5 million in value for a cash outlay of $500,000, or 20-cents on the dollar.

▶ The barter firm now finds a manufacturer of home products with a national salesforce who frequently book hotel space. They swing a deal where the barter company receives $2 million in the company's products plus $500,000 in cash in return for the $2.5 million in room space from the hotel chain.

▶ The bartering firm now has fully recovered its initial cash outlay and has $2 million in products that, even if sold at discounted prices, returns a handsome profit.

As the barter company adds more and more clients, the chances for negotiating swaps increase incrementally. The downside risks are also evident. The barter firm must employ special skills in taking only products or services that are marketable. That means the barterer must assure that the products are of good quality and backed by warranties. As for the other party, the "seller," they must gain assurances that the bartered goods will not disrupt normal sales channels. They must also assure that proper accounting for tax purposes accompanies the whole transaction. And, finally, the seller takes the risk that the goods and services received in return are of real value and help with cash flow.

Atwood Richards minimum transaction is $1 million, but there are other barter firms springing up around the United States that deal with smaller amounts. The real "revolution," according to Jerry Jasinowski, executive vice president of the National Association of Manufacturers, is among the growing number of firms who are "using it innovatively to add to their marketing capability." A 1988 survey by *Sales & Marketing Management* magazine supported this view, citing "a score or more of companies that have begun experimenting with bartering in recent months." The magazine also reported that companies as diverse as USX, Republic Airlines, 3M, Zayre, and K-Mart have reached the stage in bartering where full time executives and staffs are required.

Here are examples of international countertrade:

▶ *General Motors* sold $12 million worth of locomotive and diesel engines to the government of Yugoslavia. But, in return GM had to agree to purchase $4 million in Yugoslavian cutting tools that it brought back to the United States and sold to a tool manufacturer.

▶ *Levi-Strauss* sold the Hungarian government equipment and designs necessary to manufacture blue jeans. In return, it agreed to purchase a portion of the jeans produced in the plant.

▶ *Boeing Co.* exchanged ten 747 jet aircraft with the government of Saudi Arabia in exchange for $1 billion worth of oil.

▶ *Chrysler Corp. and General Motors* cut deals with Jamaica to deliver, during a three-year period, trucks and cars in exchange for aluminum and bauxite.

▶ In 1986, the barter unit of *Caterpiller Inc.* traded its earthmoving equipment to Venezuela, which in turn traded iron ore to Romania. Romania then sent a load of men's suits to Britain for cash, which was passed back to Caterpiller.

▶ The governments of Indonesia, Colombia, Guatemala, and Kenya have created programs under which foreign firms selling products to the government are required to purchase specified amounts of local goods or commodities such as rubber, coffee, and timber.

▶ Ghana traded diamonds, cocoa, wood, and rubber in 1985 to Bulgaria for $8 million worth of agricultural equipment and pharmaceuticals.

▶ Nigeria has tried a plan of offering the refueling, loading, and cleaning of ships in port as partial payment for imports.

Here are two detailed case studies of American firms actively involved in countertrade:

Control Data Corporation edged into countertrade in the 1970s "Because we had to," according to Jackson Hipps, head of CDC's in-house countertrade company. "Some of our foreign customers said you must buy from us if you expect to sell to us." A separate profit center was established with the first deals occurring with Eastern Europe via an office in Austria. "You absolutely must have top management support and commitment," Hipps warns. CDC soon learned it could be a risky business because it was often on the receiving end of "real dogs," products that could not be sold elsewhere. A unique trade occurred when government agencies in the U.S.S.R. bought computers from CDC who, in turn, agreed to sponsor a Soviet art exhibition in the United States. Organizationally, Hipps advises, two types of specialists are needed: first, a specialist in countertrade who knows the mechanics and methods, and second, marketing specialists who can take the products received in trade and turn them into cash.

Pepsi Trading Company is a subsidiary of PepsiCo. Inc. and received early publicity in the countertrade game when it swapped Pepsi concentrate in the U.S.S.R. for Stolichnaya vodka which it brought to the United States and marketed. Pepsi began experimenting with countertrade in 1969 in Hungary but it was not until 1973 that they realized its importance and formed a separate trading company. Reef Ivey II of Pepsi echoes the advice of Control Data in warning that any moves toward countertrade must have solid top management support. "The name of the game," Ivey says, "is the disposition of the products. Anyone can find products available for countertrade; the trick is finding a buyer and disposing of the products." Pepsi has dealt in movies made in Hungary, wines from Eastern Europe, shoes, glass, and malt. In the case of shoes, Pepsi committed to buy $17 million worth over a period of years and, in turn, was able to sell $5 million in Pepsi products into Hungary. In this case, Pepsi sent shoe designers into Hungary to supervise the production of the shoes to assure that they could be successfully sold in the United States. In another deal, Pepsi bought wine bottles from Poland and filled them with wine from Yugoslavia. This allowed Pepsi to sell its syrup into Poland while Yugoslavia paid Pepsi with excess wine. Pepsi searches for countertrade deals first within its own organization, then among its suppliers, then among barter houses in Eastern Europe, and then among the general range of U.S. companies inexperienced in countertrade but who have products or opportunities and don't know how to proceed.

TERMINOLOGY

As you have seen from the variety of deals described here, barter is just one form under an umbrella of activity that has generically come to be called countertrade. There are many variations, each with a descriptive term. Here are the terms commonly used and an explanation of each:

▶ *Barter* generally means simply trading goods for goods with no currency involved. Examples: Pepsico sold its products into Korea, Thailand, China, and Poland in exchange for toys, glassware, cashmere, and beer.

▶ *Counterpurchase* means you sell products to a sovereign nation and in return agree to purchase a quantity of other goods from that nation, either on a direct one-to-one value ratio or more likely a higher ratio, say two-to-one or three-to-one on the exporting nation's side.

▶ *Import entitlements* are a variation of counterpurchase and occur in countries like Brazil and Mexico with huge foreign debts and low reserves of hard currencies. In those countries, if you have a product that is not considered a necessity, the government will say "You can send your product here but only if you generate exports from our country in amounts equal to or greater than the value of the imports." The device used to control this is, of course, import permits.

▶ *Clearing agreements* occur when two parties agree to purchase equivalent amounts of the other's products over a period of time. In these cases, accounts are established at a central bank which records purchases and sales of the two parties using "clearing dollars."

▶ *Compensation,* or *buy-back,* usually means you offer to sell a production facility or some other technology into a certain market but also agree to buy a portion of the products produced by that facility or from that technology.

▶ *Switch* refers to bringing in a third party. For example, A wants to sell to B but B doesn't have U.S. dollars. So, B brings in C with whom they have obligations and C supplies the needed dollars to wipe out that obligation.

As you can see, countertrade not only takes many forms but can also become highly complex. It is not for amateurs.

How to Get Involved

It is estimated that over half of the Fortune 500 companies have already become involved with some form of countertrade. Most large multinational firms establish separate subsidiaries, examples being General Motors, PepsiCo, Coca-Cola, General Electric, and Control Data Corp. These may serve as independent profit centers or a breakeven service center to assist separate divisions within a conglomerate.

Smaller companies usually create countertrade divisions. These may be attached to the international trade or marketing department of the company. Three functions are required within this separate division: experienced specialists who know the ins and outs of countertrade negotiating and contracting, marketing specialists who can first assess and then sell the goods involved, and an administrative section to handle and track the transaction. In these cases, the goods are usually restricted to products produced and sold by the company and usually do not involve unrelated products produced by third parties.

For companies confronted by occasional or sporadic use of countertrade, the best resources are probably trading houses or independent consultants located both in the United States and abroad. Your trade specialist at the nearest district office of the U.S. Department of Commerce will probably know if there are any countertrade advisers in your region. Brokerage fees can be high, as much as 30 percent of the value of the goods, because of the high risks involved in countertrade. Or, if your agreement is simply to sell to a broker, be prepared for substantial discounts. Large international trading houses can be found in most European capitals, plus Japan and other major Pacific Basin trade centers. There are perhaps 20 countertrade houses within the United States, some of them specializing in commodities only, while others will handle almost any type product.

A trading house's role may range from advice on countertrade practices in developing countries, to market assessments, to assistance in negotiations, to acting as brokers, and even to possibly serving as principals in the transaction. If you should choose to investigate one or more of these trading houses to handle a transaction for you, learn the full range of services they can provide. In addition to marketing, they may also be able to assist with such things as financing and transportation. In the case of commodities, some even specialize in processing and upgrading.

SOURCES OF HELP

Aside from seeking advice from trading houses and consultants who specialize in countertrade, it is possible that banks and law firms in your area have experience to assist you. Again, check with the trade specialist at the district office of the U.S. Department of Commerce.

DoC also offers a helpful booklet entitled *Countertrade Practices in East Europe, The Soviet Union and China: An Introductory Guide to Business*. In addition, Commerce can advise and assist companies who encounter countertrade opportunities. However, they should be contacted early in the transaction. They can help collect needed information, identify options, avoid risks and problems, and locate private sector sources of assistance. For complete information on this service, contact the Office of Trade Finance, International Trade Administration, U.S. Department of Commerce, Washington, DC, (202) 377-3277.

Business International S.A. has prepared and published a book titled *101 Checklists for Coping With Worldwide Countertrade*, June 1985. This book may be found at your local library or you can write Business International S.A., 12–14, chemin Rieu, 1208 Geneva, Switzerland.

Trade Without Money: Barter and Countertrade by Leo G. B. Welt, Law & Business, Inc./Harcourt Brace Jovanovich, 1984, is one of the most widely read books in this specialized field. Welt has extensive experience, is based in Washington, DC, and represents U.S. companies in countertrade transactions particularly with the Soviet Union, Eastern Europe, and the People's Republic of China. This book explains how countertrade arrangements are structured, how financing can be arranged, how countertrade differs around the world, and provides case studies and sample contract agreements.

Winning the Countertrade War: A New Approach to America's Trade Deficit by Matt Schaffer, John Wiley, 1989, is the latest book on this timely subject and contains practical advice on doing countertrade the world over. It describes polyoptions facing the United States on both countertrade and export credit financing. The author was director of countertrade at Sears World Trade and also senior vice president for policy at the U.S. Export-Import Bank. He holds a doctorate in social anthropology and has 12 years direct experience in international business.

SUMMARY

The lessons in this chapter are fairly clear; to summarize:

▶ Countertrade already comprises an impressive share of all world commerce.

▶ It is growing each year, which makes it nearly impossible to ignore.

▶ Thus far, most countertrade has been conducted by major U.S. multinationals with the Soviet Union, other countries in Eastern Europe, African nations, and the People's Republic of China.

▶ It is a highly entrepreneurial business.

▶ Finding products for countertrade is not the problem; it is locating or creating a demand for those products.

▶ Americans, by and large, are neophytes to countertrade. The Europeans are more experienced as are the underdeveloped countries who, perforce, must engage in all forms of countertrade in order to bring nonessential but desired products into their market.

▶ Medium- and small-sized U.S. firms would be wise to quickly turn to advisers and specialists in countertrade before attempting any transaction. However, odds are that at some time in the future, an opportunity for countertrade will arise and therefore it is good to be prepared.

One observer who has spent over 30 years in international commerce counsels: "If I was a young man again, just embarking on a career, I would, first, choose international trade without hesitation. Second, I would learn everything I could about countertrade. My reasons are pretty simple. There is no doubt whatsoever that international trade must become larger and more important in the United States. Over the next few decades, no company—large, medium or small—can afford to ignore it. Furthermore, our national economy depends on more vigorous pursuit of trade, particularly exporting. And for individual companies, the world marketplace offers a potential many times greater than the U.S. market. Now, as to countertrade . . . that judgment is based on simple supply and demand. Presently, there are very few people in the United States, probably only in the hundreds, who are knowledgeable and experienced in countertrade. If one-half of all trade will involve countertrade practices by the year 2000, it becomes simple logic that it would pay to learn anything and everything I could about it."

Resources

INTERNATIONAL TRADE ADMINISTRATION/ US&FCS DISTRICT OFFICES

ALABAMA
*Birmingham—Rmk. 302, 2015 2nd Ave. North, Berry Bldg., 35203 (205 731-1331

ALASKA
Anchorage—701 C St., P.O. Box 32, 99513, (907) 271-5041

ARIZONA
Phoenix—Federal Bldg. & U.S. Courthouse, 230 North 1st Ave., Rm. 3412, 85025, (602) 261-3285

ARKANSAS
Little Rock—Suite 811, Savers Fed. Bldg., 320 W. Capitol Ave., 72201, (501) 378-5794

CALIFORNIA
Los Angeles—Rm. 800, 11777 San Vicente Blvd., 90049, (213) 209-6707
*Santa Ana—116-A W. 4th St., Suite #1, 92701, (714) 836-2461
San Diego—6363 Greenwich Dr., 92122, (619) 557-5395
*San Francisco—Fed. Bldg., Box 36013, 450 Golden Gate Ave., 94102, (415) 556-5860

COLORADO
*Denver—Rm. 119, U.S. Customhouse, 721-19th St., 80202, (303) 844-3246

CONNECTICUT
*Hartford—Rm. 610-B, Fed. Office Bldg., 450 Main St., 06103, (203) 240-3530

DELAWARE
Serviced by Philadelphia District Office

DISTRICT OF COLUMBIA
*Washington, D.C.—(Baltimore, Md. District) Rm. 1066 HCHB, Department of Commerce, 14th St. & Constitution Ave., N.W. 20230, (202) 377-3181

FLORIDA
Miami—Suite 224, Fed. Bldg., 51 S.W. First Ave., 33130, (305) 536-5267
*Clearwater—128 North Osceola Ave. 33515, (813) 461-0011
*Jacksonville—3100 University Blvd. South, 32216, (904) 791-2796
*Orlando—75 East Ivanhoe Blvd., 32804, (305) 425-1234
*Tallahassee—Collins Bldg., Rm. 401, 107 W. Gaines St., 32304, (904) 488-6469

GEORGIA
Atlanta—Suite 504, 1365 Peachtree St., N.E., 30309, (404) 347-4872
Savannah—120 Barnard St., A-107, 31402, (912) 944-4204

HAWAII
Honolulu—4106 Fed. Bldg., P.O. Box 50026, 300 Ala Moana Blvd., 96850, (808) 541-1782

IDAHO
*Boise—(Denver, Colorado District) State-house, Room 113, 83720, (208) 334-9254

ILLINOIS
Chicago—1406 Mid Continental Plaza Bldg., 55 East Monroe St., 60603, (312) 353-4450
*Palatine—W.R. Harper College, Algonquin & Roselle Rd., 60067, (312) 397-3000, x-532
*Rockford—515 North Court St., P.O. Box 1747, 61110-0247, (815) 987-8100

---

* Denotes regional office with supervisory regional responsibilities.

269

INDIANA
Indianapolis—357 U.S. Courthouse & Fed. Office Bldg., 46 East Ohio St., 46204, (317) 269-6214

IOWA
Des Moines—817 Fed. Bldg., 210 Walnut St., 50309, (515) 284-4222

KANSAS
*Wichita—(Kansas City, Missouri District) River Park Pl., Suite 565, 727 North Waco, 67203, (316) 269-6160

KENTUCKY
Louisville—Rm. 636B, U.S. Post Office and Courthouse Bldg., 40202, (502) 582-5066

LOUISIANA
New Orleans—432 World Trade Center, No. 2 Canal St., 70130, (504) 589-6546

MAINE
*Augusta—(Boston, Massachusetts District) 1 Memorial Circle, Casco Bank Bldg., 04330, (207) 622-8249

MARYLAND
Baltimore—415 U.S. Customhouse, Gay and Lombard Sts., 21202, (301) 962-3560

MASSACHUSETTS
Boston—World Trade Center, Suite 307 Commonwealth Pier Area, 02210, (617) 565-8563

MICHIGAN
Detroit—1140 McNamara Bldg., 477 Michigan Ave., 48226, (313) 226-3650
*Grand Rapids—300 Monroe N.W., Rm. 409, 49503, (616) 456-2411

MINNESOTA
Minneapolis—108 Fed. Bldg., 110 S. 4th St., 55401, (612) 348-1638

MISSISSIPPI
Jackson—328 Jackson Mall Office Center, 300 Woodrow Wilson Blvd., 39213, (601) 965-4388

MISSOURI
*St. Louis—7911 Forsyth Blvd., Suite 610, 63105, (314) 425-3302-4
Kansas City—Rm. 635, 601 East 12th St., 64106, (816) 426-3141

MONTANA
Serviced by Denver District Office

NEBRASKA
Omaha—11133 "O" St., 68137, (402) 221-3664

NEVADA
Reno—1755 E. Plumb Ln., #152, 89502, (702) 784-5203

NEW HAMPSHIRE
Serviced by Boston District Office

NEW JERSEY
*Trenton—3131 Princeton Pike Bldg. 6, Suite 100, 08648, (609) 989-2100

NEW MEXICO
Albuquerque—517 Gold, S.W., Suite 4303, 87102, (505) 766-2386

NEW YORK
Buffalo—1312 Fed. Bldg., 111 West Huron St., 14202, (716) 846-4191
*Rochester—121 East Ave., 14604, (716) 263-6480
New York—Fed. Office Bldg., 26 Fed. Plaza, Rm. 3718, Foley Sq., 10278, (212) 264-0634

NORTH CAROLINA
*Greensboro—324 W. Market St., P.O. Box 1950, 27402, (919) 333-5345

NORTH DAKOTA
Serviced by Omaha District Office

OHIO
*Cincinnati—9504 Fed. Office Bldg., 550 Main St., 45202, (513) 684-2944
Cleveland—Rm. 600, 666 Euclid Ave., 44114 (216) 522-4750

OKLAHOMA
Oklahoma City—5 Broadway Executive Park, Suite 200, 6601 Broadway Extension, 73116, (405) 231-5302
*Tulsa—440 S. Houston St., 74127, (918) 581-7650

OREGON
Portland—Rm. 618, 1220 S.W. 3rd Ave., 97204, (503) 221-3001

PENNSYLVANIA
Philadelphia—9448 Fed. Bldg., 600 Arch St., 19106 (215) 597-2866
Pittsburgh—2002 Fed. Bldg., 1000 Liberty Ave., 15222, (412) 644-2850

PUERTO RICO
San Juan (Hato Rey)—Rm. 659-Fed. Bldg., 00918, (809) 753-4555

RHODE ISLAND
*Providence—(Boston, Massachusetts District) 7 Jackson Walkway, 02903, (401) 528-5104, ext. 22

SOUTH CAROLINA
Columbia—Strom Thrumond Fed. Bldg.,
Suite 172, 1835 Assembly St., 29201
(803) 765-5345
*Charleston—17 Lockwood Dr., 29401,
(803) 724-4361

SOUTH DAKOTA
Serviced by Omaha District Office

TENNESSEE
Nashville—Suite 1114, Parkway Towers,
404 James Robertson Parkway,
37219-1505, (615) 736-5161
*Memphis—555 Beale St., 38103,
(901) 521-4137

TEXAS
*Dallas—Rm. 7A5, 1100 Commerce St.,
75242, (214) 767-0542
*Austin—P.O. Box 12728, Capitol Station,
78711, (512) 472-5059
Houston—2625 Fed. Courthouse, 515
Rusk St., 77002, (713) 229-2578

UTAH
Salt Lake City—Rm. 340 U.S. Courthouse,
350 S. Main St., 84101, (801) 524-5116

VERMONT
Serviced by Boston District Office

VIRGINIA
Richmond—8010 Fed. Bldg., 400 North
8th St., 23240, (804) 771-2246

WASHINGTON
Seattle—3131 Elliott Ave., Suite 290,
98121, (206) 442-5616
*Spokane—P.O. Box 2170, 99210,
(509) 456-4557

WEST VIRGINIA
Charleston—3309 Fed. Bldg., 500 Quarrier
St., 25301, (304) 347-5123

WISCONSIN
Milwaukee—Fed. Bldg., U.S. Courthouse,
517 E. Wisc. Ave., 53202, (414) 291-3473

WYOMING
Serviced by Denver District Office

INTERNATIONAL TRADE DIRECTORS OF THE NATIONAL ASSOCIATION OF STATE DEVELOPMENT AGENCIES

ALABAMA
Fred F. Denton, Jr., Director
International Development
Alabama Development Office
135 S. Union Street
Montgomery, Alabama 36130
(205) 263-0048

ALASKA
Robert G. Poe, Director
Office of International Trade
Department of Commerce and Economic
Development
3601 C Street, Suite 798
Anchorage, Alaska 99503
(907) 561-5585

ARIZONA
Jim Ferguson, Director, International Trade
Department of Commerce
1700 West Washington Street
Phoenix, Arizona 85007
(602) 255-5371

ARKANSAS
Maria Haley, Director, International
Marketing
Department of Economic Development
One Capitol Mall
Little Rock, Arkansas 72201
(501) 682-7678

CALIFORNIA
Gregory Mignano, Executive Director
California State World Trade
Commission
1121 L Street, Suite 310
Sacramento, California 95814
(916) 324-5511
Janice McEntee, Washington
Representative
California State World Trade
Commission
444 North Capitol Street, N.W.
Suite 305
Washington, D.C. 20001
(202) 347-6894

Fargo Wells, Director
Export Finance Office
107 South Broadway, Room 8039
Los Angeles, California 90012
(213) 620-2433

COLORADO
Bea Celler, Interim Director, International
    Trade Office
Department of Commerce and
    Development
1625 Broadway
Suite 1710
Denver, Colorado 80202
(303) 892-3840

CONNECTICUT
Gary H. Miller, Director, Investment
    Attraction
International Business Development
Department of Economic Development
210 Washington Street
Hartford, Connecticut 06106
(203) 566-3842

DELAWARE
Larry Windley, Assistant to Director,
International Operations
Delaware Development Office
Division of Economic Development
99 Kings Highway
Box 1401
Dover, Delaware 19903
(302) 736-4271

Claire D. Wilson, International Trade
    Specialist
Delaware Development Office
World Trade Section
Carvel State Office Building
820 French Street
Wilmington, Delaware 19801
(302) 571-6262

FLORIDA
Tom Slattery, Bureau Chief
Florida Department of Commerce
107 West Gaines Street
Tallahassee, Florida 32301
(904) 487-1399
Hilda Thompson
Trade/Export Group
Florida Department of Commerce
107 West Gaines Street
Tallahassee, Florida 32301
(904) 487-1399

Gerald Wilson
Foreign Investment
Florida Department of Commerce
107 West Gaines Street

Tallahassee, Florida 32301
(904) 487-1399

GEORGIA
Kathleen Kleeman, Director, Division of
    Trade
Department of Industry and Trade
P.O. Box 1776
Atlanta, Georgia 30301
(404) 656-3538

HAWAII
Kenneth Kwak, Chief, International
    Services Branch
Department of Planning and Economic
    Development
P.O. Box 2359
Honolulu, Hawaii 96804
(808) 548-3048 or 4621

IDAHO
Jay Engstrom, Manager of Economic
    Development
Division of Economic and Community
    Affairs
State Capitol
Room 108
Boise, Idaho 83720
(208) 334-2470

ILLINOIS
Hendrik Woods, Manager, International
    Business Division
Illinois Department of Commerce and
    Community Affairs
100 West Randolph, Suite C-400
Chicago, Illinois 60601
(312) 917-7164

Robert H. Newtson, Director
Illinois Export Council
214 State House
Springfield, Illinois 62706
(217) 782-7884

INDIANA
Phillip M. Grebe, Director, International
    Trade Division
Department of Commerce
One North Capitol
Indianapolis, Indiana 46204-2248
(317) 232-8846

IOWA
Max L. Olsen, Marketing Manager,
    International Trade
Iowa Department of Economic
    Development
200 East Grand Avenue
Des Moines, Iowa 50309
(515) 281-3138

KANSAS
Jim Kadel, Director, International
    Marketing
Department of Commerce
400 Southwest 8th Street
Topeka, Kansas 66603
(913) 296-4027

Larry Childs, Director, Trade Services
Department of Commerce
400 Southwest 8th Street
Topeka, Kansas 66603
(913) 296-4027

KENTUCKY
William Savage, Executive Director
Office of International Marketing
Kentucky Commerce Cabinet
Capitol Plaza Tower
24th Floor
Frankfort, Kentucky 40601
(502) 564-2170

LOUISIANA
Stan Fulcher, International Marketing
    Specialist
Louisiana Office of International Trade,
    Finance, and Development
P.O. Box 94185
Baton Rouge, Louisiana 70804-9185
(504) 342-9232
(504) 342-5389 FAX

MAINE
Michael Naylor-Davis, President,
    International Trade
Maine World Trade Association
77 Sewall Street
Augusta, Maine 04330-6332
(207) 289-5700

MARYLAND
Harold R. Zassenhaus, Executive Director
Office of International Trade
World Trade Center
401 East Pratt Street
Suite 752
Baltimore, Maryland 21202
(301) 333-4295

MASSACHUSETTS
Mary Ellen Sutherland, Program Director
Office of International Trade
100 Cambridge Street
Room 902
Boston, Massachusetts 02202
(617) 367-1830

MICHIGAN
Greg Main, Director, Foreign Investment
U.S./International Division

Manufacturing Development Group
Michigan Department of Commerce
P.O. Box 30225
Lansing, Michigan 48909
(517) 373-6390

Randy Harmson, Executive Director
World Trade Services
P.O. Box 30017
Lansing, Michigan 48909
(517) 373-6390

MINNESOTA
Sandra Renner, Director, Export Services
Minnesota Trade Office
1000 MN World Trade Center
30 East 7th Street
St. Paul, Minnesota 55101-4902
(612) 297-4222

MISSISSIPPI
William A. McGinnis, Director, Marketing
    Division
Department of Economic
    Development
P.O. Box 849
Jackson, Mississippi 38205
(601) 359-3444

MISSOURI
Bob Black, Business Development Director
Economic Development Programs
P.O. Box 118
Jefferson City, Missouri 65102
(314) 751-4855

Angie Kenworthy, Senior Trade Specialist
Economic Development Programs
P.O. Box 118
Jefferson City, Missouri 65102
(314) 751-4999

MONTANA
John Maloney, International Trade Officer
Montana Department of Commerce
State Capitol
Helena, Montana 59620
(406) 444-3923

NEBRASKA
Susan Rouch
International Trade Promotion
Department of Economic
    Development
301 Centennial Mall South
P.O. Box 94666
Lincoln, Nebraska 68509
(402) 471-3111

NEVADA
Julie Wilcox, Director
International Program

Nevada Commission on Economic
   Development
Capital Complex
Carson City, Nevada 89710
(702) 885-4325

NEW HAMPSHIRE
William Hernan, Programs Information
   Officer
Department of Resources and Economic
   Development
105 Loudon Road, Building 2
Concord, New Hampshire 03301
(603) 271-2591

NEW JERSEY
Ming Hsu, Governor's Special Trade
Representative and Director
Division of International Trade
Department of Commerce and Economic
   Development
744 Broad Street, Room 1709
Newark, New Jersey 07102
(201) 648-3518

NEW MEXICO
David S. Henkel, Jr., Director
Economic Development Division
Economic Development and Tourism
   Department
1100 St. Francis Drive
Montoya Building
Santa Fe, New Mexico 87503
(505) 827-0272

NEW YORK
R. Barry Spaulding, Deputy
   Commissioner,
International Division
Department of Commerce
230 Park Avenue, Room 2240
New York, New York 10169
(212) 309-0502

NORTH CAROLINA
Gordon McRoberts, Director, International
   Marketing
International Division
Department of Commerce
430 North Salisbury Street
Raleigh, North Carolina 27611
(919) 733-7193

Steve Stevenson, Director, International
   Division
Department of Commerce
430 North Salisbury Street
Raleigh, North Carolina 27611
(919) 733-7193

NORTH DAKOTA
Jack Minton, International Trade
   Consultant
Economic Development Commission
Liberty Memorial Building
Bismarck, North Dakota 58505
(701) 224-2810

OHIO
Marnie Shaul, Deputy Director
International Trade Division
Department of Development
30 East Broad Street, 25th Floor
P.O. Box 1001
Columbus, Ohio 43266-0101
(614) 466-5017

OKLAHOMA
Bill Maus, Director
International Trade Division
Oklahoma Department of Commerce
6601 Broadway Extension
Oklahoma City, Oklahoma 73116-8214
(405) 521-3501

OREGON
Jim Raske, Director
International Trade Division
Oregon Economic Development
   Department
1500 SW First Avenue
Suite 620
Portland, Oregon 97201
(503) 229-5625
(1-800-452-7813)

PENNSYLVANIA
Alberta Norton, Director
International Projects
Bureau of International Commerce
489 Forum Building
Harrisburg, Pennsylvania 17120
(717) 787-7190

Anthony Amorosi, Acting Director
International Projects
Bureau of International Commerce
489 Forum Building
Harrisburg, Pennsylvania 17120
(717) 787-7190

Laila Cully, Director
Office of Economic Policy, Planning and
   Research
486 Forum Building
Harrisburg, Pennsylvania 17120
(717) 787-4088

RHODE ISLAND
Christine Smith, Business and Industry
   Representative

International Trade
Department of Economic Development
7 Jackson Walkway
Providence, Rhode Island 02903
(401) 277-2601

SOUTH CAROLINA
Dr. James A. Kuhlman, Associate Director
International Business Development
South Carolina State Development
    Board
P.O. Box 927
Columbia, South Carolina 29202
(803) 734-1400

SOUTH DAKOTA
John Huminski, Director
South Dakota International Trade Center
USD-School of Business
414 East Clark Street
Vermillion, South Dakota 57069-2390
(605) 677-5536

TENNESSEE
Thomas Turner, Director
Export Promotion Office
Department of Economic and Community
    Development
320 6th Avenue, North, 7th Floor
Nashville, Tennessee 37219
(615) 741-5870

TEXAS
Bill Luttrell, Director, International
    Business Development Department
Texas Department of Commerce
P.O. Box 12728
Austin, Texas 78711
(512) 472-5059

Rebecca Reynolds, Director, International
    Trade
Texas Department of Commerce
P.O. Box 12728
Austin, Texas 78711
(512) 472-5059

UTAH
Osamu Hoshimo, Director
International Business Development
Economic and Industrial Development
    Division
6150 State Office Building
Salt Lake City, Utah 84114
(801) 538-3036

VERMONT
Graeme Freeman, Director, International
    Business
Department of Economic Development

Pavilion Office Building
Montpelier, Vermont 05602
(802) 828-3221

VIRGINIA
Ron Renchard, Director of International
    Marketing
1000 Washington Building
Richmond, Virginia 23219
(804) 786-3791

WASHINGTON
Don Lorentz, Director
Domestic & International Trade Division
Department of Trade and Development
312 First Avenue, North
Seattle, Washington 98109
(206) 464-7143

Dan Cudaback, Director
Domestic & International Trade
    Investment
Department of Trade and Development
312 First Avenue, North
Seattle, Washington 98109
(206) 464-6282

WEST VIRGINIA
Steve Spence, Director and Trade
    Representative
Governor's Office of Community and
    Industrial Development
State Capitol, Room M-146
Charleston, West Virginia 25306
(304) 348-0400

WISCONSIN
Ralph H. Graner, Director
Bureau of International Development
Wis. Department of Development
123 W. Washington Ave.
Madison, Wisconsin 53703
(608) 266-1767

WYOMING
Peter Cunningham
State Planning Coordinator's Office
International Trade Division
Economic Development and Stabilization
    Board
Herschler Building
3rd Floor, East Wing
Cheyenne, Wyoming 82202
(307) 777-7285

---

* *Source:* This list provided through the
    courtesy of the National Association of
    State Development Agencies,
    Washington D.C.

DIRECTORS OF SMALL BUSINESS DEVELOPMENT CENTERS

STATES HAVING SBDCs

Alabama
Jeff D. Gibbs, Director
UNIVERSITY OF ALABAMA IN
   BIRMINGHAM
School of Business
1717-11th Avenue, South
Medical Towers Bldg.-Suite 419
Birmingham, AL 35294
(205) 934-7260

Alaska
Janet Nye, Director
SMALL BUSINESS DEVELOPMENT
   CENTER OF ALASKA
430 West 7th Avenue
Anchorage, AK 99501
(907) 274-7232

Arkansas
Paul McGinnis, Director
UNIVERSITY OF ARKANSAS AT
   LITTLE ROCK
Small Business Development
   Center
100 South Main
Suite 401
Little Rock, AR 72204
(501) 371-5381

Connecticut
John O'Connor, Director
UNIVERSITY OF CONNECTICUT
School of Business Administration
Box U-41D
Storrs, CT 06268
(203) 486-4135

Delaware
Helene Butler, Director
UNIVERSITY OF DELAWARE
005 Purnell Hall
Newark, DE 19711
(302) 451-2747

District of Columbia
Nancy Flake, Director
HOWARD UNIVERSITY
Small Business Development Center
P.O. Box 748
Washington, DC 20059
(202) 636-5150

Florida*
Gregory L. Higgins, Jr. Directors
State Coordinator's Office
Florida Small Business Development Center
THE UNIVERSITY OF WEST FLORIDA
Building 38
Pensacola, FL 32514-5752
(904) 474-3016

Georgia*
Frank Hoy, Director
UNIVERSITY OF GEORGIA
Small Business Development Center
Chicopee Complex
Athens, GA 30602
(404) 542-5760

Idaho
Ronald R. Hall
BOISE STATE UNIVERSITY
College of Business
1910 University Drive
Boise, ID 83725
(208) 385-1640

Illinois
Jeff Mitchell, Administrator
Small Business Development Center
DEPARTMENT OF COMMERCE AND
   COMMUNITY AFFAIRS
620 East Adams Street, 5th Floor
Springfield, IL 62701
(217) 785-6174

Indiana
Stephen G. Thrash, Director
One North Capitol, Suite 200
Indianapolis, Indiana 46204-2248
(317) 634-1690

Iowa
Ronald A. Manning, Director
IOWA SMALL BUSINESS
   DEVELOPMENT CENTER
Chamberlynn Building
137 Lynn Avenue
Ames, IA 50010
(515) 292-6351

Kansas
Susan K. Osborne-Howes, Director
WICHITA STATE UNIVERSITY
College of Business Administration
1845 Fairmount
Wichita, KS 67208
(316) 689-3193

Kentucky
James (Jerry) G. Owen, Director
UNIVERSITY OF KENTUCKY
18 Porter Building
Lexington, KY 40506-0205
(606) 257-1751

Louisiana
John Baker, Director
NORTHEAST LOUISIANA UNIVERSITY
College of Business Administration
Administration Bldg. 2-57
Monroe, LA 71209-6345
(318) 342-2464

Maine*
Bob Heard, Director
UNIVERSITY OF SOUTHERN MAINE
246 Deering Avenue
Portland, ME 04102
(207) 780-4420

Massachusetts*
John Ciccarelli, Director
UNIVERSITY OF MASSACHUSETTS
School of Business Management
Room 205
Amherst, MA 01003
(413) 549-4930 Ext. 310

Michigan*
Norman J. Schlafmann, Director
WAYNE STATE UNIVERSITY
2727 Second Avenue-MCHT
Detroit, MI 48201
(313) 577-4848

Minnesota
Jerry Cartwright, Director
Minnesota SBDC
1107 Hazeltine Blvd., Suite 452
Chaska, MN 55318
(612) 448-8810

Mississippi
Robert D. Smith, Director
MISSISSIPPI SBDC
3825 Ridgewood Road
Jackson, MS 39211
(601) 982-6760

Missouri*
Fred O. Hale, Director
ST. LOUIS UNIVERSITY
3642 Lindell Blvd.
St. Louis, MO 63108
(314) 534-7204

Nebraska
Robert Bernier, Director
Nebraska Business Development Center
UNIVERSITY OF NEBRASKA AT OMAHA
Omaha, NB 68182
(402) 554-2521

Nevada
Samuel Males, Director
Nevada Small Business Development Center
College of Business Administration
UNIVERSITY OF NEVADA RENO
Reno, NV 89557-0010
(702) 784-1717

New Hampshire
James E. Bean, Director
New Hampshire Small Business
    Development Center
University Center, Room 311
400 Commercial Street

Manchester, NH 03101
(603) 625-4522

New Jersey
Janet Holloway, Director
RUTGERS UNIVERSITY
Ackerson Hall, Third Floor
180 University Street
Newark, NJ 07102
(201) 648-5950

New York
James L. King, Director
NYS/SBDC
State University of New York
Suny Plaza, Room S-523
Albany, NY 12246
(518) 443-5398

North Carolina*
Scott R. Daugherty, Director
SMALL BUSINESS AND
    TECHNOLOGY DEVELOPMENT
    CENTER
820 Clay Street
Raleigh, NC 27605
(919) 733-4643

North Dakota
Terry Stallman
NORTH DAKOTA SMALL BUSINESS
    DEVELOPMENT CENTER
North Dakota Economic Development
    Commission
Liberty Memorial Building
Bismarck, ND 58505
(701) 224-2810

Ohio
Jack Brown, Director
OHIO SMALL BUSINESS
    DEVELOPMENT CENTER
P.O. Box 1001
Columbus, OH 43266-0101
(614) 466-5111

Oklahoma
Lloyd B. Miller, Director
SOUTHEASTERN OKLAHOMA STATE
    UNIVERSITY
517 West University
Durant, OK 74701
(405) 924-0277

Oregon
Edward (Sandy) Cutler, Director
LANE COMMUNITY COLLEGE
Oregon Small Business Development
    Center Network
1059 Willamette Street
Eugene, OR 97401
(503) 726-2250

Pennsylvania
Susan M. Garber, Director
UNIVERSITY OF PENNSYLVANIA
The Wharton School
3201 Steinberg Hall-Dietrich Hall/6374
Philadelphia, PA 19104
(215) 898-1219

Puerto Rico
Jose M. Romaguera
UNIVERSITY OF PUERTO RICO
P.O. Box 5253
College Station
Mayaguez, PR 00709
(809) 834-3590 or 834-3790

Rhode Island*
Doug Jobling, Director
BRYANT COLLEGE
Smithfield, RI 02917
(401) 232-6111

South Carolina
W. F. Littlejohn, Director
UNIVERSITY OF SOUTH CAROLINA
College of Business Administration
Columbia, SC 29208
(803) 777-4907

South Dakota
Donald Greenfield, Director
UNIVERSITY OF SOUTH DAKOTA
School of Business
414 East Clark Street
Vermillion, SD 57069
(605) 677-5272

Tennessee
Leonard Rosser, Director
MEMPHIS STATE UNIVERSITY
Tennessee Small Business Development
   Center
Memphis, TN 38152
(901) 454-2500

Texas-Dallas***
Norbert Dettmann, Director
Small Business Development Center
DALLAS COUNTY COMMUNITY
   COLLEGE
Business & Professional Institute
302 N. Market Street, Suite 300
Dallas, TX 75202-1806
(214) 747-0555

Texas-Houston
Jon P. Goodman, Director
UNIVERSITY OF HOUSTON
Gulf Coast SBDC
401 Louisiana, 8th Floor
Houston, TX 77002
(713) 223-1141

Texas-Lubbock***
J.E. (Ted) Cadou
Small Business Development Center
TEXAS TECH UNIVERSITY
2005 Broadway
Lubbock, TX 79417
(806) 744-5343

Texas-San Antonio***
Rudolfo Ramirez
UNIVERSITY OF TEXAS AT
   SAN ANTONIO
San Antonio Small Business
   Development Center
San Antonio, TX 78285
(512) 224-0791

Utah
Kumen Davis, Director
Utah Small Business Development Center
660 South 200 East, Suite 418
Salt Lake City, UT 84111
(801) 581-4869

Vermont
Norris Elliott, Director
UNIVERSITY OF VERMONT
Extension Service-Morrill Hall
Burlington, VT 05405
(802) 656-4479

Virgin Islands
Solomon S. Kabuka, Jr., Director
UNIVERSITY OF THE VIRGIN ISLANDS
Grand Hotel Building, Annex B
P.O. Box 1087
St. Thomas, VI 00801
(809) 776-3206

Washington
Lyle Anderson, Director
WASHINGTON STATE UNIVERSITY
College of Business and Economics
Pullman, WA 99164-4740
(509) 335-1576

West Virginia
Eloise Jack, Director
SMALL BUSINESS DEVELOPMENT
   CENTER DIVISION
GOCID, State Capital Complex
Charleston, WV 25305
1-800-225-5982

Wisconsin
Peggy Wireman, Director
UNIVERSITY OF WISCONSIN
602 State Street, 2nd Floor
Madison, WI 53703
(608) 263-7794

Wyoming
Mac Bryant, Director
WYOMING SMALL BUSINESS
    DEVELOPMENT CENTER
130 North Ash, Suite A
Casper, WY 82601
(307) 235-4825

---

*ASBDC Executive Committee
***Not a Member of ASBDC

Neece, Cator & Associates
Tom Cator
Allen Neece
Shawn Browning
1050 17th Street, NW, Suite 810
Washington, DC 20036
(202) 887-5599-Telephone
(202) 223-8608-Telefax

SMALL BUSINESS ADMINISTRATION FIELD OFFICES

Alabama
2121 8th. Ave. N. Suite 200 Birmingham,
    AL 35203-2398 (205)731-1344

Alaska
8th. & C Streets Room 1068 Anchorage,
    AK 99501 (907)271-4022

Arizona
2005 N. Central Ave. 5th. Floor Phoenix,
    AZ 85004 (602)261-3732
300 W. Congress St. Box FB-33 Tucson,
    AZ 85701 (602)629-6715

Arkansas
320 W. Capitol Ave. Room 601 Little Rock,
    AR 72201 (501)378-5971

California
1825 Bell Street Suite 208 Sacramento,
    CA 95825 (916)978-4578
901 W. Civic Ctr. Dr. Room 160 Santa Ana,
    CA 92703 (714)836-2494
660 J Street Room 215 Sacramento,
    CA 95814 (916)551-1445
211 Main Street 4th. Floor San Francisco,
    CA 94105-1988 (415)974-0642
880 Front Street Room 4-S-29 San Diego,
    CA 92188 (619)557-5440
350 S. Figueroa St. 6th. Floor Los Angeles,
    CA 90071 (213)894-2956
2202 Monterey St. Suite 108 Fresno,
    CA 93721 (209)487-5189
450 Golden Gate Avenue San Francisco,
    CA 94102 (415)556-7487

Colorado
999 18th. Street Suite 701 Denver,
    CO 80202 (303)294-7001
721 19th. St. Room 407 Denver,
    CO 80202-2599 (303)844-2607

Connecticut
330 Main Street 2nd. Floor Hartford,
    CT 06106 (203)240-4700

Delaware
844 King St. Room 5207 Wilmington,
    DE 19801 (302)573-6294

District of Columbia
1111 18th. St. Room 3015 Washington,
    DC 20036 (202)634-4950

Florida
700 Twiggs Street Room 607 Tampa,
    FL 33602 (813)228-2594
5601 Corporate Way S. Suite 402 W. Palm
    Beach, FL 33407 (305)689-3922
1320 S. Dixie Highway Suite 501 Coral
    Gables, FL 33146 (305)536-5521
400 W. Bay St. Room 261 Jacksonville,
    FL 32202 (904)791-3782

Georgia
120 Ralph McGill St. 14th. Floor Atlanta,
    GA 30308 (404)347-3771
1720 Peachtree Rd, NW 6th. Floor Atlanta,
    GA 30309 (404)347-2441
52 N. Main Street Room 225 Statesboro,
    GA 30367-8102 (912)489-8719
1375 Peachtree St., NE 5th. Floor Atlanta,
    GA 30367-8102 (404)347-2797

Guam
Pacific Daily News Bdg. Room 508 Agana,
    GM 96910 (671)472-7277

Hawaii
300 Ala Moana Room 2213 Honolulu,
    HI 96850 (808)541-2990

Idaho
1020 Main Street Suite 290 Boise,
    ID 83702 (208)334-1696

Illinois
230 S. Dearborn Street Room 510 Chicago,
    IL 60604-1593 (312)353-0359
219 S. Dearborn Street Room 437 Chicago,
    IL 60604-1593 (312)353-4528

511 W. Capitol Street Suite 302
Springfield, IL 62704 (217)492-4416

Indiana
575 N. Pennsylvania St. Room 578
Indianapolis, IN 46204-1584
(317)269-7272

Iowa
373 Collins Road NE Room 100 Cedar
Rapids, IA 52402-3118 (319)399-2571
210 Walnut Street Room 749 Des Moines,
IA 50309 (515)284-4422

Kansas
110 E. Waterman St. 1st. Floor Wichita,
KS 67202 (316)269-6571

Kentucky
600 Federal Place Room 188 Louisville,
KY 40202 (502)582-5976

Louisiana
500 Fannin St. Room 8A-08 Shreveport,
LA 71101 (318)226-5196
1661 Canal St. Suite 2000 New Orleans,
LA 70112 (504)589-6685

Maine
40 Western Ave. Room 512 Augusta,
ME 04330 (207)622-8378

Maryland
10 N. Calvert St. 3rd. Floor Baltimore,
MD 21202 (301)962-4392

Massachusetts
60 Batterymarch Street 10th. Floor Boston,
MA 02110 (617)451-2030
10 Causeway Street Room 265 Boston,
MA 02114 (617)565-5590
1550 Main Street Room 212 Springfield,
MA 01103 (413)785-0268

Michigan
477 Michigan Ave. Room 515 Detroit,
MI 48226 (313)226-6075
300 S. Front St. Marquette, MI 49885
(906)225-1108

Minnesota
100 N. 6th. Street Ste 610 Minneapolis,
MN 55403-1563 (612)370-2324

Mississippi
100 W. Capitol Street Suite 322 Jackson,
MS 39269-0936 (601)965-4378
One Hancock Plaza Suite 1001 Gulfport,
MS 39501-7758 (601)863-4449

Missouri
911 Walnut Street 13th. Floor Kansas City,
MO 64106 (816)426-2989

1103 Grand Avenue 6th. Floor Kansas City,
MO 64106 (816)374-3419
815 Olive Street Room 242 St. Louis,
MO 63101 (314)539-6600
620 S. Glenstone St. Suite 110 Springfield,
MO 65802-3200 (417)864-7670

Montana
301 S. Park Room 528 Helena, MT 59626
(406)449-5381

Nebraska
11145 Mill Valley Rd. Omaha, NB 68154
(402)221-4691

Nevada
50 S. Virginia St. Room 238 Reno,
NV 89505 (702)784-5268
301 East Stewart St. Room 301 Las Vegas,
NV 89125 (702)388-6611

New Hampshire
55 Pleasant St. Room 210 Concord,
NH 03301-1257 (603)225-1400

New Jersey
2600 Mt. Ephrain Ave. Camden, NJ 08104
(609)757-5183
60 Park Place 4th. Floor Newark, NJ 07102
(201)645-2434
15-01 Broadway 1st. Floor Fairlawn,
NJ 07410 (201)794-8195

New Mexico
5000 Marble Ave., NE Room 320
Albuquerque, NM 87100 (505)262-6171

New York
26 Federal Plaza Room 31-08 New York,
NY 10278 (212)264-7772
445 Broadway Room 261 Albany,
NY 12207 (518)472-6300
100 State Street Room 601 Rochester,
NY 14614 (716)263-6700
26 Federal Plaza Room 3100 New York,
NY 10278 (212)264-4355
100 S. Clinton St. Room 1071 Syracuse,
NY 13260 (315)423-5383
111 W. Huron Street Room 1311 Buffalo,
NY 14202 (716)846-4301
333 E. Water Street 4th. Floor Elmira,
NY 14901 (607)734-8130
35 Pinelawn Rd. Room 102E Melville,
NY 11747 (516)454-0750

North Carolina
222 S. Church St. Room 300 Charlotte,
NC 28202 (704)371-6563

North Dakota
657 2nd. Ave. N. Room 218 Fargo,
ND 58108-3086 (701)239-5131

Ohio
550 Main Street Room 5028 Cincinnati,
  OH 45202 (513)684-2814
85 Marconi Blvd. Room 512 Columbus,
  OH 43215 (614)469-6860
1240 E. 9th. Street Room 317 Cleveland,
  OH 44199 (216)522-4180

Oklahoma
200 N.W. 5th. Street Suite 670 Oklahoma
  City, OK 73102 (405)231-4301

Oregon
1220 S. W. Third Ave. Room 676 Portland,
  OR 97204-2882 (503)221-2682

Pennsylvania
20 N. Pennsylvania Ave. Room 2327
  Wilkes-Barre, PA 18701 (717)826-6497
100 Chestnut St. Suite 309 Harrisburg,
  PA 17101 (717)782-3840
960 Penn Ave. 5th. Floor Pittsburgh,
  PA 15222 (412)644-2780
475 Allendale Rd. Suite 201 King Prussia,
  PA 19406 (215)962-3846

Puerto Rico
Carlos Chardon Ave. Room 691 Hato Rey,
  PR 00918 (809)753-4002

Rhode Island
380 Westminster Mall 5th. Floor
  Providence, RI 02903 (401)528-4856

South Carolina
1835 Assembly Street Room 358 Columbia,
  SC 29202 (803)765-5376

South Dakota
101 S. Main Ave. Suite 101 Sioux Falls, SD
  57102-0527 (605)336-2980

Tennessee
404 James Robertson Pkwy. Ste. 1012
  Nashville, TN 37219 (615)736-5881

Texas
8625 King George Dr. Bldg. C Dallas,
  TX 75235-3391 (214)767-7643
800 E. 8th. Street Room 520 Austin,
  TX 78701 (512)482-5288
505 E. Travis Room 103 Marshall,
  TX 75670 (214)935-5257
1100 Commerce Street Room 3C-36
  Dallas, TX 75242 (214)767-0605
10737 Gateway W. Suite 320 El Paso,
  TX 79902 (915)541-7586
222 E. Van Buren St. Room 500 Harlingen,
  TX 78550 (512)427-8533
2525 Murworth Suite 112 Houston, TX
  77054 (713)660-4401

1611 Tenth Street Suite 200 Lubbock, TX
  79401 (806)743-7462
7400 Blanco Road Suite 200 San Antonio,
  TX 78216 (512)229-4535
400 Mann Street Suite 403 Corpus Christi,
  TX 78401 (512)888-3331
819 Taylor Street Room 10A27 Ft. Worth,
  TX 76102 (817)334-3613
2306 Oak Lane Suite 110 Grand Prairie,
  TX 75051 (214)767-7571

Utah
125 S. State Street Room 2237 Salt Lake
  City, UT 84138-1195 (801)524-5800

Vermont
87 State Street Room 205 Montpelier,
  VT 05602 (802)828-4474

Virginia
400 N. 8th. Street Room 3015 Richmond,
  VA 23240 (804)771-2617

Virgin Islands
4C & 4D Este Sion Frm Room 7 St. Croix,
  VI 00820 (809)778-5380
Veterans Drive Room 283 St. Thomas,
  VI 00801 (809)774-8530

Washington
2615 4th. Avenue Room 440 Seattle, WA
  98121 (206)442-5676
915 Second Avenue Room 1792 Seattle,
  WA 98174-1088 (206)442-5534
W. 920 Riverside Ave. Room 651 Spokane,
  WA 99210 (509)456-3783

West Virginia
168 W. Main Street 5th. Floor Clarksburg,
  WV 26301 (304)623-5631
550 Eagan Street, NW 6th. Floor
  Charleston, WV 25301 (304)347-5220

Wisconsin
500 S. Barstow Common Room 37 Eau
  Claire, WI 54701 (715)834-9012
212 E. Washington Ave. Room 213
  Madison, WI 53703 (608)264-5261
310 W. Wisconsin Ave. Suite 400
  Milwaukee, WI 53203 (414)291-3941

Wyoming
100 East B. Street Room 4001 Casper, WY
  82602-2839 (307)261-5761

COUNTRY DESK OFFICERS*

Country	Desk Officer	Phone	Room
Afghanistan	Stan Bilinski	377-2954	2029B
Albania	Naomi Norden	377-2645	3414
Algeria	Jeffrey Johnson	377-4652	2039
Angola	John Crown	377-0357	3317
Argentina	Mark Siegelman	377-1548	3021
ASEAN	Linda Droker	377-3875	2032
Australia	Gary Bouck/		
	Barbara Korthals-Altes	377-3647	2308
Austria	Philip Combs	377-2920	3415
Bahamas	Americo Tadeu	377-2527	3314
Bahrain	Claude Clement	377-5545	2039
Bangladesh	Stan Bilinski	377-2954	2029B
Barbados	Tom Klotzbach	377-2527	3314
Belgium	Boyce Fitzpatrick	377-5401	3415
Belize	Kirsten Baumgart	377-2527	3314
Benin	Reginald Biddle	377-4388	3317
Bermuda	Randy Mye	377-2527	3314
Bhutan	Stan Bilinski	377-2954	2029B
Bolivia	Laurie McNamara	377-2521	3029
Botswana	Tim Gilman	377-5148	3317
Brazil	Roger Turner/		
	Larry Farris/		
	Robert Bateman	377-3871	3017
Brunei	Joan Sitnik	377-3875	2308
Bulgaria	Naomi Norden	377-2645	3414
Burkina Faso	Reginald Biddle	377-4564	3317
Burma	Kyaw Win	377-5334	3820
Burundi	John Crown	377-0357	3317
Cambodia	Craig Allen	377-2462	2317
Cameroon	Ian Davis	377-0357	3033
Canada	Kenneth Fernandez/		
	Stephen Jacobs/		
	William Cavitt	377-3101	3033
Cape Verde	Philip Michelini	377-4388	3317
Caymans	Randy Mye	377-2527	3314
Central African Rep.	Ian Davis	377-0357	3317
Chad	Ian Davis	377-0357	3317
Chile	Brian Hannon	377-1495	3021
Colombia	Herbert Lindow	377-4303	3029
Comoros	James Robb	377-4564	3317
Congo	Ian Davis	377-0357	3317
Costa Rica	Brigit Helms	377-2527	3314
Cuba	Ted Johnson	377-2527	3314

*As in most government offices, people change jobs frequently. This list includes the current names of Country Desk Officers at the time of publication, but if you are told that the person on this list is no longer working at the Department of Commerce, make sure that you request to speak to the specific country desk officer.

The area code for telephoning desk officers is 202. Letters should be addressed to the individual at his or her room number, U.S. Department of Commerce, Washington, DC 20230.

Country	Desk Officer	Phone	Room
Cyprus	Ann Corro	377-3945	3044
Czechoslovakia	Kate Scanlan	377-2645	3414
Denmark	Maryanne Lyons	377-3254	3413
D'Jibouti	James Robb	377-4564	3317
Dominica	Tom Klotzbach	377-2527	3314
Dominican Republic	Kirstin Baumgart	377-2527	3314
East Caribbean	Tom Koltzbach	377-2527	3314
Ecuador	Herbert Lindow	377-4303	3029
Egypt	Jeffrey Johnson	377-4652	2039
El Salvador	Brigit Helms	377-2527	3314
Equatorial Guinea	John Crown	377-0357	3317
Ethiopia	James Robb	377-4564	3317
European Community	Charles Ludolph	377-5276	3036
Finland	Maryanne Lyons	377-3254	3413
France	Maria Aronson/		
	Kelly Jacobs	377-8008	3042
French Guiana	Americo Tadeu	377-2527	3314
Gabon	Ian Davis	377-0357	3317
Gambia	Philip Michelini	377-4388	3317
Germany (East)	Naomi Norden	377-2645	3414
Germany (West)	Velizar Stanoyevitch/		
	Greg O'Connor	377-2434	3411
Ghana	Reginald Biddle	377-4388	3317
Greece	Ann Corro	377-3945	3044
Grenada	Tom Klotzbach	377-2527	3314
Guadeloupe	Americo Tadeu	377-2527	3314
Guatemala	Americo Tadeu	377-2527	3314
Guinea	Philip Michelini	377-4388	3317
Guinea-Bissau	Philip Michelini	377-4388	3317
Guyana	Tom Klotzbach	377-2527	3314
Haiti	Americo Tadeu	377-2527	3314
Honduras	Brigit Helms	377-2527	3314
Hong Kong	JeNelle Matheson	377-2462	2317
Hungary	Karen Ware	377-2645	3414
Iceland	Maryanne Lyons	377-3254	3413
India	Richard Harding/		
	Polly Holcombe/		
	Cheryl McQueen	377-2954	2029B
Indonesia	Don Ryan/Linda Droker	377-3875	2032
Iran	Claude Clement	377-5545	2039
Iraq	Thomas Sams	377-5767	2039
Ireland	Brenda Fisher	377-4104	3045
Israel	Cherie Loustaunau/		
	Shelley Galbraith/		
	Doris Nelmes	377-4652	2039
Italy	Brenda Fisher	377-2177	3045
Ivory Coast	Philip Michelini	377-4388	3317
Jamaica	Kirsten Baumgart	377-2527	3314
Japan	Phil Agress/		
	Mike Benefiel/		
	Bob Francis	377-4527	2318

Country	Desk Officer	Phone	Room
Jordan	Thomas Sams	377-5767	2039
Kampuchea	Craig Allen	377-2462	2317
Kenya	Elizabeth Brown	377-4564	3317
Korea (North)	Liliana Monk	377-3583	2323
Korea (South)	Karen Chopra/		
	Scott Goddin	377-4958	2034
Kuwait	Thomas Sams	377-5767	2039
Laos	JeNelle Matheson	377-2462	2317
Lebanon	Thomas Sams	377-5757	2039
Lesotho	Tim Gilman	377-5148	3317
Liberia	Philip Michelini	377-4388	3317
Libya	Simon Bensimon	377-5737	2039
Luxembourg	Boyce Fitzpatrick	377-5401	3415
Macao	JeNelle Matheson	377-2462	2317
Madagascar	John Crown	377-0357	3317
Malawi	Fred Stokelin	377-5148	3317
Malaysia	Joan Walsh	377-3875	2308
Maldives	Stan Bilinski	377-2954	2029B
Mali	Reginald Biddle	377-4564	3317
Malta	Robert McLaughlin	377-3748	3049
Martinique	Americo Tadeu	377-2527	3314
Mauritania	Reginald Biddle	377-4564	3317
Mauritius	John Crown	377-0357	3317
Mexico	Jim Holbein	377-4464	3028
Mongolia	Liliana Monk	377-3583	2323
Morocco	Simon Bensimon	377-5737	2039
Mozambique	Tim Gilman	377-5148	3317
Namibia	Emily Solomon	377-5148	3317
Nepal	Stan Bilinski	377-2954	2029B
Netherlands	Boyce Fitzpatrick	377-5401	3415
Netherlands Antilles	Randy Mye	377-2527	3314
New Zealand	Gary Bouck/		
	Barbara Korthals-Altes	377-3647	2308
Nicaragua	Ted Johnson	377-2527	3314
Niger	Reginald Biddle	377-4564	3317
Nigeria	Reginald Biddle	377-4388	3317
Norway	James Devlin	377-4414	3413
Oman	Claude Clement	366-5545	2039
Pacific Islands	Gary Bouck	377-3647	2310
Pakistan	Cheryl McQueen	377-2954	2029B
Panama	Brigit Helms	377-2527	3314
Paraguay	Mark Siegelman	377-1548	3021
Peoples' Rep. of China	Jeffrey Lee	377-3583	2317
Peru	Laurie MacNamara	377-2521	3029
Phillippines	George Paine	377-3875	2308
Poland	Kate Scanlan	377-2645	3414
Portugal	Ann Corro	377-3945	3044
Puerto Rico	Ted Johnson	377-2527	3314
Qatar	Claude Clement	377-5545	2039
Romania	William Winter	377-2645	3414
Rwanda	John Crown	377-0357	3317

Country	Desk Officer	Phone	Room
Sao Tome & Principe	John Crown	377-0357	3317
Saudia Arabia	Cynthia Anthony	377-4652	2039
Senegal	Philip Michelini	377-4388	3317
Seychelles	James Robb	377-4564	3317
Sierra Leone	Philip Michelini	377-4388	3317
Singapore	Joan Walsh	377-3875	2032
Somalia	James Robb	377-4564	3317
South Africa	Davis Coale/		
	Emily Solomon	377-5148	3317
Spain	Richard Humbert	377-4508	3042
Sri Lanka	Stan Bilinski	377-2954	2029B
St. Bartholemey	Americo Tadeu	377-2527	3314
St. Kitts-Nevis	Tom Klotzbach	377-2527	3314
St. Lucia	Tom Klotzbach	377-2527	3314
St. Maarten	Americo Tadeu	377-2527	3314
St. Vincent-Grenadines	Tom Klotzbach	377-2527	3314
Sudan	James Robb	377-4564	3317
Suriname	Tom Klotzbach	377-2527	3314
Swaziland	Tim Gilman	377-5148	3317
Sweden	James Devlin	377-4414	3413
Switzerland	Philip Combs	377-2920	3415
Syria	Thomas Sams	377-5767	2039
Taiwan	Dan Duvall/Jeff Hardee	377-4957	2034
Tanzania	James Robb	377-4564	3317
Thailand	Donald Ryan/		
	Linda Droker	377-3875	2032
Togo	Reginald Biddle	377-4388	3317
Trinidad & Tobago	Randy Mye	377-2527	3314
Tunisia	Simon Bensimon	377-4652	2039
Turkey	Geoffrey Jackson	377-3945	3042
Turks & Caicos Islands	Americo Tadeu	377-2527	3314
Uganda	James Robb	377-4564	3317
United Arab Emirates	Claude Clement	377-5545	2039
United Kingdom	Robert McLaughlin	377-3748	3048
Uruguay	Brian Hannon	377-1495	3021
USSR	Valentine Zabitjaka/		
	Susan Lewenz	377-4655	3414
Venezuela	Marie Haugen	377-1659	3025
Vietnam	Craig Allen	377-2462	2317
Virgin Islands (UK)	Tom Klotzbach	377-2527	3314
Virgin Islands (US)	Ted Johnson	377-2527	3314
Yeman (North)	Cynthia Anthony	377-4652	2039
Yemen (South)	Cynthia Anthony	377-4562	2039
Yugoslavia	Jeremy Keller	377-5373	3046
Zaire	Ian Davis	377-0357	3317
Zambia	Emily Solomon	377-5148	3317
Zimbabwe	Emily Solomon	377-5148	3317

WORLD TRADE CENTERS ASSOCIATION
MEMBERSHIP CITIES

WTCA HEADQUARTERS

WTCA Headquarters, located at The World Trade Center in New York, coordinates the administrative and financial activities of the WTCA. It also produces WTCA News, membership directories and other publications and disseminates a a variety of materials and information to current and prospective WTCA Members. Contacts include:

Guy F. Tozzoli, President
World Trade Centers Association
One World Trade Center, Suite 7701
New York, NY 10048
Telephone: (212)313-4600
Fax: (212)488-0064
Telex: 285472 WTNY UR
WTC NETWORK: WTCA

Christine A. Secola
WTCA Administrator
World Trade Centers Association
One World Trade Center, Suite 7701
New York, NY 10048
Telephone: (212)313-4610
Fax: (212)488-0064
Telex: 285472 WTNY UR
WTC NETWORK: CHRIS

Thomas J. Kearney
Secretary General
World Trade Centers Association
One World Trade Center,
Suite 63 North
New York, NY 10048
Telephone: (212)466-8278
Fax: (212)488-0064
Telex: 285472 WTNY UR
WTC NETWORK: TKEAR

Nona Haimer
Assistant to the President
Editor, WTCA News
World Trade Centers Association
One World Trade Center, Suite 63 North
New York, NY 10048
Telephone: (212)466-8287
Fax212)488-0064
Telex: 285472 WTNY UR
WTC NETWORK: NONA

CITIES WORLDWIDE WITH MEMBERSHIP OFFICES

Aarhus, Denmark
Abidjan, Ivory Coast
Albany, New York
Amsterdam, The Netherlands
Anchorage, Alaska
Antwerp, Belgium
Archamps, Switzerland
Atlanta, Georgia
Bahrain, Arabian Gulf
Baltimore, Maryland
Bangkok, Thailand
Barcelona, Spain
Basel, Switzerland
Beijing, PRC
Bogota, Colombia, S.A.
Bombay, India
Boston, Massachusetts
Brisbane, Queensland
Brugge, Belgium
Brussels, Belgium

Budapest, Hungary
Buenos Aires, Argentina, S.A.
Cairo, Egypt
Calgary, B.C. Canada
Cape Verde, Republic of Cape Verde
Cardiff, Wales, U.K.
Cedar Rapids, Iowa
Charlotte, North Carolina
Chengdu, Sichuan, PRC
Chicago, Illinois
Chongqing, Sichuan Province, PRC
Cincinnati, Ohio
Cologne, Federal Republic of Germany
Colorado Springs, Colorado
Columbus, Ohio
Curacao, Caribbean
Cyprus, Nicosia, Cyprus
Denver, Colorado
Des Moines, Iowa
Detroit, Michigan

Dubai, United Arab Emirates
Dusseldorf, Switzerland
Edmonton, Canada
Eindhoven, The Netherlands
Fort de France, French West Indies
Fort Lauderdale, Florida
Frankfurt, Switzerland
Geneva, Switzerland
Genoa, Italy
Ghent, Belgium
Glasgow, United Kingdom
Gothenburg, Sweden
Greensboro, North Carolina
Guangzhou, PRC
Halifax, Nova Scotia, Canada
Hamburg, Federal Republic of Germany
Hangzhou, PRC
Hartford, Connecticut
Havana City, Cuba
Hefei, PRC
Hong Kong, Causeway Bay, Hong Kong
Honolulu, Hawaii
Houston, Texas
Istanbul, Turkey
Jacksonville, Florida
Jakarta, Indonesia
Jamaica, West Indies
Jeddah, Kingdom of Saudi Arabia
Johannesburg, Republic of South Africa
Kansas City, Missouri
Karachi, Pakistan
Kuala Lumpur, Malaysia
Lagos, Nigeria
Las Vegas, Nevada
Le Havre, France
Leiden, The Netherlands
Lexington, Kentucky
Lille, France
Lima, Peru
Lisbon, Portugal
Ljubljana, Yugoslavia
London, United Kingdom
Long Beach, California
Luxembourg,
Lyon, France
Macau,
Madrid, Spain
Maimo, Sweden
Manchester, United Kingdom
Manila, Philippines
Marseille, France
Melbourne, Australia
Mexico City, Mexico
Miami, Florida
Milan, Italy
Milwaukee, Wisconsin
Mmabatho, Republic of South Africa
Montreal, Canada
Moscow, USSR

Munich, Switzerland
Nairobi, Kenya
Nanjing, PRC
Nantes, France
New Delhi, India
New Orleans, Louisiana
New York, New York
Norfolk, Virginia
Orlando, Florida
Ottawa, Canada
Oxnard, California
Panama, Republic of Panama
Paris, France
Philadelphia, Pennsylvania
Pointe-a-Pitre, Guadeloupe
Pomona, California
Ponce, Puerto Rico
Portland, Oregon
Porto, Portugal
Port Said, Egypt
Rio de Janeiro, Brazil
Rotterdam, The Netherlands
Ruhr Valley, West Germany
San Antonio, Texas
San Francisco, California
San Juan, Puerto Rico
Santa Ana, California
Sao Paulo, Brazil
Seattle, Washington
Seoul, Korea
Shanghai, PRC
Shenzhen, PRC
Singapore, Republic of Singapore
Sofia, Bulgaria
St. Louis, Missouri
St. Paul, Minnesota
Stockholm, Sweden
Strasbourg, France
Sydney, Australia
Tacoma, Washington
Taipei, Taiwan
Tampa, Florida
Tel-Aviv, Israel
Tokyo, Japan
Toledo, Ohio
Toronto, Canada
Trinidad and Tobago, Port of Spain,
   Trinidad
Tunis, Tunisia
Valencia, Spain
Vancouver, B.C. Canada
Vienna, Austria
Washington, D.C.
Wichita, Kansas
Wilmington, Delaware
Wilmington, North Carolina
Winnipeg, Canada
Xiamen, PRC
Xi'an, PRC

Glossary of Selected Common International Terms

Acceptance—This term has several related meanings: (1) A time draft (or bill of exchange) which the drawee (the Payer) has accepted and is unconditionally obligated to pay at maturity. The draft must be presented first for acceptance—the drawee becomes the "acceptor"—then for payment. The word "accepted" and the date and place of payment must be written on the face of the draft. (2) The drawee's act in receiving a draft and thus entering into the obligation to pay its value at maturity. (3) (Broadly speaking) Any agreement to purchase goods under specified terms.

Ad Valorem (According to Value)—One of the generic methods used to establish actual duty charges on shipments, using monetary valuation as a basis for calculation rather than non-monetary standards (e.g., fixed amount per unit, ton, bushel, etc.) which are known as "specified" duties.

Advance Against Documents—A loan secured by shipment documents of title, which remain in control of the creditor; an alternative to acceptance financing.

Advising Bank—A bank which informs a party (the seller) that another bank has created (opened) a letter of credit on behalf of the latter bank's customer (the buyer) in favor of the seller. The advising bank's primary duty is to describe accurately the conditions under which payment will be made to the seller. Often the advising bank will also later "negotiate" the letter of credit with the seller, which then makes the bank responsible for determining that the seller has satisfactorily complied with the terms of the letter of credit. Under this arrangement, the letter of credit beneficiary (the seller) receives only the "conditional" promise to pay from the bank which opened the letter of credit originally, and the advising bank performs these services without responsibility on its own part. A "confirming bank," however, not only performs the above services, but also strengthens the letter of credit by "lending its name" to the conditional promise to pay.

Advisory Capacity—A term indicating that a shipper's agent or representative is not empowered to make definitive decisions or adjustments without approval of the group or individual represented. Compare **Without Reserve**.

Affreightment (Contract of)—An agreement between steamship line (or similar carrier) and an importer or exporter in which cargo space is reserved on a vessel for a specified time and at a specified price. The importer/exporter is obligated to make payment whether or not the shipment is made.

After Date—A phrase indicating that payment on a draft or other negotiable instrument is due a specified number of days after presentation of the draft to the drawee or payee. Compare **After Date, at Sight.**

After Sight—A phrase indicating that payment on a draft or other negotiable instrument is due a specified number of days after presentation of the draft to the drawee or payee. Compare **After Date, at Sight.**

Agent—See **Foreign Sales Agent.**

Air Waybill—A bill of lading which covers both domestic and international flights transporting goods to a specified destination. Technically, it is a non-negotiable instrument of air transport which serves as a receipt for the shipper, indicating that the carrier has accepted the goods listed therein and obligates itself to carry the consignment to the airport of destination according to specified conditions. Compare **Inland Bill of Lading, Through Bill of Lading.**

Alongside—A phrase referring to the side of a ship. Goods to be delivered "alongside" are to be placed on the dock or lighter within reach of the transport ship's tackle so that they can be loaded aboard the ship.

Antidiversion Clause—See **Destination Control Statement.**

Arbitrage—The process of buying foreign exchange, stocks, bonds, and other commodities in one market and immediately selling them in another market at higher prices.

At Sight—A phrase indicating that payment on a draft or other negotiable instrument is due upon presentation or demand. Compare **After Sight, After Date.**

Authority to Pay—A letter used mostly in the Far Eastern trade, addressed by a bank to a seller of merchandise, notifying him that it is authorized to purchase, with or without recourse, drafts up to a stipulated amount drawn on a certain foreign buyer in cover of specified shipments of merchandise.

Balance of Trade—The monetary difference between a country's total imports and exports; if the exports exceed the imports, a "favorable" balance of trade exists.

Bank Affiliate ETC—An ETC partially or wholly owned by a banking institution as provided under the ETCA.

Bankers' Bank—A bank that is established by mutual consent by independent and unaffiliated banks to provide a clearinghouse for financial transactions.

Bank Holding Company (BHC)—Any company which directly or indirectly owns or controls, with power to vote, more than five percent of voting shares of each of one or more other banks.

Barratry—Negligence or fraud on the part of a ship's officers or crew resulting in injury or loss to the ship's owners.

Barter—Trade in which merchandise is exchanged directly for other merchandise without use of money. Barter is an important means of trade with countries using currency that is not readily convertible.

Bilateral Trade Agreement—A reciprocal commerce arrangement between two governments outlining tradeable goods, categories, and respective quantities, stating time limitations under the basic agreement's validity, and providing for remittance of balances due directly between the two countries.

Bill of Lading—A document that establishes the terms of a contract between a shipper and a transportation company under which freight is to be moved between specified points for a specified charge. Usually prepared by the shipper on forms issued by the carrier, it serves as a document of title, a contract of carriage, and a receipt for goods. Also see **Air Waybill, Inland Bill of Lading, Ocean Bill of Lading, Through Bill of Lading**.

Blocked Exchange—Exchange which cannot be freely converted into other currencies.

Bonded Warehouse—A warehouse authorized by customs authorities for storage of goods on which payment of duties is deferred until the goods are removed.

Booking—An arrangement with a steamship company for the acceptance and carriage of freight.

Broker—See **Export Broker**.

Brussels Tariff Nomenclature (BTN)—See **Nomenclature of the Customs Cooperation Council**.

Buying Agent—See **Purchasing Agent**.

Carnet—A customs document permitting the holder to carry or send merchandise temporarily into certain foreign countries (for display, demonstration, or similar purposes) without paying duties or posting bonds.

Cash Against Documents (C.A.D.)—Payment for goods in which a commission house or other intermediary transfers title documents to the buyer upon payment in cash.

Cash in Advance (C.I.A.)—Payment for goods in which the price is paid in full before shipment is made. This method is usually used only for small purchases or when the goods are built to order.

Cash With Order (C.W.O.)—Payment for goods in which the buyer pays when ordering and in which the transaction is binding on both parties.

CCCN (The Customs Cooperation Council Nomenclature)—The customs tariff used by many countries worldwide, including most European nations but not the United States. It is also known as the Brussels Tariff Nomenclature. Compare **Standard Industrial Classification, Standard International Trade Classification, Tariff Schedule, Commodity Groupings**.

Certificate of Inspection—A document certifying that merchandise (such as perishable goods) was in good condition immediately prior to its shipment.

Certificate of Manufacture—A statement (often notarized) in which a producer of goods certifies that the manufacturing has been completed and the goods are now at the disposal of the buyer.

Certificate of Origin—A document, required by certain countries for tariff purposes, certifying as to the country of origin of specified goods.

Certificate of Review—See **Export Trade Certificate of Review**.

C & F—"Cost and Freight." A pricing term indicating that these costs are included in the quoted price.

Chamber of Commerce—An association of businesspeople organized to promote local business interests.

Charter Party—A written contract, usually on a special form, between the owner of a vessel and a "charterer" who rents use of the vessel or a part of its freight space. The contract generally includes the freight rates and the ports involved in the transportation.

C & I—"Cost and Insurance." A pricing term indicating that these costs are included in the quoted price.

C.I.F.—"Cost, Insurance, Freight." A pricing term indicating that these costs are included in the quoted price.

C.I.F. & C.—"Cost, Insurance, Freight, and Commission." A pricing term indicating that these costs are included in the quoted price.

C.I.F. & E.—"Cost, Insurance, Freight, and (Currency) Exchange." A pricing term indicating that these costs are included in the quoted price.

Claused Bill Lading—One on which the common carrier has noted exceptions to having accepted a shipper's merchandise for transportation in "apparent good order and condition."

Clayton Act—A major U.S. antitrust law passed in 1914 to supplement the Sherman Act. The Clayton Act dealt primarily with the prohibition of price discrimination among buyers by sellers in the sale of commodities and the acquisition of the company's stock by a competitor.

Clean Bill of Lading—A receipt for goods issued by a carrier with an indication that the goods were received in "apparent good order and condition," without damages or other irregularities. Compare **Foul Bill of Lading**.

Clean Draft—A draft to which no documents have been attached.

Collection Papers—All documents (invoices, bills of lading, etc) submitted to a buyer for the purpose of receiving payment for a shipment.

Commercial Invoice—An itemized list of goods shipped, usually included among an exporter's **Collection Papers**.

Commission Agent—See **Purchasing Agent**.

Commodity Credit Corporation—A government corporation controlled by the Department of Agriculture to provide financing and stability to the marketing and exporting of agricultural commodities.

Commodity Groupings—A numerical system used by the U.S. Bureau of the Census to group imports and exports in broader categories than are provided by the **Tariff Schedules**. Currently, Schedule A is used to categorize imports, Schedule E for exports. Schedule B was replaced by Schedule E in 1978. Compare **The Customs Cooperation Council Nomenclature, Standard Industrial Classification, Tariff Schedules**.

Common Carrier—A firm (or individual) offering the general public passenger and/or cargo transportation services, and which is governed by special laws and regulations.

Confirmed Letter of Credit—A letter of credit, issued by a foreign bank, whose validity has been confirmed by an American bank. An exporter whose payment terms are a confirmed letter of credit is assured of payment even if the foreign buyer of the foreign bank defaults. See **Letter of Credit**.

Consignment—Delivery of merchandise from an exporter (the consignor) to an agent (the consignee) under agreement that the agent sell the merchandise for the account of the exporter. The consignor retains title to the goods until the consignee has sold them. The consignee sells the goods for commission and remits the net proceeds to the consignor.

Consular Declaration—A formal statement, made to the consul of a foreign country, describing goods to be shipped.

Consular Invoice—A document, required by some foreign countries, describing a shipment of goods and showing information such as the consignor, consignee, and value of the shipment. Certified by a consular official of the foreign country, it is used by the country's customs officials to verify the value, quantity, and nature of the shipment.

Convertibility—The degree to which a particular currency may be traded for another in foreign exchange markets. "Hard" currencies enjoy nearly universal acceptance and are thus said to have (good) convertibility.

Countervailing Duty—An extra duty imposed by the Secretary of Commerce to offset export grants, bounties, or subsidies paid to foreign suppliers in certain countries by the government of those countries as an incentive to exports.

Credit Risk Insurance—Insurance designed to cover risks of nonpayment for delivered goods. Compare **Marine Insurance**.

Customs—The authorities designated to collect duties levied by a country on imports and exports. The term also applies to the procedures involved in such collection.

Customhouse Broker—An individual or firm licensed to enter and clear goods through Customs.

Date Draft—A draft which matures a specified number of days after the date it is issued, without regard to the date of **Acceptance** (Definition 2). Compare **Sight Draft, Time Draft**.

Demand Draft—An instrument which is payable upon presentation.

Demurrage—Excess time taken for loading or unloading a vessel. Demurrage refers only to situations in which the charterer or shipper, rather than the vessel's operator, is at fault.

Destination Control Statement—Any one of various statements which the U.S. Government requires to be displayed on export shipments and which specify the destinations for which export of the shipment has been authorized.

Devaluation—The official lowering of the value of one country's currency in terms of one or more foreign currencies. Thus, if the U.S. dollar is devalued in relation to the French franc, one dollar will "buy" fewer francs than before.

DISC—"Domestic International Sales Corporation." The DISC incentive was created by the Revenue Act of 1971. Taxpayers are permitted to establish corporations (called Domestic International Sales Corporations) to conduct their export activities. The DISC legislation provides for deferral of Federal income tax on 50 percent of the export earnings allocated to the DISC, with the balance treated as dividends to the parent company (export income allocated to the parent company is taxed in the normal manner). The DISC must obtain 95 percent or more of its receipts from "qualified exports receipts." At least 95 percent of the DISC's assets must be "qualified export assets." The Tax Reduction Act of 1975 removed the tax deferral for export earnings attributed to the sale of products in short supply in the U.S. and also removed DISC benefits for earnings from certain natural resources. The Tax Reform Act of 1976 added an additional requirement that tax deferral benefits could be applied only to income from export gross receipts exceeding 67 percent of average export gross receipts during a four-year period. As a result of pressure from its trading partners in the General Agreement on Tariffs and Trade (GATT), the U.S. promised in 1982 to develop a GATT-acceptable substitute for the DISC mechanism. See **FSC**.

Dispatch—An amount paid by a vessel's operator to a charterer if loading or unloading is completed in less time than stipulated in the charter party. See **FSC**.

Distributor—A foreign party who sells directly for a supplier and maintains an inventory of the supplier's products.

Dock Receipt—A receipt issued by an ocean carrier to acknowledge receipt of a shipment at the carrier's dock or warehouse facilities. Also see **Warehouse Receipt**.

Documents Against Acceptance (D/A)—Instructions given by a shipper to a bank indicating that documents transferring title to goods should be delivered to the buyer (or drawee) only upon the buyer's acceptance of the attached draft.

Documents Against Payment (D/P)—Instructions given by a shipper to a bank indicating that documents transferring title to goods should be delivered to the buyer (or drawee) only upon the buyer's payment of the attached draft.

Domicile—The place where a draft or acceptance is made payable.

Draft (or Bill of Exchange)—An unconditional order in writing from one person (the drawer) to another (the drawee), directing the drawee to pay a specified amount to a named payee at a fixed or determinable future date.

Drawback—A refund of duties paid on imported goods which is provided at the time of their reexportation.

Drawee—The individual or firm on whom a draft is drawn and who owes the indicated amount. Compare **Drawer**. Also see **Draft**.

Drawer—The individual or firm that issues or signs a draft and thus stands to receive payment of the indicated amount from the drawee. Compare **Drawee**. Also see **Draft**.

Dumping—Importing merchandise into a country (e.g., the United States) at low prices that are detrimental to local producers of the same kind of merchandise.

Duty—A tax imposed on imports by the customs authority of a country. Duties are generally based on the value of the goods (ad valorem duties), some other factor such as weight or quantity (specific duties), or a combination of value and other factors (compound duties).

Edge Act Corporation—Banks that are subsidiaries either to bank holding companies or other banks established to engage in foreign business transactions. They were established by Act of Congress in 1919.

EMC—See **Export Management Company**.

ETC—See **Export Trading Company**.

ETCA—See **Export Trading Company Act**.

Eurodollar Trading (Euro-Currency)—The practice of accepting (buying) deposits from overseas holders of "local" currencies and relending (selling) such deposits with the intent of retaining a positive interest spread. This is often practiced by overseas offices of U.S. banks acting as U.S. dollar banks, such time deposits being effectively a type of "purchased funds" for the U.S. dollar. The term "Eurodollar" merely signifies a U.S. dollar on deposit in a bank outside the United States. The bank need not necessarily be located in Europe; it may be located anywhere outside the United States. The Eurodollar market attracts money from depositors in countries with excess funds, low interest rates, or currency devaluation risks, and channels funds to borrowers in countries with tight credit and low liquidity, higher interest rates, and currencies that may appreciate in value. The key factors that determine the volume and movement of funds are interest rates and availability of lendable funds.

EX-"From"—When used in pricing terms such as "Ex Factory" or "Ex Dock," it signifies that the price quoted applies only at the point of origin (in the two examples, at the seller's factory or a dock at the import point). In practice, this kind of quotation indicates that the seller agrees to place the goods at the disposal of the buyer at the specified place within a fixed period time.

Exchange Rate—The price of one currency in terms of another i.e., the number of units of one currency that may be exchanged for one unit of another currency.

Export—To send or transport goods out of a country for sale in another country. In international sales, the exporter is usually the seller or the seller's agent. Compare **Import**.

Export Broker—An individual or firm that brings together buyers and sellers for a fee but does not take part in actual sales transactions.

Export/Import Bank—An independent U.S. Government Agency created to facilitate U.S. trade relations primarily by providing financing, insurance, and feasibility studies.

Export License—A government document which permits the "Licensee" to engage in the export of designated goods to certain destinations.

Export Management Company—A private firm that serves as the export department for several manufacturers, soliciting and transacting export business on behalf of its clients in return for a commission, salary, or retainer plus commission.

Export Merchant—A company that buys products directly from manufacturers, then packages and marks the merchandise for resale under its own name.

Export Trade Certificate of Review—A certification of partial immunity from antitrust laws that can be granted based on the ETCA legislation by the Department of Commerce with Department of Justice concurrence. Any prospective or existing exporter may apply by filling out the appropriate form describing the anticipated method of trade and other trade activities.

Export Trading Company—An ETC is a company doing business in the United States principally to export goods or services produced in the United States or to facilitate such exports by unaffiliated persons. It can be owned by foreigners and can import, barter, and arrange sales between third countries, as well as export.

Export Trading Company Act—The law passed on October 8, 1982, creating a special legal status for Export Trading Companies. It established an Office of Export Trading Company Affairs in Commerce, permitted bankers' banks and bank holding companies to invest in ETC's, reduced the restrictions on export financing provided by financial institutions, and modified the application of the antitrust laws to certain export trade.

Factoring—A method used by businesses including trading companies to obtain cash for discounted accounts receivables or other assets.

F.A.S.—**"Free Alongside (VESSEL)."** A pricing term indicating that the quoted price includes the cost of delivering the goods alongside a designated vessel.

FCIA—See the **Foreign Credit Insurance Association.**

F.I.—**"Free In."** A pricing term indicating that the charterer of a vessel is responsible for the cost of loading goods onto the vessel.

F.I.O.—**"Free In and Out."** A pricing term indicating that the charterer of a vessel is responsible for the cost of loading and unloading goods from the vessel.

F.O.—**"Free Out."** A pricing term indicating that the charterer of a vessel is responsible for the cost of loading goods from the vessel.

F.O.B.—**"Free On Board."** A pricing term indicating that the quoted price includes the cost of loading the goods into transport vessels at the specified place.

Force Majeure—The title of a standard clause in marine contracts exempting the parties for non-fulfillment of their obligations as a result of conditions beyond their control, such as earthquakes, floods, or war.

Foreign Credit Insurance Association (FCIA)—An association of fifty insurance companies which operate in conjunction with the EXIMBANK to provide comprehensive insurance for exporters against nonpayment. FCIA underwrites the commercial credit risks. EXIMBANK covers the political risk and any excessive commercial risks.

Foreign Exchange—The currency or credit instruments of a foreign country. Also, transactions involving purchase and/or sale of currencies.

Foreign Freight Forwarder—See **Freight Forwarder.**

Foreign Sales Agent—An individual or firm that serves as the foreign representative of a domestic supplier and seeks sales abroad for the supplier.

Foul Bill of Lading—A receipt for goods issued by a carrier with an indication that the goods were damaged when received. Compare **Clean Bill of Lading.**

F.P.A.—**"Free of Particular Average."** The title of a clause used in marine insurance, indicating that partial loss or damage to a foreign shipment is not covered. Note: Loss resulting from certain conditions, such as the sinking or burning of the ship, may be specifically exempted from the effect of the clause. Compare **W.P.A.**

Free Port—One which is open to all traders on equal terms and in which goods may be stored duty-free while awaiting re-export or sale within the country where the port is located.

Free Trade Zone—A port designated by the government of a country for entry of any non-prohibited goods. Merchandise may be stored, displayed, used for manufacturing, etc., within the zone and reexported without duties being paid. Duties are imposed on the merchandise (or items manufactured from the merchandise) only when the goods pass from the zone into an area of the country subject to the Customs Authority.

Freight Forwarder—An independent business which handles export shipments for compensation. A freight forwarder is among the best sources of information and assistance on U.S. export regulations and documentation, shipping methods, and foreign import regulations.

FSC—**"Foreign Sales Corporation."** The Reagan Administration initiated the proposal for Foreign Sales Corporations (FSCs) which replaces DISCs. Under the proposal, to qualify for special tax treatment, a FSC must be a foreign corporation, maintain an office outside the U.S. territory, maintain a summary of its permanent books of account at the foreign office, and have at least one director resident outside of the U.S. A portion of the foreign sales corporation's income (generally corresponding to the tax deferred income of a DISC) is exempt from U.S. tax at both the FSC and the U.S. corporate parent levels. This exemption is achieved by allowing a domestic corporation that is a FSC shareholder a 100 percent deduction for a portion of dividends received from a FSC attributable to economic activity actually conducted outside the U.S. customs territory. Interest, dividends, royalties, or other investment income of a FSC are subject to U.S. tax.

GATT—**"General Agreement on Tariffs and Trade."** A multilateral treaty whose purpose is to help reduce trade barriers between the signatory countries and to promote trade through tariff concessions.

General Export License—Any of various export licenses covering export commodities for which validated Export Licenses are not required. No formal application or written authorization is needed to ship exports under a General Export License. Compare **Validated Export Licenses**.

Gross Weight—The full weight of a shipment, including goods and packaging. Compare **Tare Weight**.

Hard Currency—Any currency which enjoys a high degree of international convertibility.

Hedging—The sale or purchase of foreign exchange, usually on a forward basis, in order to avoid a loss in the event of an unfavorable change in the foreign exchange rate. Such action naturally also acts to preclude windfall profits when rates move in a favorable direction. Hedging is simply a mechanism for transferring some or all undesired or speculative foreign exchange rate risks to banks (and others) that make such risk management their livelihood.

Horizontal ETC—An ETC which exports a range of similar or identical products supplied by a number of manufacturers or other producers. Webb-Pomerene Organizations, trade-grouped organized ETCs, and an ETC formed by an association of agricultural cooperatives are the prime examples of horizontally organized ETCs. See also **Webb-Pomerene Associations**.

Import—To bring foreign goods into a country. In international sales, the importer is usually the buyer or an intermediary who accepts and transmits goods to the buyer. Compare **Export**.

Import License—A document required and issued by some national governments authorizing the importation of goods into their individual countries.

Inherent Vice—An insurance term referring to any defect or other characteristics of a product which could result in damage to the product without external cause. Insurance policies may specifically exclude losses caused by inherent vice.

Inland Bill of Lading—A bill of lading used in transporting goods overland to the exporter's international carrier. Although a through bill of lading can sometimes be used, it is usually necessary to prepare both an inland bill of lading and ocean bill of lading for export shipments. Compare **Air Waybill, Ocean Bill of Lading, Through Bill of Lading.**

International Freight Forwarder—See **Freight Forwarder.**

International Trade Administration (ITA)—The ITA is a division of the Department of Commerce designed to promote world trade and to strengthen the international trade and investment position of the United States.

Irrevocable Letter of Credit—A letter of credit in which the specified payment is guaranteed by the bank if all terms and conditions are met by the drawee. Compare **Revocable Letter of Credit.**

ITA—See **International Trade Administration.**

Joint Venture—A business undertaking in which more than one firm share ownership and control.

Letter of Credit—An instrument created by a financial institution designed to serve as a conduit for commercial transaction documentation movement from buyer to seller. The role played by the financial institution is beneficial to both buyer and seller insofar as: (1) the buyer, normally working with his own bank as issuer of the letter of credit, stipulates the documentation he requires to be reasonably certain of actually receiving the goods he intends to order (though his bank pays solely against apparently valid documentation, never against the merchandise itself) and, (2) the seller must only demonstrate to the financial institution that he has fully complied with the terms of its letter of credit in order to be paid directly by the institution, which in turn settles accounts between itself and the buyer.

Licensing—A business arrangement in which the manufacturer of a product (or a firm with proprietary rights over certain technology, trademarks, etc.) grants permission to some other group or individual to manufacture that product (or make use of that proprietary material) in return for specified royalties or other payment.

Lighter—An open or covered barge towed by a tugboat and used mainly in harbors and inland waterways.

Marine Insurance—Insurance covering loss or damage of goods at sea. Marine insurance will typically compensate the owner of merchandise for losses sustained from fire, shipwreck, piracy, and various other causes, but excludes losses which can be legally recovered from the carrier. Compare **Credit Risk Insurance.**

Marking (or Marks)—Letters, numbers, and other symbols placed on cargo packages to facilitate identification.

Ocean Bill of Lading—A bill of lading (B/L) indicating that the exporter consigns a shipment to an international carrier for transportation to a specified foreign market. Unlike an inland B/L, the ocean B/L also serves as a collection document. If it is a "Straight B/L," the foreign buyer can obtain the shipment from the carrier by simply showing proof of identity. If a "Negotiable B/L" is used, the buyer must first pay for the goods, post a bond, or meet other conditions agreeable to the seller. Compare **Air Waybill, Inland Bill of Lading, Through Bill of Lading.**

Open Account—A trade arrangement in which goods are shipped to a foreign buyer without guarantee of payment. The obvious risk this method poses to the supplier makes is essential that the buyer's integrity be unquestionable.

Open Insurance Policy—A marine insurance policy that applies to all shipments made by an exporter over a period of time rather than to only one shipment.

OPIC—Overseas Private Investment Corporation. A wholly owned government corporation designed to promote private U.S. investment in developing countries by providing political risk insurance and some financial assistance.

Packing List—A list showing the number and kind of items being shipped, as well as other information needed for transportation purposes.

Parcel Post Receipt—The postal authorities' signed acknowledgment of delivery of a shipment made by parcel post.

Par Value—The official rate of exchange for a currency, as registered with international bodies, such as the IMF (International Monetary Fund). Actual foreign exchange trading frequently takes place within "bands" (e.g. $+/-1\%$) around par values. However, market forces have increasingly influenced real currency values as manifested by today's multitude of "floating rates."

Phytosanitary Inspection Certificate—A certificate, issued by the U.S. Department of Agriculture to satisfy import regulations of foreign countries, indicating that a U.S. shipment has been inspected and is free from harmful pests and plant diseases.

Pro Forma Invoice—An invoice provided by a supplier prior to the shipment of merchandise, informing the buyer of the kinds and quantities of goods to be sent, their value, and important specifications (weight, size, etc.).

Purchasing Agent—An agent who purchases goods in his/her own country on behalf of large foreign buyers such as government agencies and large private concerns.

Procuring Agent—See **Purchasing Agent**.

Quota—The quantity of goods of a specific kind that a country will permit to be imported without restriction or imposition of additional duties.

Quotation—An offer to sell goods at a stated price and under specified conditions.

Recourse—The rights of a holder to force prior endorsers to meet their legal obligations to pay on a negotiable instrument if it is dishonored by the maker or acceptor.

Remittance—The forwarding of money from one party to another in the form of cash or by a negotiable instrument.

Revocable Letter of Credit—A letter of credit which can be cancelled or altered by the drawee (buyer) after it has been issued by the drawee's bank. Compare **Irrevocable Letter of Credit**.

S.A. (Societe Anonyme)—French expression meaning a corporation.

Sales Representative—An agent who distributes, represents, services, or sells goods on the behalf of foreign sellers.

Sherman Act—This act prohibits any contract, combination, or conspiracy that (1) unreasonably interferes with the ordinary and freely competitive pricing or distribution system of the open-market in interstate trade or (2) has a direct, substantial, and reasonably foreseeable effect on domestic trade or commerce or on the export commerce of a person engaged in such commerce in the U.S.

Shipper's Export Declaration—A form prepared by a shipper and required by the U.S. Treasury Department for all shipments which indicates the value, weight, destination, and other basic information about an export shipment.

Ship's Manifest—An instrument in writing, signed by the captain of a ship, that lists the individual shipments constituting the ship's cargo.

SIC—See **Standard Industrial Classification.**

Sight Draft—A draft which is payable upon presentation to the drawee. Compare **Date Draft, Time Draft.**

SITC—See **Standard International Trade Classification.**

Soft Currency—Currency which is not fully convertible to all currencies but only perhaps to some other "weak" currencies.

Spot Exchange—Foreign exchange for delivery by the seller and payment by the buyer at the time the transaction is arranged. This "immediate" transaction is understood by convention to mean actual consummation two business days hence.

Standard Industrial Classification (SIC)—A standard numerical code system used by the U.S. Government to classify products and services. Compare **Commodity Groupings, The Customs Cooperation Council Nomenclature, Standard International Trade Classification.**

Standard International Trade Classification (SITC)—A standard numerical code system developed by the United Nations and used in international trade to classify commodities. Compare **Commodity Grouping, The Customs Cooperation Council Nomenclature, Standard Industrial Classification, Tariff Schedules.**

State-controlled Trading Company—In a country with a state trading monopoly, a trading entity empowered by the country's government to conduct export business.

Steamship Conference—A group of steamship operators that operate under mutually agreed upon freight rates.

Swaps—The purchasing of foreign exchange for spot delivery, with the simultaneous sale of equivalent foreign exchange for forward delivery.

Tenor—The nature of a draft's maturity, being either (a) a "sight" draft (payable upon presentation), or (b) a "time" draft (payable at some determinable future date, e.g., 30 days after sight or 60 days after bill of lading date).

Tare Weight—The weight of a container and/or packing materials without the weight of the goods it contains. Compare **Gross Weight.**

Tariff Schedules of the United States (TSUS)—A standard numerical system used by the U.S. Customs Bureau to classify imports and exports. Compare **Standard Industrial Classification, Customs Cooperation Council Nomenclature, Standard Industrial Trade Classification.**

TDP—See **Trade and Development Program.**

Through Bill of Lading—A single bill of lading covering both the domestic and international carriage of an export shipment. An air waybill, for instance, is essentially a through bill of lading used for air shipments. Ocean shipments, on the other hand, usually require two separate documents—an inland bill of lading for domestic carriage and an ocean bill of lading for international carriage. Through bills of lading, therefore, cannot be used. Compare **Air Waybill, Inland Bill of Lading, Ocean Bill of Lading.**

Time Draft—A draft which matures either a certain number of days after acceptance or a certain number of days after the date of the draft. Compare **Date Draft, Sight Draft.**

Trade and Development Program (TDP)—This program is designed to promote economic development in the Third World and the sale of U.S. goods and services to these developing countries. It operates as part of the International Development Cooperative Agency.

Trade Mission—A mission to a foreign country organized to promote trade through the establishment of contacts and exposure to the commercial environment. They are frequently organized by Federal, State, or local agencies.

Tramp Steamer—A ship not operating on regular routes or schedules.

Trust Receipt—Release of merchandise by a bank to a buyer in which the bank retains title to the merchandise. The buyer, who obtains the goods for manufacturing or sales purposes, is obligated to maintain the goods (or the proceeds from the sales) distinct from the remainder of his/her assets and to hold them ready for repossession by the bank.

Turnkey—A method of construction whereby the contractor assumes total responsibility from design through completion of the project.

Validated Export License—A document issued by the U.S. Government authorizing the export of commodities for which written export authorization is required by law. Compare **General Export License**.

Vertical ETC—An ETC that sells a diverse range of products overseas. The mix can range from agricultural commodities to high technology products. It is not organized around product line or specific industry.

W.A.—**"With Average."**—A marine insurance term meaning that a shipment is protected from partial damage whenever the damage exceeds 3 percent (or some other percentage).

Warehouse Receipt—A receipt issued by a warehouse which lists the goods deposited there; it may be negotiable (to bearer) or non-negotiable.

Webb-Pomerene Association—Institutions engaged in exporting that combine the products of similar producers for overseas sales. These associations have partial exemption from U.S. anti-trust laws but may not engage in third country trade. See also **Horizontal ETCs**.

Wharfage—A charge assessed by a pier or dock owner for handling incoming or outgoing cargo.

Without Reserve—A term indicating that a shipper's agent or representative is empowered to make definitive decisions and adjustments abroad without approval of the group or individual represented. Compare **Advisory Capacity**.

World Traders Data Reports—Reports issued by the Bureau of International Commerce of the U.S. Department of Commerce that give credit-type information on individual foreign firms regarding the type of organization, method of operation, sales volumes, territory, product lines, etc.

FOREIGN TRADE ABBREVIATIONS

A.A.R.	Against All Risks
Ad Val.	Ad Valorem (duty on the value of the merchandise)
A.I.D.	Agency for International Development
A.B.	Swedish term for "Incorporated"
A.G.	German term for "Incorporated"
B/E	Bill of Exchange
B/L	Bill of Lading
B.M.	Board Measure
C.A.D.	Cash Against Documents
C.C.C.	Commodity Credit Corporation
C. & F.	Cost and Freight
CANDF	Same as above, as used in cables
Cla.	Spanish term for "company" (abbrev.)

C.I.F.	Cost, Insurance, Freight
C.I.F. & C.	Cost, Insurance, Freight & Commission (or charges)
C.I.F.C & I	Cost, Insurance, Freight, Commission (or charges) and Interest
C. & I.	Cost and Insurance
C.L.	Carload
CWT	Hundredweight (112 lb. in Great Britain)
D/A	Documents Against Acceptance
D/D	Days After Date
D.F.	Dead Freight
D/N	Debit Note
D/P	Documents Against Payment
D/R	Dock Receipt
D/S	Days After Sight
E. & O.E.	Errors and Omissions Excepted
F.A.S.	Free Along Side (vessel)
F.C. & S.	Free from Capture and Seizure
F.C.I.A.	Foreign Credit Insurance Association
F.O.B.	Free on Board
F.O.R.	Free on Rails
F.P.A.	Free of Particular Average
G.A.	General Average
GmbH	German for "Limited Liability Company"
G.T.	Gross Ton
L/C	Letter of Credit
L.C.L.	Less than Carload
Ltd.	Limited. British term for "Limited Liability Company"
Ltda. or Lda.	Same as above in Portuguese and Spanish
L/T	Long Ton (2240 lb.)
M.E.C.	Marine Extension Clause
M.I.P.	Marine Insurance Policy
M/R	Mate's Receipt
M/T	Metric Ton (2205 lb.)
M/V	Motor Vessel
N.O.E.	Not Otherwise Enumerated
N.V.	Dutch term for "Incorporated"
O.C.P.	Overland Common Points
O.R.L.	Owner's Risk of Leakage
P.L. 480	Public Law 480 (of 1954) which for specific cases permits U.S. agricultural exporters to sell in the currency of the country of destination.
PTY.	Proprietary (type of company in certain British Commonwealth countries)
R.O.D.	Refused on Delivery
S.A.	French, Italian, Spanish, and Portuguese for "Incorporated"
S.L. & C.	Shipper's Load and Count
S.R.&C.C.	Strikes, Riots, and Civil Commotion
S.S.	Steamship
S/T	Short Ton (2000 lb.)
T.T.	Telegraphic Transfer
W.A.	With Average
W.R.	War Risk

Index